Big picture questions

14. Family likeness
Who in the family are you most like?

Ways to ask it
As a family, we've given so much to each other. Who do you think you are most like – your mum or your dad?
Who have you inherited your sense of humour from? What about your creativity or your organisational skills? Think about the way you approach a challenge, conflict or failure. How would you change or improve on the faults/qualities you see in us?

What to try and avoid
This is not a 'who is the better parent?' contest. This is about inspiring reflection concerning what we are like, where we learn our character traits from and what we would change if we could. Avoid being hurt if they spot something you'd rather not confront. This isn't about you, it's about your child's awareness of who they are, their strengths and what is needed to move forward.

What it will give
The apple doesn't fall far from the tree, but it can be moved! This question will provide keen self-awareness. Success comes from knowing ourselves.

15. The Generation Game
Can you guess what Grandma and Grandpa were like before big games (or pressure moments) with me?

Ways to ask it
As I try my best to support you, can you guess what your grandparents were like at supporting me? From what you know about their character, what do you think they were like? How do you think I responded to their support? How do you think their support affected me? What differences do you think there are between the way my parents supported me and how they now support you? Why do you think there is that difference? (If possible, have the grandparents in the room when you ask these questions.)

What to try and avoid
This isn't about shaming grandparents or suggesting that our children have it easier or harder. This is about encouraging reflection, which leads to learning and gratitude. Avoid feeling guilty if there are any differences between you and your parents, and be wise about letting your children see any anger you might harbour regarding your upbringing. We shouldn't hide our anger, however, make sure you don't put your children in an awkward position. Something else to avoid is presenting our parents as perfect! That's not helpful either.

What it will give
Connection to our wider story helps to create deeper roots, even if there is pain in that story. Our children can learn so much about who they are by listening to their family's stories. Deeper roots give us a stronger base from which to grow our character, and they help us make more informed choices about how we develop. What other stories can you tell about the different generations, especially those that will highlight good character?

16. Annual appraisal

Over the last year, how have you improved regarding the ways you approach your sport?

Ways to ask it

I've gained so much from watching you play over the last year, and there have been so many highlights. I'm curious to know how you think you have improved over the last 12 months in the way you approach your sport? How have those steps forward improved your game?

What to try and avoid

This is a character question, not a coaching one. The number of goals or running speed is not our focus here. Instead, look at determination, sportsmanship, effort and responses to setbacks. However, this is not meant to be a guilt trip if your child has not progressed in these areas. Perhaps you could highlight times when progress was made.

What it will give

Growth involves more than winning and goals. This will give you the chance to help your child see how they are growing in the area that really matters – character. It reinforces that your child is not the 'finished' article. This also gives you the chance to think about the future, with follow-up questions such as, "Where would you like to develop next?", "What would help support your growth in these areas?" or "What would hinder that development?"

17. What's the big dream?
What are your sporting dreams and what will you need to get there?

Ways to ask it
I am thrilled to watch you play, but I've been wondering what your sporting dreams are. What sporting achievements will really give you a thrill? My dream is that you will always enjoy playing and taking part, but what is your dream? (You might want to write this one down with them.)

What to try and avoid
There are loads of dangers in this question. Number one: squashing their dream by saying or implying, "You'll never get that far." Number two: puffing up their ego with no reality by saying or implying, "You are the best, national captain should be your target." Number three: pushing your sporting dream for your children onto them, saying something like, "This is what I think you should aim for …" Be willing to accept their answer and help them break it down, even if you are not sure about their response.

What it will give
The opportunity to get a feel for what your child really wants, and you'll be surprised at the range of answers they'll give. You'll also be able to help your child see how their character will help them achieve these goals. I encourage you to avoid making loads of comments focused on what they need to do. Instead, encourage them to sit down with you and their coach to talk about what is required in order to move forward.

18. Sticks and stones may break my bones, but bullying in sport is real

What does bullying look like in sport?

Ways to ask it
I know you have been told loads about bullying at school, but has anyone ever talked to you about what it looks like on the sports field? How could a fellow team member bully you? How could a coach or manager bully you?

What to try and avoid
This question may open a can of worms – good! Try to give examples of the actions of a coach or team member and ask your child to decide if it would constitute bullying. Most people don't realise that coaches shouting at players is a form of bullying and isn't acceptable. If your child describes being bullied themselves, try not to fly into action or anger (easier said than done). Listen and take notes and then consult the team's safeguarding policy.

What it will give
This will give your child an understanding of what boundaries are acceptable in sport. Having good character means having respect for yourself and the courage to speak out. This is never easy to do when you are being bullied. Having this conversation will make it clear to your child that you are open to talking about it with them. Should they go on to play professional sport, it's also essential they understand that bullying can happen to adults too.

Joy in France

Bon Journeys

Also by the author

Motorcycle Trips for Mortals

Joy in Europe

CONTENTS

ÎLE-DE-FRANCE 3
   Paris 3
   Montmartre 4
   Bastille 10
   Montparnasse 11
   Madeleine 15

BOURGOGNE FRANCHE-COMTÉ 20
   Dijon 20
   Beaune 29
   Besançon 33
   Auxerre 35

PROVENCE 38
   Antibes 39
   Grasse 46
   Juan-les-Pins 47
   Monaco 50
   Villefranche sur-mer. 52
   Nice 57
   Menton 62
   Toulon 68

OCCITANIE 74
   Sète 74
   Marseillan Plage 79
   Mus 85
   Le Grau du Roi 87

Rodez 88
Figeac 90
LANGUEDOC/ROUSILLON 91
Le Somail 91
Sallèllas-d'-Aude 93
Minerve 99
Narbonne 101
Saint-Pierre-la-Mer 103
Sigean African Nature Reserve 106
Bages 106
Gruissan Plage 107
Carcassonne 109
Limoux 115
PYRENEES ORIENTALES 120
Argelés-sur-Mer 121
Banyuls 124
Port Vendres 126
Collioure 130
Toulouse 134
AQUITAINE 145
Bordeaux 145
Arcachon 150
Dunes du Pilat 151
Biscarrosse Plage 152
Cap Ferret 153
BRITTANY 157

    Huelgoat 160

    Locquirec 161

    Morlaix 163

NORMANDY 166

    Honfleur 166

    Veulettes-sur-mer 167

    St Valery-en-Caux 168

    Evreux 170

LOIRE 178

    Touraine 178

    Villeloin-Coulange 179

    Chenonceau 180

    Montrésor 182

    Beauval Zoo 183

    Loches 185

    Château de Villandry 186

    Saumur 187

    Amboise 189

    Bourges 190

    Sancerre 193

    Chavignol 194

PICARDY 196

    Albert 196

    Amiens 198

    Delville Wood 204

    Longueval 206

Mametz Wood	206
Lochnagar	207
Beaumont Hamel	208
Thiepval	209
Fréchencourt	210
Fouilloy	211
Vimy Ridge	212
BELGIUM	**215**
Tyne Cot	215
Ypres	216
Langemark	219
Poperinge	220
PAS-DE-CALAIS	**222**
St Omer	222
La Coupole	223
GRAND EST	**225**
Nancy	225
Metz	231
Luxembourg	232
Toul	234
Strasbourg	236
Basel, Switzerland	243
Obernai	244
Colmar	245
HAUTE-DE-FRANCE	**250**
Lille, Christmas Shopping	250

FINAL NOTE 257
ACKNOWLEDGEMENTS 259
ABOUT THE AUTHOR 261

Dedication

In memory of Rose.

It was a privilege to have shared some of these journeys with you.

PREFACE

Travel is the only thing you buy that makes you richer
(Anon)

During my working career I spent a lot of time interviewing people for jobs. Aside from their expertise in their profession, I asked them to tell me what their interests were. Very few did not say 'travel'. When I delved a little more into what sort of travel; where they had been and just as importantly, where would they like to go, France often cropped up.

It's our nearest foreign neighbour after all, but it's undoubtedly, also the most diverse, being loved or criticised in equal parts. It's a love-hate relationship in many ways. I always cringed when I heard the reply, "I've been to Paris, the people are always rushing around, and so rude, I hate the French." From just one visit, and the misfortune to have a negative experience, and the whole of France is condemned. In this book, where we have travelled a little farther than a suburban arrondissement of the Capital city, I think I can dispel such cursory condemnation.

My affection for France began during the days of the 'booze cruise' trips, when half the population of Kent would pile onto a ferry from Dover to Calais and return the same day laden with cheap wine, beer and fags. It wasn't the booty that appealed to me but the feeling that I was actually standing in a foreign country for the first time in my life. The restaurant we sat in all afternoon, and half the evening, had a completely different feel to it than the Wimpy bar in Walthamstow. The food, the décor and the easy-going attitude of the staff were all very new, and I liked it.

This book came about much by accident. I've been fortunate to have been able to travel to France, and other countries, a lot since those limited opportunities of the 1970's. I wrote about my travels, in part, because a disabled friend of mine, who sadly, is no longer with us, was unable to travel at all. I would write up my notes, cast political correctness aside and, in his words, 'take him on holiday with me.' Interest grew with other colleagues and I could barely go to a rock concert or a football match without being asked if I'd written something about it.

When I decided to write this book, I had in mind to include all the European countries I had visited, but when Joy, my long suffering wife and I, put together all the notes I had made on France, we decided we had more than enough material to write entirely about this one country. OK, there's a couple of chapters that include a part of Belgium, Luxembourg and Switzerland, but that is easily explained when the reader reaches those segments.

It is important to clarify how the book is laid out. Most travelogues tend to concentrate on a linear format, using time: a year in Provence for example. It is easy to follow the changes of the seasons and the events that evolve over the period in question. Here, we begin the journey in the spring, (what better time is there to visit Paris?) and end with Christmas shopping in Lille. However, it took more than a single year to complete this sojourn. We also had to travel back and forth from England as time and work commitments allowed.

We found the most convenient form of transport to be the train. Crossing under the English Channel is convenient if you have adequate access to the Eurostar terminals. Once there, connections from Paris or Lille are very straightforward. We also took our own car on occasion. The rail link and the many ferry ports offer lots of choice. We did resort to travel once or twice by air but preferred to spend as much time as possible on the ground, enjoying the views.

There were some places we visited on more than one occasion, resulting in the need to compress experiences into one chapter. The flow of the book follows a geographical progression and not so much a chronological one. It would explain why a short journey from one place to another suddenly changed in season with surprising speed. There were times we would visit a city in the height of the season, spend a day in a nearby town and pledge to return later in the year to explore in more detail.

Although the route taken in each chapter is geographically linked by proximity, the reader is not obligated to follow the same pattern. Apart from an occasional reference to a previously mentioned experience, or character, the chapters can be selected as the reader wishes.

This is neither a guide book nor an academic text book. Whilst every effort is made to ensure any facts or figures I have included are accurate and cross-checked, there may be oversights. I actually found an official website for a museum that claimed a French King was responsible for a certain action, when in fact, he had yet to be born! My entries of such facts and statements have been made in good faith and I would recommend that scholars and pedants who take an interest in certain factual claims cross reference through their own efforts.

The aim of this book is to enlighten, inform and most importantly, to entertain. Whereas it is always nice to preach to the converted, my hope is to change a few minds of those who err towards the negative end of the spectrum of opinion about France and its people.

France is almost 3 times the size of the UK, with a comparable population, so many parts are remote, yet still very accessible. I cannot claim that this book is a definitive exploration of the beauty spots. We still have many more to see.

ÎLE-DE-FRANCE

Paris

Paris in the springtime. They sing songs about it. Perhaps the best way to begin a tour of France, is to start with arguably, the most iconic and famous foreign city in the whole world.

We set off at 5am on Monday morning and caught the train from Birmingham New Street to Derby and changed there for a direct service to London St Pancras. Arriving in good time, we picked a café in the station for coffee and a snack before checking in at the Eurostar terminal. It was all hassle free and leisurely, as we waited in the departure lounge whilst passengers quickly filled up the hall and stared at the departure screens. When the call came for us to head for the gates to board, the mad rush began. People crowded around the still closed doors to the escalators that take you up to the platform. When the doors finally opened, it was like watching engine oil pouring too quickly into a funnel then trickling too slowly out of the other end. We didn't move, but sat patiently for 25 minutes before sauntering onboard without queuing at all. I can't understand the mentality of crushing a gangway to get to a seat that's already reserved for you.

We set off exactly on time and it was merely moments before we were hurtling into long dark tunnels. 25 minutes later as we emerged from the tunnel at Dartford, Joy was taken in as I told her we had now crossed the channel and were already in France. Geography, and that time, space continuum concept has not improved since I met her.

We had reserved seats in the carriage that provided a meal during the journey. The treatment the Eurostar staff provided was wonderful. The hostesses and their male counterparts attended to our every need. Champagne was offered to begin with and then a choice of red or white wine. Joy chose white, which was immediately sent back as it was awful, and the girl brought us three sealed mini bottles of red as recompense. For the meal, I chose salmon with a Waldorf salad followed by lemon meringue. Joy had a very nicely presented shish kebab. Coffee and chocolate biscuits filled the small gaps and the journey was over before you could take it all in. Speeding across the plains of northern France instantly makes you realise how pretty the British countryside really is. It's just big and boring through here. Racing along at 150mph is the best thing the driver could have done.

Arrival at the Gare du Nord and setting off into Paris from the station puts airport practices to shame. We are already in the middle of the city and barely ten minutes after arriving in the French capital we were heading for the underground metro. I am beginning to love this rail travel lark in preference to airport shenanigans.

Montmartre

I had already tested the metro system on a previous trip, so it took only moments to fill my pockets with 20 journey tokens for use on public transport. It works out much cheaper than buying a single ticket each time. Each trip requires one ticket regardless of the number of station-stops along the way.

20 minutes later and we emerged into the sunlight at Blanche. Joy's little face lit up like a Christmas tree. Right in front of us was the windmill façade of the Moulin Rouge. This was her first trip to Paris and I wanted her to enjoy every landmark available. A couple of photos later, we walked barely 200 metres up the hill and into a side street to reach our chosen hotel for the week. The Hotel le Relais. A few flights up, we were shown to our garret room. Chintzy,

Liberty print style furnishings, a ceiling beam and a large bathroom offering plenty of elbow room. This is not always the case in Parisian boutique hotels. The outside world was shut away and it was as silent to us as an Augustinian priory. The perfect setting for a relaxing week in springtime Paris. Arriving by Eurostar to the Gare du Nord, as opposed to flying into Charles de Gaul airport meant we had gained a whole afternoon to now go and explore the immediate surroundings.

The Montmartre district is home to the Sacré-Coeur Basilica and is just a short stroll up the hill behind the hotel. Stopping for a coffee along the way we discovered two things. 1 - The weather was anything like springtime, as showers showered us at random moments, rendering everywhere drenched and dripping. 2 - The price of everything from coffee to clothes is astronomical. We had to memorise the correct phrases in French when ordering coffee. Joy is not an espresso drinker and in Paris, the espresso can arrive thick as black treacle. It was an expensive mistake but I can drink two and stay awake all night. With the rains still pouring down as we headed on to the basilica, we found we had to fight our way through the scores of smokers crowding under the shop awnings and in doorways, as they puffed away on their lip-stuck pyres.

The Sacré Coeur is very impressive to look at and walk around. The first thing that struck me when we entered the building was the domed ceiling. It resembles a painted egg shell, but on the inside. The actual décor and fittings had a nice calming effect on me. I'm usually in and out of a cathedral or church within three minutes, except at weddings and funerals. It's quite dramatic in here throughout. Outside, the views across the city are amazing. All the major buildings of Paris seem to be visible from here.

Behind the basilica is the Artists' Quarter. There is so much history and lovely architecture in these streets, but we didn't get lulled in to the trap of stopping for coffee or purchasing any of the trinkets and wares on show. It's a tourist trap like no other. Street artists cram the squares, offering to sketch your portrait within seconds. From the samples on display, each artist would have you looking like Donald Duck on a bad hair day. The tiny shops were stuffed to the gunnels with the type of tat and tourist trash you would expect to find in Blackpool. It was far too crowded for comfort as well, so we returned to enjoy the views across Paris from the front of the basilica before heading down a to find a tucked away café for some essential, cheaper refreshment.

The rain poured, stopped, poured again, then slowly dissolved to a constant drizzle. Oh, well, what did we care. This is Paris.

The streets in and around Montmartre are lovely and about as Parisian as it gets, with narrow passageways, high walls and artisan shops lining both sides. We settled for supper in a nearby restaurant and ordered beef bourguignon and a red Touraine to wash it down, which won me Brownie points from Joy for the choice. The service was friendly and the atmosphere cosy. Afterwards, we strolled along the main boulevard of Blanche where the Moulin Rouge and the streets thronged with late evening revellers. Joy was slightly surprised to note that many of the shops sold lingerie, and strappy, stilettos. That was until she peeked closer to discover they were all fetish shops. Unwittingly, she'd been wandering past the clubs and parlours, smiling at the doormen and enjoying the atmosphere without realising exactly what went on behind these curtain fronted doors.

Rejecting several invitations to go inside Joy had decided enough was enough. She thought the Moulin Rouge was merely a vaudeville dance hall, not a modern-day peep show venue. We giggled and commented on sights as we strolled back towards our perfectly prim and proper hotel. We occasionally noticed girls standing alone in doorways, then disappearing with a suited bloke up an alleyway, in the blink of an eye. It was strange but reassuring to note our little abode was so close yet so far from such decadent debauchery.

The next morning it was still raining. Searching out a café for petit-déjeuner took a little while as prices varied. Some places appeared way too expensive.

It was touring time. A trip up the Ave. de Champs-Élysées and back again. Ignore the rain. This is Paris. The Arc de Triomphe is massive. It's London's Marble Arch on steroids. The views down the avenue and north west towards the business quarter are exceptional. Banks, shops and car show rooms line the pavements down both sides of the Champs-Élysées. The car show rooms were displaying Formula One cars and other un-obtainables. Every crossroads offered sideways views of even more landmarks and resplendent buildings. It's a long, long road but every step is worth the blisters.

The roundabout at the Place de la Concorde is huge as we approached on foot. It's the largest square in Paris. It's constantly busy, handling at least four lanes of traffic. Government buildings line one side, the Seine runs close by and the Palais Bourbon stares back from the opposite bank. The grand entrance to the Tuileries Gardens completes the panorama. We had to stop and allow our brains to take it all in. Here, was the final view Marie Antoinette had of Paris as she knelt to place her head on the guillotine. The monument, now standing in the centre of the square is the 3,000-year-old Luxor obelisk, which was given to France in 1833. The obelisk is one half of a pair, taken from the tomb of Ramesses II. In return the French sent Egypt a clock that didn't work and apparently, still doesn't to this day.

We walked through the gardens of the Tuileries and stopped for lunch in a classical Parisian restaurant close to the Louvre. I wanted French onion soup. What else is as appropriate in such a propitious location?

We then made our way along the bank of the Seine to the Cathedral of Notre Dame. The route we took didn't look all that different to a wander along the banks of the Thames at Westminster. We have traipsed almost 4 miles already today. There were long queues to enter this most famous of all French cathedrals. We sneaked in through the out-door, and strolled around the opposite way to the flow. It's a very imposing building from the outside but appeared very disappointing inside. Those in higher places had elected to install vending machines, offering a choice of candles, rosaries and other iconic knick-knacks. I would not be surprised if they installed machines where you have to steer the claws of a crane to 'win' your chosen icon. The crush and cacophony coming from the hundreds of visitors that flocked around everything at every step made it an unpleasant experience. The Sacré-Coeur took higher marks for presentation than here. The famous organ, which was first built in the 15th century makes up for any disappointment. It holds the attention of all those that look up to the stained-glass windows beyond. The surrounding balconies and arches holding up the roof, would be every bit as calming as the Sacré-Coeur, if there were far less people jostling for elbow room.

Onwards we trudged to the Latin quarter where street markets proffered plants and trees in small pots at exorbitant prices. We looked at books in famous bookshops. The Latin Quarter is as popular as any attraction in Paris but it's in danger of being too brash with its attitude to tourists and ripping folk off.

We strolled by the Sorbonne, and carried on, hoping to find a good restaurant for dinner. Most of them were closed this early in the evening, the door signs suggesting they opened at 9pm.

We decided to take the metro to the Place d'Italie and in the fading light we strolled back up the Ave. des Gobelins, enjoying the evening bustle from the bistros and brasseries as we passed, until we found an old-style French restaurant tucked down a side street. As we entered, it looked like there was no room, as we hadn't booked ahead. The delightful lady in charge squeezed us into a dark corner and produced the day's menu. She informed us the menu is only created once they have purchased the fresh meats and produce each morning. The wine list was extensive and the meal expensive, but tucked away restaurants in Paris are *the* places to eat out, when you can grab a table.

We ambled back to the metro and returned to our hotel feeling we had accomplished a great many things today.

We were greeted by rain once again in the morning. We rode the metro to Châtelet. Much of this journey was overland. It gave a good insight into various districts. Some nice, some slums. We alighted close to the Pompidou Centre. A carbuncle of monstrous proportions. It looks so out of place. We hid from the rain under a clear Perspex awning of a café. We made a run for a shopping precinct but that was almost deserted. We need to make a decision. We concluded, today was an indoor day. The rain lashed more frequently than a leaking puppy on your living room carpet, with the same depressing results.

The Louvre was the place we chose to visit. Despite many other museums and galleries of high reputation it's a magnet for everyone. It's an amazing complex of buildings but once inside, on a busy day you might as well be in Debenhams on the first day of the sales. It's manic. There is little or no chance to enjoy looking at the spectacular works on display. People just barged their way through, recording images on their phones without looking up. The noise in every hall is more like a cattle market auction room, than a sanctuary of priceless art.

In addition, there's far too much to see in one visit. There are enormous paintings that require an uninterrupted view to see them properly. We did our best to get around and enjoy the works. I don't get the many biblical pieces, depicting severe violence and horror. What's the idea of painting a picture of a bloke with an axe sticking out of his head? Or bare breasted women holding up a severed head (John the Baptist) over a dinner plate? There are countless depictions of naked men lolling all over each other in sham biblical settings, with cherubic angels gathering at their feet. It's no wonder the religiously vigorous were so screwed up in the middle to late ages. I had to find a section where the art is more aesthetic and pleasing to the soul. Thank goodness for Giovani Panini. His depictions of Rome's architecture are absolutely beautiful. Once we had entered the halls displaying the great Renaissance and Baroque artists, the ambience changed and we could take more time over the works. For myself and Joy, these are well worth seeking out. We could not get up close to see Mona Lisa and her unfathomable smile, the area around her was totally packed with voyeurs. Such a small painting, so much fuss? I guess her eyes followed us as we passed by, they have that ability. What I do know, is that her husband was known to be a slave trader.

We had to leave too soon, due to the crush. It was stifling, like being stuck in the underground waiting for a delayed train. Besides, we peeked through a window and it looked like it had stopped raining. It took 25 minutes to find an actual exit. It's like the Crystal Maze in there. You see a sign that says sortie, but then after passing through a few doors and down stairwells we were no nearer an exit. Eventually, we made our way back to the main entrance. The queues to enter were out the doors. And so were we. It had stopped raining.

We next took the metro to the Eiffel Tower. Joy's eyes lit up once more as the pinnacle, from ground level, is miles up those tapering girders. From underneath, it is an awesome sight. So was the queue for tickets and the lifts. I reckon an hour or more at least just to get to the box office.

We could not wait if we wanted to. A hailstorm shattered the skies and our ears were nipped by flying pellets of ice as we legged it back to a subway and cover. That was as close as we got to ascending this most famous of all landmarks. But at least we managed to stand underneath and look up and marvel.

Bastille

The train we now took dumped us at Austerlitz station. I'd passed through here a couple of years ago on my way to the Loire. The temptation to board a train and supper in some distant village was almost too much to resist but we decided to walk to the nearby Gare de Lyon instead. After a short coffee break, we headed to the Bastille area. There was an art exhibition on in a market square and since we'd cut our visit to the Louvre a bit short, we had a mosey around in a more peaceful setting. The works on display included impressionist, cubist and a nice selection of Dutch and Norwegian artists from the Baroque era. Several of which could have adorned the walls of our home, if only we had the finances.

There are a lot of hippies, bikers and layabouts at the Bastille. It was entertaining, as the streets buzzed with police sirens and street artists. We bought bread from a popular artisan boulangerie, and a few bits of ham and cheese for supper tonight in our hotel room. We wandered, almost aimlessly, around the district for the rest of the afternoon. It's an easy way to get a bit lost but there's always something to attract the eye. We ended up at Voltaire metro and returned to our hotel. Along with the red wine we had kept from the Eurostar journey this proved to be a fantastic supper. Rustic and wholesome. We stared out across the rooftops from the open window of our garret room. If I knew the words I could have burst into song and an aria to my very own Mimi from Puccini's La Bohème.

After supper we wandered out in the cool evening air. The rain stayed away and as we circumnavigated a very high walled cemetery, we stumbled upon a café called Flunch. It was a buffet kitchen place where the real Parisians eat out. School tables and self-service stalls, offering all types of food stuffs. It was here we had dessert. We noted this as a potential venue for lunch on our final day.

Montparnasse

The easiest way to plot territories to explore in Paris is to begin at a railway terminal. There are so many to choose from. Today, we elected to head to Gare Montparnasse. It is an enormous complex. With my bundle of underground tickets, we can pick and choose wherever we fancy in the city. Once we reached the station, we could not find our way to the surface. There were plenty of sortie signs but most just led us to another platform. There must be a dozen exits from this place but if you emerge into the daylight at the wrong point you might be several, wide, and very busy streets away from your intended destination. We eventually followed a scruffy looking lad through a metal sheeted door that looked more like an entrance to an abattoir than an exit from a railway station. However, it did bring us to the surface, squinting into the sunlight.

We are in the 14th Arrondissement. This area was once outside the confines of Paris and was somewhat run down back in the day. Now, it's very much a part of the metropolis and has a healthy student population and is a magnet for nightlife and entertainment. We however, are looking for just a few hours of daylight distraction as we wander the streets.

The Rue del la Gaite was a good place to start our mini tour. It is crammed with bars, clubs, small theatres and mid-priced trattorias. Boutique hotels proliferate so it's just the place for a short break weekend, a show, dinner and revelry. The bright sky-blue frontage of La Comedie Italienne stands out amongst the predictable façades of the surrounding businesses. It's a legacy of when this street lived up to its name in colour as well as activities. Crossing the junction at Blvd. Edgar Quinet, we were spoilt for choice, as alleyways lead in different directions. This whole area is popular among students and visitors alike and has more than your average number of creperies. The galettes they serve have a distinctive Breton bias. I'm normally one for sweet toppings on my crepe but the darker flour used to make the galettes are ideal for savoury lunches.

We took a break in a shopping centre on the corner of Rue Montparnasse and Rue de l'Arrivee. Inside the precinct there was a shop chock full of cowboy boots and other American leather wear. I could even buy a ten-gallon hat (what's that in litres?). In C&A we spotted a coat that fitted Joy perfectly. What is it with the C&A chain that the Brits don't fancy? Branches proliferate in Europe but not in the UK.

From the roof of this precinct, we could watch the traffic below as youngsters sat around, chatting or skateboarding. Behind a glass wall was a cluster of beehives, a children's garden and other unusual curiosities on this city centre roof top. The sun was finally warming, and the café bars beckoned. Joy fled to a postcard rack and I ordered soft cooling drinks. We then sat and people watched in the afternoon sun.

On the roads, scooters and motorbikes flashed by, when traffic lights allowed. They were everywhere. Every centimetre of kerbside and pavement space was taken up with hundreds, probably thousands of bikes throughout the district. Cars and buses all got along nicely with these two and sometimes three wheeled contraptions. It certainly looks like the best way to get around Paris if quantity was the deciding factor. Walking along Rue Montparnasse, we passed the restaurant La Coupole, opened in 1927 and famous, due to the patronage of artists and writers, such as Picasso, Hemmingway and Joyce. It has retained an Art Nuevo décor inside and serves the most amazing fruits de mer.

Turning right into Blvd. Raspail we walked to the Place Denfert-Rochereau. Here is where the Catacombs containing human bones and skulls are stacked along the underground walls and caves. The Museum of Liberation is based here too, and still more bars and cafes along many of the side roads. As an Emergency Nurse Practitioner, Joy has seen enough bones in her life time, (although they were for the most part, still attached to the rest of the body). So, we chose to just take in the scenery outside and made our way back along Rue Froidevoux. We had circumnavigated the exterior walls of the Montparnasse cemetery. This is worthy of a visit. It might seem morbid, but there is something enlightening about paying respects to those that perished during war times. This is an exceptionally well-kept and designed park and cemetery. The paths have street names and it is all very orderly, without being regimental. It's like a solemn version of Central Park in New York. It's so peaceful in here. Along the paths, well-maintained crypts and headstones occupy the lawns. There are memorials of all shapes and designs. Some modern constructions are amongst the traditional stonework for the wealthy deceased. There are quite a few famous names in here, which add to the occasion. Jean Paul Sartre, Serge Gainsbourg and Alfred Dreyfus for starters.

Oddly, it's a triumph to note that these three guys appear in book form on my shelf at home.

The bars and cafes along the route back to the metro were beginning to fill with young revellers. We finally headed back to Montmartre, once the afternoon began to change into its own evening wear.

As we travelled on the metro, there are overland sections which give an elevated view of many streets. We passed one building that had grass laid on the outside of vertical walls. The Seine looked majestic in the twinkling twilight. Paris was the first city in the world to have electric lighting and it is why it is called the City of Light. The Eifel tower was glittering with a thousand light bulbs, reminding everyone of this pioneering achievement.

We found a small brasserie on the corner and dined simply. An elderly French couple sat at the next table. The man struck up a conversation with us and we could tell he loved his wife so much. Sixty years of marriage he said, his watery eyes, proud as a lion. He held her hand and spoke softly while looking into her eyes. They paid their bill and got up to leave. The old fellow could hardly walk, as the octogenarian lovers helped each other slowly to the kerbside, he straightened and buttoned their jackets, waved a farewell to us and turned away into the night. Paris.

In the morning the rains had stopped, so we headed out early, back to the Bastille district. We walked along the side of the Saint Martin canal. It's very pleasant along here. The moored boats, two-deep in places, gave a seaside feel, rather than the centre of a city. The blossom was evident on the trees and the weak sunshine felt so much better on our faces despite the chill air. The canal flows via a lock and a tunnel, into the Seine. In our tourist book we noted a street market operates daily somewhere near here, but we couldn't find it. However, wandering at random sometimes pays off and we stumbled upon an ethnic African street market, just off a main road. It was much like London's Brick Lane, with many colourful and unfamiliar fruits and vegetables on the stalls. The traders that hassled us as we passed, added an edge to the ambience that we didn't like. I did find some amazing lavas puff bread in a Turkish shop behind the market stalls. It was a cross between a Naan bread and a big sticky bun. I also bought some other bread that looked delicious, but it was far too quirky on the tongue as it was infused with jasmine flowers and salty spices. Weird!

We did note, as we drifted away from the market and zig zagged through back street shopping alleys that most, if not all the shops were closed. 'Pressures of the economy,' I surmised. We did find a café open for lunch which served a fabulous ham salad with apricots and a deliciously curious cheese included. Before we finished eating, a strong wind had kicked up and we had to huddle behind the café awnings for a while. Once we made our way to our next point of interest however, we noticed folk were either selling or carrying little bunches of lily-of-the-valley flowers. Curious. As we made our way back across the city this vision was repeated everywhere. Very curious.

Madeleine

We made our way to the upmarket district of Madeleine, which is close to the Place de la Concorde. The focal point here is the Greek styled church building, in the middle of a square. The reason for the deviation from the Parisian style of architecture was because the building was originally built, in honour of the triumphs of Napoleon Bonaparte. What drew my attention more were the underground public toilets, which are worth a visit beyond purely bladder relief. The décor is decidedly Parisian, with ornate tiled walls and it is beautifully maintained.

This busy traffic interchange is home to a cluster of classy shops. Most of them shut today! What the hell is going on? It's a Thursday, the first of May. Aaaaaah, the centime dropped. It's the May Day holiday and unlike the Brits, who always wait until Monday for a Bank Holiday, the French drop everything on the specific date. Typical French impetuosity. This also explains the Lily-of-the-valley incursion. It's been tradition for centuries for 'peasants' to flock into the city at this very moment to flog the stuff.

We were now standing in the posh bit of Paris with no place to go. The caviar shop, the chocolate shop and the honey shop were all closed for the day. Even a brilliant looking German clothing store with lederhosen clad mannequins in the window was zumachen.

We shall return.

The sun finally forced the rain clouds to stop assaulting us so we could wend our way back to the hotel via Gare de Lazare and the Place de Clichy. Incidentally, part of my attraction to railway stations is to note the destinations, when we return to explore more of France via the iron horse. This is the beginning of a sojourn that will take us to so many places all across this amazing country. I have trouble working out the Arrondissements in Paris. It can be confusing when checking out guide books. Montparnasse for example, is often referred to as in the 14th or the 15th arrondissement. Place de Clichy is the border for no less than four of these invisible territorial boundaries.

Our last tango in Paris was booked for this very evening. A French cuisine restaurant, away from the beaten track and frequented by locals was our plan. We'd found it the night before on our little wander, and reserved a table. OK, it was Italian, not French, but it suited our desires in every other way.

It turned out to be the perfect finale. The waitress at our table was a dizzy student with all the charm of young dizzy students. She had a beautiful smile and a disarming innocence of all things culinary. Her grasp of the English language was thin. Our French, thinner. We could only communicate cryptically through the words on the menu. She tried to describe vegetables as she did not know their equivalent translation. We were none the wiser and they didn't appear in our French phrase book. We ordered a glass of Prosecco as an aperitif and a bottle of Gavi with the meal. The Gavi never showed up. The food, as with every meal we'd eaten this week, was perfect. Langoustines with risotto for me. These guys were bigger than a claw hammer. Joy's two veal escalope came only in size tens. Simply cooked and superbly presented. As we ate, many people entered the restaurant only to be turned away. Everyone else was gathered round their tables in perfect harmony, to eat, drink, enjoy and not annoy other diners with loud cackling and flying bread rolls. Our waitress got a little flustered when we asked for the un-delivered wine to be removed from the final bill but it didn't detract from the enjoyment at all.

Strolling back to the hotel, Joy and I reflected on something else memorable and possibly very Parisian. Before the meal, we had stopped in a bar close by. Sitting at a table beside us was an elderly woman. Her face, painted in glaring theatrical colours, like a peacock gone blotchy. Her wrinkled complexion added to the regrets of a beauty long since passed. She sipped Dubonnet from a schooner. A short time later, a guy came into the bar to greet her and sat beside her. He was perhaps about 45 years old. As he embraced her respectfully and gently, he had tears rolling down his cheeks. Evidently, he had not seen her for a long time, they were certainly compatriots from a bygone era. He was humbled in her presence and could not but wipe tears from his smiling cheeks.

It was a classic moment to witness, like a film we had inadvertently become extras in. Such a sensitive, powerful and emotive moment. It sums up Paris. A bit haggard, over daubed in parts but real warmth and style still peeking through the fascia. It has charm, decorum, decadence and decay. It's such an emotive city. You cannot fail to be impressed, despite its tired old limbs and oversubscribed tourist community.

A morning without rain. We're going home today. We wandered off down towards the city centre once more. Breakfast near Opera. It's a massive building with statues of all the great composers lining the top tier. I don't think I saw Sasha Distel up there but nevertheless, it's very impressive.

We stumbled to the Colonne Vendôme and spotted the Ritz hotel, where Princess Diana revolved through the doors for the very last time. Black windowed limos sidled up to the entrance with regular monotony. Scruffy oiks emerged and disappeared though the famous doors. We strutted the square taking photos of me in front of all the classy watch shops. It confirms I don't spend nearly enough on the watches I buy.

Then it was back to Madeleine and the specialist shops. Everywhere was open and so expensive that you could soon exceed your credit card limit on just frippery. Caviar, champagne, foie gras. Even chocolate was prohibitively expensive, but the honey shop made the trip all worthwhile. The old hag in the shop said I could taste only three different types for free. How ridiculous! The younger sales guy that subsequently appeared however, kept opening sample jars and digging a teaspoon in for me to try. 7 or more wonderful gargles later I picked two to buy. I smiled for the rest of the day and my haul was added to a (rare) white Balsamic vinegar I had purchased from a market stall the day before. My international kitchen becomes more exotic with every trip.

Back now to Flunch for lunch, before we make our way to the Gare du Nord and the Eurostar to England. Just down the road from the Gare du Nord, along the Rue de Maubeage is a row of shops catering exclusively for wedding wear. There are suits here that would dim a firework display and dresses that would make hot air balloons look bulimic. But if you looked more carefully, there's some decent outfits there as well.

As we waited for our train to take us back under the English Channel, we decided to visit more of France at every opportunity. We would make more use of the railway network whenever possible. Paris would only be a hub for us from now on. We can fly into France or bring the car. The best plan would be to take the train when possible and hire a car to get us to the tucked away places.

We are due to come back in less than a month's time. It is now our ambition to reach the farthest corners and the loveliest interiors of France and pass on what we experience for others to enjoy. We might even change an opinion or two.

BOURGOGNE FRANCHE-COMTÉ

The Duchy of Burgundy was once so large and so strong it threatened to rule the whole of France. Territories were gobbled up as successive rulers expanded the boundaries that at one time or another absorbed Geneva, Grenoble, Worms, Basel, Bruges, Brussels, Luxembourg and Lyon. Nowadays, the leading cities are restricted to the likes of Dijon, Auxerre and Beaune. With such a rich history, there are too many places to visit than a mere chapter could cope with. We have chosen the well-travelled railway tracks, that have more than a hint of bias towards the wine growing centres of Burgundy.

Dijon

We took the Eurostar from London St Pancras to the Gare du Nord, and then the metro to the Gare de Lyon. I already had metro tickets, purchased during a previous trip to Paris, which made for a quick transfer between the two terminals. However, our scheduled departure from here to Dijon was delayed for around 30 minutes. Announcements and departure boards changed their minds more than once as to which platform our train would eventually leave from. Finally, two trains were coupled together and we were informed of the appropriate platform. This had everyone flocking to scramble on board. Both trains were heading to Dijon but would then be split, one continuing to the South Eastern Coast while the other headed for the South Western shores. Well, at least we won't be on the wrong service when that happens. We alight at Dijon. We found our seat reservations easily, so all was well.

It was a delightful journey from Paris, as we passed through forested valleys and gentle pastural slopes. The two dominating basilicas of Auxerre could be seen in the distance. That's Chablis country. The views in this region are far more appealing than the ones the carriage windows reveal on the way to Paris from Calais. As we approached Gare Dijon, we were given a glimpse of the Parc de la Toison d'Or, which has a large lake and surrounding walking routes. It is a feature in the brochures to this Capital of the Côte D'or.

As we alighted with our cases on the platform at Dijon, there was a cluster of rail staff handing out envelopes containing a form for us to apply for a refund due to the lateness of this service!

At the top of the stairs just outside the exit was a massed choir of purple apparelled songsters belting out some familiar tunes. Now that's something eh? Your train is only thirty minutes late and they lay on a gospel choir to welcome you to Dijon!

It was barely 6pm. The heat had followed us all day. We stood and marvelled at the choir for a few minutes before slipping away. Joy asked if I knew exactly where the hotel we had booked might be. I muttered something about it not being far, or I would have definitely printed off a map. As she scanned a billboard with a town plan on it, I spotted in the near distance above her head the neon light that read 'Hotel Jura'. It must be all of 200 metres away.

Oh, how we laughed.

We announced our arrival to Julian, the hotel receptionist. He was so helpful and his command of the English language was very reassuring. We asked him if he could recommend a restaurant for us to dine in this evening, and if possible, could he telephone and reserve a table, while we emptied our cases. We were directed to a lovely room on the ground floor. The large window looked across an inner courtyard, with tables, flower beds and sunlight splashing off the walls. When we were ready to head out, we returned to the reception. Julian said that the town was already very busy because there was a wine festival all weekend, so, many restaurants were fully booked. Despite this he still managed to get a table for us at one of his favourite restaurants. Oh, what bad luck. We'd stumbled on a town in Burgundy right in the middle of a wine festival!

Following the map Julian gave us we made it to the very centre of town in search of the restaurant Le Chabrot. It is located at the popular Place Emile. We were served a beautiful meal outside, in true French fashion. The square was mobbed with diners, strolling couples and happy groups in the bars, all enjoying the balmy weather, without a care in the world.

Joy chose Beef Bourguignon (the local speciality). I chose the wine, Crozes Hermitage, which went down easier than Ronaldo in full flight in the penalty box, and a dish of pork cooked in 4 different ways in 4 different sauces. Absolute heaven.

After dinner we strolled through the streets and lanes, taking in our new surroundings. The noises from the crowd in the square grew more distant as we walked along quiet alleyways. In one short street, as we passed an open window, we heard music. Inside, a group of people were sitting round a table, enjoying a private family gathering. We walked a little further and as a melodic folk song drifted in the night air, Joy and I danced together in our own private world.

Our first day was almost over. This felt perfect in every sense. We headed back to the hotel for a nightcap and to thank Julian for a superb choice of restaurant and for booking our table. He was given the task of repeating this feat for tomorrow night. 'Somewhere even better,' he promised.

Glorious sunshine greeted us as we stepped out onto the street on Sunday morning. The second thing to please us were the prices in the cafes for breakfast. Paris really does cost you a small fortune to eat, but here the very same choice of croissant, juice and coffee is less than half that in the capital.

We'd decided to explore more of the town of Dijon for the day. Sunday being still a day of rest in these parts it ought to be quiet enough. We'd met a Japanese woman and her daughter at the restaurant the night before, who recommended we take a bus tour with them, to a vineyard in the countryside. At the price they were willing to pay, I had already consigned that proposition to the dustbin. As the day unfolded, we found we had more than our share of wine and fun, for the princely sum of nothing.

Joy had spotted on the pavement, a line of brass markers with an owl emblem, every 20 metres or so. The tourist map in our hand highlighted these markers and a circuit could be seen dotted around many landmarks throughout the town. She suggested we follow in the footsteps of these strange objects and see where it should take us. We meandered around and up to various impressive buildings and a few statues with interesting histories. In addition, the roof tile designs on the older buildings caught our eye. They pop up everywhere. The polychrome patterns were intended as a sign of wealth and status throughout Burgundy. A bit like Nick Faldo with his Pringle jumpers and socks in his golfing days. They look much more attractive on the roofs of these wonderful buildings.

The first big church we came to was the Cathedral of Saint Bénigne. Outside, a uniformed brass band were mustering and in the corner of the square, a group of small children were playing, dressed in traditional Burgundian costumes. Elsewhere, older folk were hanging about in traditional costumes. Dutch, Flemish and French. I got my camera at the ready and asked if I could photograph the children as we stood waiting. Before I could focus my camera, the rest of this gorgeous little troupe of about a dozen primary school children all ran to gather for a photo call. The parents agreed it was okay and joined in the smiles all round as I clicked a couple of frames of happy, cheerful, innocent faces. It brings a tear to the eye and anger at the caution one must now take when attempting anything as innocent as enjoying the company and laughter of young children.

A few minutes later, the doors to the church were opened and a procession of people, dressed in various traditional costumes emerged into the sunlight to the backing of the now assembled brass band. At the head of each group a proud faced marcher held a placard aloft revealing the origins of the troop. There were people from Poland, Holland, Germany and countries in Latin America as well as numerous regions in France.

There must have been more than a dozen groups heading down the street, with the brass band giving chase. Joy's smile was as wide as the smiles on the children in their costumes, watching the procession. Mine was not far behind. At the bottom of the street, several coaches waited to collect the marchers and whisk them away.

How good was that? A bit of colour and celebration. We walked on, zigging streets, zagging lanes but keeping within eye shot of the little owls on the brass markers. The streets here have been retained since Medieval times, very clean and full of eye-catching frontages, rooftops, windows and balconies.

We eventually came to the Place de la Liberation. Here, the pedestrianised square has fountains that shoot straight out of the ground. Cafés line the semicircle that face the Ducal Palace. This was the home of the Dukes of Burgundy in the 15th century. It has been renovated several times since but it still retains the sheer grandeur of the homes of the ruling classes. It is now the Town Hall but it also houses the fine-arts museum. I had recently read a great crime thriller by Aaron Elkins which was centred on this particular gallery, although he gave it a fictional name. It brought a little intrigue to my overall interest. The museum holds collections of sculptures, paintings and artefacts from all over the world. I couldn't resist taking a look at some of the old masters they have on display. Sadly, the place was closed today. We shall return.

It was time for coffee and the sight of the palace as a backdrop to our midmorning snack could not be passed by. We had a light lunch of Croque Monsieur for me and a pizza for Joy, which she regretted, since my choice was fabulously light and tasty. I had ordered in French as well and my cold milk with a raw egg and a sprig of lavender was the talk of the café for days afterwards!

Dijon, being famous for mustard, meant that I would normally have purchased a jar to take home, but home was going to be a few weeks away. So, I settled for a bottle of rather fine local pinot noir and a tee shirt embroidered with a small bunch of grapes, underscored with a slogan in French. At least I hope it was a bunch of grapes and the slogan doesn't actually translate as; 'Piles, needn't be this big'.

The next church we came to was the Notre Dame, at the bottom of the hill. It's tucked in the Rue de la Chouette. On the north wall is a stone carving of an owl (chouette). It is quite polished in appearance due to the fact, that people passing are supposed to press their left hand on the statue to bring them luck. The owl is the symbol of Dijon and that explains why the brass markers Joy has been following all day feature an owl. What was more striking were the rows of gargoyles that are erected on the wall. There are over 50 of them. All defined, distinctive and very ugly. Legend has it that the gargoyle represents evil money lenders. In the 13th century a groom arrived for his wedding and before he entered, a gargoyle broke free and dropped on his head. His occupation, (the groom, not the gargoyle) was 'money lender'. That's what I call paid back with interest.

I made a gargoyle face at Joy when she passed an ice cream vendor without stopping. I had hardly wiped the melted bits from my shirt when we entered another square, this time with stalls set up for folk to taste and buy wine. This was fun. For a few Euros I was handed an embossed tasting glass and a few samples to try. I did my swirling and swallowing bit and got to keep the tasting glass, which had an image painted on the side with the same small bunch of grapes as the one on my new tee shirt. Perhaps I'd translated the slogan wrong after all.

Happy as Hooray Henrys in the hospitality tent at Henley, the brass markers led us to the High Street. Joy had hardly stepped more than a foot or so adrift of these treasure hunt tokens all the way round. The High street was lined with people. Banners hung from the lamp posts and bunting stretched over our heads from one side of the road to the other. We sat on the edge of the pavement to see what it was all about. After about 20 minutes and several deliberations as to whether I needed more ice cream or more wine, we caught sight of a brass band marching down the street from away up the hill. It was not the same brass band we'd spotted a couple of hours before. They marched by, they played, everyone clapped and then nothing. 5 minutes later, another group came down the street. This time it was Indian music. This troupe had a fire eater, a dervishly attractive female dancer and a few guys blowing karna trumpets and banging daya drums to an identifiably Indian rhythm. 5 minutes went by and yet another group. Different costumes, different nationality and so on. This tempo kept up for over an hour. The parade we had witnessed in the morning reappeared. Each party held up a banner displaying their origin. We were entertained by clog dancers in peasant dress, Samba dancers in garish orange and yellow costumes and all the children, proud but self-conscious, trying to keep in step with the slow march. At the very end, from Britain, a pipe band, from Shirley near Birmingham. Kilted and marching with gusto as only bagpipe bands can do. Goose bump time for me.

Each troupe had a few minutes to themselves with the crowds before the next lot shuffled up behind. The folks crowding the pavements were good natured, friendly and loving it. Especially one couple we'd both noticed. They were standing opposite us on the other side of the road. They must have been in their late 30's. He, a tall balding type and she with short blonde hair. We never saw their faces. They were kissing and snogging the whole time. Stuck together at the lips like glue. I got a photo and I'm going to send a copy to his wife. Those two were definitely not married to each other.

On Daddy's shoulders, close to the kissing couple, perched a poppet of a tiny child. She had a perfect view of the procession from her lofty lair. As the bands approached it was obvious that they were a little loud for her tender ears. She spent the whole time pressing her palms to the side of her head as she enjoyed the spectacle. After the pipe band played the crowds began to disperse. We too headed back towards the hotel, still following the brass markers of course. What a day? What a find!

Our Japanese friends would no doubt return from their trip, delighted with their vineyard tour, but a whole barrel short of the vintage memories we drank in today.

We had time for a coffee and Kataifi from a Turkish café and then back to the hotel to change for dinner. Julian promised the restaurant he'd chosen for us would top last night's experience. Just a little further along from where we ate last night, is the Hotel le Sauvage. We were led into the courtyard, which was as old as your great granny's granny. Vines covered the beams; climbers scaled the walls to tiny windows and underfoot we tackled cobbled paving. Our table was located under the vines. The service was perfect, champagne equally so and the wine gorgeous, Saint Veran for Joy, while I opted for the Côte de Nuits. The food was utterly wonderful. Joy had puff pastry with leeks and scallops for starters, while I, had crayfish the size of giraffes and frogs' legs all in a stunning sauce.

For the main course, Joy ordered lamb cutlets with jacket potato. I had duck with a potato and cheese sauce. The perfect complement to my choice of red wine. It's times like these your heart is fit to burst, if your stomach doesn't do it first.

On the way home we witnessed a tremendous lightning storm. No rain, just the skies sparking up like neon every few seconds. We made it safely back to the hotel and thanked Julian once again for his brilliant choice in eating houses. Could he do it once more for tomorrow night? He said he was up to the challenge.

Holidays don't get better than this, I'm sure. It definitely beats the week I spent at my auntie's in Gillingham when I was a kid.

After breakfast we headed off, away from the city centre back through the railway station and to the botanical gardens. There's a natural history museum here as well as a very pleasant walk around the arboretum. The tram service is excellent and it took about ten minutes to get us from the centre of town to the Toison d'Or park on the northern edge of the city. It's a recreation centre with a large lake that stages competitions and training schools for lovers of water sports. There is an amusement park here too. It was nice to take a break from city centre activities for a few hours. We walked along the sandy beach that was freshly raked that morning. Rubbish bins were placed every twenty metres apart, deck chairs, a life guard hut and refreshment house. There's even volleyball and tennis courts. On the lake, canoeists were floating about and all against the backdrop of the Burgundian hills. Many people use this facility to picnic and sunbathe. It's such a great setting.

Instead of taking the tram we chose to walk back to the centre, it was the equivalent of a day's hiking. Evening came quickly.

Le Smart was the restaurant we'd been recommended and it proved to be a bit le Disappointment. It resembled a converted night club inside. Snazzy zebra cloth stools and purple fabric over the chairs and settees. A disco dance floor in the corner and a flash git for a waiter. He could speak good English and ridiculed us mercilessly at our poor performance with his native dialect. He left us waiting for 40 minutes with our pre meal drinks before showing us to a table. The restaurant was almost empty. In the corner, a gaggle of girls drinking cocktails got his undivided attention.

I was inclined to get up and walk away, but Joy said to give him a few more minutes. Four more people entered the restaurant, waited at the bar for five minutes without being acknowledged and left. I left enough euros on the table to cover the drinks and we followed them out. We found a small creperie along the street and dined on galettes and coffee. It was absolutely lovely. Poor Julian, he was so eager to hear our report. He felt personally embarrassed. We assured him it was nothing of the sort. It just reminds us to remember to appreciate the good restaurants.

Beaune

Today we plan to take a train ride to Beaune. It's the administrative centre of the Burgundy wine business. The city itself is a sort of Taj Mahal of the Côte D'or. The route the train takes to Beaune is a wine lover's wet dream. The view changes with each mile. Vineyards reach up into the hills and sunflower fields jostle for attention, like crowds in Vatican Square. The villages we passed through all have magical names: Marsannay le Côte, Fixin, Gevrey Chambertin, Vosne Romanee and Nuit St George, to name just a few. It's better than walking along the aisle at a wine merchant and reeling off the names on the labels, that's for sure.

The stroll to the centre of Beaune dazzles the senses with crumbling but homely dwellings, with shuttered windows and the ubiquitous tessellated rooftops. Beaune prospered in the middle ages due to the weavers and leather makers, but fell in to serious decline when the persecution of the Huguenots forced them to flee. The growing popularity for better wines in the 18th century led to its revival and to the 5-star status it enjoys today.

The city has a walled perimeter, everything inside is photogenic. Tiny alleyways, neat, clean and inviting. The shop windows display tempting products, and that's not just the patisseries with their seductive creations. Inside the ramparted city is the Hotel-Dieu. It's the most popular attraction for visitors as it was built in the 15th century as a hospital, following the end of the Hundred Years war. The cobbled streets lead to many interesting corners and historical landmarks. There are wine tastings and cheese sampling events almost every day in the summer months.

We came here for a special wine tasting event that was being held at les Halles. The building is right in the centre of the town and is like a large cottage, with a sloping roof and flower boxes, filled with colour under the row of upstairs windows. As we waited in the queue, we were approached by a twenty something Australian who introduced himself as John and said he noticed we spoke English and asked us what the queueing was for. We told him about the event, and he said he fancied trying some wines but since he's not an expert he would feel out of place. We told him we are no experts either, he was welcome to join us, and we'd show him the ropes.

We paid our entrance fee of about €10 each and were rewarded with a proper tasting glass and a plastic plate. The plate was required for the many samples of cheese on offer along with pieces of bread. There were at least 30 tables lined up, each with a selection of red and white and sparkling wines for us to sample. We've only got all afternoon, so we had better make a start. The place was very busy.

John turned to me and said he was still a little worried about all this as he knows nothing about wine and spoke no French. I took him to the first stand and suggested he hold his glass out and request a sample from one bottle. This he did, drank the contents and gave it a poor rating. He asked for a sample from the next. He quite liked that one. Then he tried the third. He loved it.

I told him he was now an expert. That is all that is needed. The only other requirement is the memory, or a pencil and paper to remind him which ones he likes. Hey presto, within half an hour he was fishing in his pocket to pay for a bottle or two to take back to his hotel or camper van. I hardly saw him again as he worked his way almost methodically round each stand. I found a few new types that I didn't care much for and bought a couple from the suppliers of those I did like. I was drawn to the Beaujolais producers, Joy disappeared under the crush, or, was it a table, where the white wines were. We came away from there much the wiser and slightly less sober than when we went in.

Back in Dijon in the evening we found another very inviting restaurant within a courtyard and were soon shown to a table to dine al fresco. I ordered a glass of vintage Les Champs Gains Montrachet premier cru, to accompany our carafe of water. Oh, yes, and we ordered food as well. Simple fare really, beef for Joy and lamb for me with dauphin potato.

As we waited for our meal, Joy startled ever so slightly. Across the yard, underneath the garage door, scuttled a discreet creature. The guy behind me at the next table saw it too. Joy acknowledged his eagle-eyed prowess and confirmed it was a rat. Then she saw another. "Did you see that?" she said. "Sort of." I replied. "It was a rat, I'm sure." said Joy. "Shame." I responded, "I've already ordered the lamb."

We saw several more, or maybe it was the same one doing relays. Perhaps it was a rat race! It is to be expected I suppose. It did take away the utopian romance of it all. At least when our food arrived the rat, or rats, stayed out of sight. We strolled back utterly satisfied and the rat was forgiven. We floated gently down into bed with the glow of a day well spent still pulsating in our veins. Or was that just the wine?

Walking to the market hall late the next morning, we were greeted by the familiar sounds of a gospel choir. A stage had been erected and many canvas tents stood around the square. The very same choir that greeted us at the railway station on the day we arrived were now performing to a gathering crowd. For the rest of this week Dijon is hosting a cultural food festival in partnership with hotels and restaurants from Louisiana. There was a craft fair in amongst all this as well. And to add to the misery, a wine tasting spectacle. A Dixie band was marching around entertaining everyone and the atmosphere was really buzzing.

Chefs and culinary artisans manned every stall. They were from some of the top hotels in both countries. Each chef was preparing little trays of some delightful delicacy for us to try. The routine was, we needed to purchase a book of tickets and in return could sample a serving of whatever was on offer from the various stalls. Yesterday, was our wine tasting indulgence, today we will try the foods. Okay, I admit, I did sample a few Cremants.

First, I tried the pound cake from Louisiana. The pastry chef was a young woman with her own version of this famous USA dessert. It came with a fig and was wonderful. There were so many types of food here. Savoury dishes galore, gumbos and spicy chicken, as well as desserts and some things in between. I stuck mostly to the sweet stuff. I did try an oyster which was set in glacê jelly with a tiny leaf, like a mint leaf. I have no idea what the jelly was but it was superb. Next, I tried a chocolate mousse affair with extra chocolate, 'other' stuff and a jet of liquid chocolate over it all just in case you think it might have lacked chocolate.

I had room for one more sample. A second portion of a summer fruits dish with a raspberry yoghurt type dollop smothered in a raspberry sauce. Ha, ha, I had the very last one. The guy behind the counter pouted to the queue that it was now all gone. The queue behind me then pouted back.

It wasn't all food. I did chat to a great bunch of French lads working on a stall stashed with American Football regalia. Joy had been indulging too but she was dazzled by the Dixie Jazz Band playing all that ragtime stuff as they strolled through the crowds. It felt like we were on a trip through New Orleans. It was fabulous. The band stopped occasionally to receive gratuities. We circumnavigated this market of tented delicacies three times. I was fit to burst with all my treats. We finally retired to a café for a cool refreshment of the lemonade kind and watched a band on the stage play a few tunes. A couple of guys from the Dixie jazz band joined them to rattle off a few impromptu blues and R&B numbers with a ragtime twist.

Meandering back towards our hotel, the day and the heat and food and was beginning to take its toll. We rested in the cool of our hotel room for a while before heading out for the evening.

Besançon

It's almost time for us to move on from Dijon. We decided today that we would take a train ride to Besançon which is in the neighbouring district of Franche-Comté. The journey took about 70 minutes through some lovely countryside, that revealed towns with attractive stonework, tiled rooftops and towering steeples. The city is located close to the Jura mountains, and less than 50 miles from the Swiss border.

The pathway from the station took us through a park filled with trees, flower beds and a large memorial dedicated to the fallen during war time. We descended along a path to a viewing platform that overlooks the old city. The history of Besançon dates back to 1,500 B.C.E. when it was possibly named Vesontio, which has Celtic connections. A couple of invasions and subtle name changes later, the 'V' became a 'B' and by 1243 C.E. it secured its current moniker. The river Doubs bends like a horseshoe here, which provides extra protection to this fortified city. It's a great view from the platform.

We made our way down to the road and crossed via the bridge into the old city, passing a large synagogue, built in 1871 in the unusual orientalist neo-Moorish style, especially for a Jewish place of worship. Along the opposite bank the fascia of what is now part of the university campus is one long, multi-windowed, three storey building, that was most likely the barracks of this was once military garrison. As we entered the confines of the old city, we were transported back 300 years. Except of course for the contemporary frontages of the shops and cafés and the absence of plague-ridden rats and revolutionaries. It was a jaw dropping moment. This is another jewel in the treasure chest that is France's country towns.

There are many churches and landmarks to pick out and several cobbled alleyways dating back to the middle ages and the Renaissance. At the far end from which we entered is a rising road that led to the Roman amphitheatre, possibly dating back to the 2nd century. Two giant pillars from the same period guard the access to the cathedral of St Jean and associated buildings. The interior of which, was interesting enough but a side room grabbed our attention. It housed a very old astronomical clock. We had to wait 40 minutes before we could witness the next session of chimes. This gave us time to attempt the steep climb up to several viewing points and reach the citadel behind the cathedral. The views across the valley and to the river below were worth the wheezing attack. The city is surrounded by hills so the views in all directions were enrapturing. The citadel was designed by Sébastien Le Prestre de Vauban, like so many throughout France. He was to France's civil and military projects what Isambard Kingdom Brunel was to British constructions.

We made it back just in time to witness this monstrously sized clock with all its functions, strike up a motion. It is an amazing piece of work. Made in 1860 by a friar by the name of Auguste Lucien Verité. He was the son of a wood engraver and was commissioned to replace the previous clock that had become irreparable. For its size, it is beautiful and remarkable in its ingenuity. It is almost 6 metres tall and over 2 metres wide and contains 30,000 components. 70 dials show 122 indications including tidal times for several French and English ports. It also shows the movement of the known planets of the time. Neither of us are much into such horology but it was fascinating to see it whirring away nonetheless.

We took our time to walk back into town, taking in the beautiful scenery and the locks along the canal section. Eventually, we turned away from the riverbank and headed back into the centre of the old city, to stop a while in a beckoning bar to bring relief to our aching limbs and parched throats. Another successful foray into the unknown. Tomorrow, we will pack our bags, check out and take the train 100 miles, North West to Auxerre.

Auxerre

The rail service from Dijon to Auxerre requires a change of train at Migennes. Years ago, while Auxerre was a prosperous industrial giant, the local authorities refused permission to extend the inter-city route through the town. Industry drastically declined as a result and the small village of Migennes said thank you very much. We are still in Burgundy, but this is Chablis country where the main grape grown is chardonnay. Our B&B for the next two nights is the Hôtel des Marechaux. With circa 19th century decorated rooms, a rambling rear garden, a small bar and lounge area and the most helpful staff. It is lovely.

The old city spills down the side of the hill that reaches the River Yonne, where working boats and pleasure cruisers berth and pass. There are three churches that dominate the vista. The largest being the cathedral of St Etienne, but the oldest church is the St Eusébe, which was founded in the 7th century. The other religious building of distinction is the Abbey of St Germaine. They almost line up in a row overlooking the river. The many narrow passageways weaving amongst shops and dwellings, make up the rest of the backdrop and promise an entertaining adventure for our short stay here. We wandered a little through the main shopping area just to get our bearings and tacked through the alleys down to the riverside. We could easily have got lost. Away from the shops and amongst all the private dwellings, we noticed that the streets were all but deserted. We should be used to that in France by now. We did find a great little restaurant close to the riverbank. It was almost empty inside but cosy and welcoming. The food was simple and tasty and the table wine more than adequate.

We made the hike back up the hill to our hotel slowly with full tummies and a feeling of tranquillity in this delightful old city. Our room had shutters over the windows, so light, and sound, (if there were any) from the street was nullified. It's just a shame that other guests on our floor bundled in and out of their rooms all night like barrow boys in a fruit market.

For the next two days, the sun shone brightly as we explored the old city. The lanes were so narrow, twisting between medieval, half-timbered buildings and stone cottages. Some list and lean so much that the furniture inside must need nailing down. The small window frames completed the Dickensian image. Each of the religious buildings too, have so many features that defy logic and gravity. Some archways have beams built into the side walls just above head height and inhabited rooms constructed above them. It was like this down most of the many alleyways.

In the shopping area, there's the astronomical clock, that is a feature in all the brochures about Auxerre. It has been ticking since 1483. The unique aspect of this clock is that one hand indicates the time and the other, the moon phase. Nearby, is a very curious statue which is like something from Disneyworld. It's a plinth with a colourful couple sitting together, the woman has one arm on the man's shoulder and another on his thigh. He is reading a book. The inscription on the plinth reads, Nicolas Retif de la Bretonne. A little research reveals that the character is a French novelist who was born in nearby Sacy. He was known as Retif. This may be just incidental, but the term used in France for someone with a shoe fetish is retif. He wrote more than 200 books and was offered a job by Napoleon. I hope it wasn't as a Footman!

During our wanderings we had a few bright moments that added to the fun of it all. I ordered a hot chocolate in a 'hip' café and when asked if I wanted cream, I replied that he should put everything on offer, including a cocktail umbrella. What arrived at the table was Montblanc in a flower pot. Down one lane was a workshop where I spotted a couple of guys working hard at renovating a very ornate table with gold leaf. They were unrolling sheets of gold, like baking foil and 'painting' it into all the curly embellishments. It was an education to see such craftsmanship. We later crossed over the river to visit the railway station to sort out tickets to travel south the following day. On the way, we passed a garden that was filled with an eclectic array of ornaments and random regalia. The army of idols included Batman, gnomes, the Pillsbury Doughboy, fairies, a saxophonist, Teletubbies and a bomber aircraft. It was a fascinating distraction.

We sat by the river reading and soaking up the beautiful surroundings. The churches behind us, parkland with walkways around us and the wide and languid river Yonne glistening as it flowed by. All boats were safely harnessed to the bank and folk that walked past smiled or waved. As did a crocodile of infants, creating an image of calm and peace. We had the feeling that nowhere else in the world was of any consequence.

Before heading out to dinner we explored the grounds of the hotel which was an oasis of tranquillity. A small secluded copse that in its unkempt and neglected condition was wonderful. We could sit and relax in perfect privacy with only the sounds of birds in the trees for company. For supper we settled on a small Moroccan restaurant tucked down a side street, where the owner was a gentle, kindly man. The slow cooked lamb with fresh figs was superb and topped off a very delightful stay in Auxerre.

Auxerre can be mastered in a day if you set out early. With a car, the very best of this region can be found in the surrounding countryside. St Bris-le-Vineux is 10 minutes away and Chablis, 20 minutes. A wine tour or just hunt through the valleys for places of interest would augment what would otherwise be a stopover here. We had other plans. We've had such an amazing time in Burgundy already.

We had booked a taxi to take us to the station at the ungodly hour of 6am. As we set off it started raining. We have made the right decision at the right time to head south for the sun.

We travelled amongst silent commuters to Migennes, and changed trains for the service that took us to Dijon. Once there, we had time to enjoy breakfast and purchase provisions for the journey ahead. Destination; the south coast and the Côte d'Azur.

PROVENCE

The rail journey from Dijon was comfortable, quiet and swift. At around midday in typical French fashion, everyone around us began to open their bags containing the food they had brought with them for lunch. There was a great deal of apple peeling, sandwich unwrapping and cups of refreshment being poured. It was as if a silent dinner bell had shrilled throughout the carriage. Seeing as we were doing exactly the same it made us feel almost native.

However, no long-distance journey on public transport would be complete without some interesting distraction from a random episode with other passengers. Today was no exception. A conversation, albeit very one sided, was being carried out between a father and son, sitting at a table across the aisle from us. The father resembled a cross between Michael Foot, and a whacky science teacher, who was badly in need of a haircut and wash. His cheekbones and sunken eye sockets had that skeletal look. His nicotine-stained teeth belied the upper-class sophistication of his vocabulary. He suddenly ripped into an equally unkempt and mop haired son of about 16, in a 1950's school master's supercilious frenzy.

He raised his voice so much the whole carriage went silent. He was remonstrating to the boy that he was 'So in the wrong' about something he had said to his sibling, whose name was Tudor.

This paternalistic paddy persisted, even beyond the boy's submission to his father's wishes to 'stop' whatever it was that irked him so. Phrases continued like "You defied my instruction. You did not carry out my order. A contravention of my clear insistence." The boy spent a while pressing his palms downwards and looking around, as if gesticulating to encourage a reduction in the volume of his father's voice. The mother, somewhat more respectably attired, was embarrassed beyond control, and eventually fled to another part of the carriage to sit alone. This left the old man looking even more foolish than his cheap, crumpled and mottled safari suit, (with grey socks and sandals) had achieved already. The mother stayed put down the carriage while the father spent the rest of the journey crouched over in his seat as if suffering stomach cramps, with his hands clasped against his forehead.

I felt sorry for the boy he had berated so publicly, but not as sorry as I did for the other kid named TUDOR. I wonder if his surname is Toffee!

The scenery changed dramatically after we passed Valence, and crossed the hilltops that separate Burgundy from Provence. Descending towards Avignon, the landscape lost its lush pastoral greens, giving way to Mediterranean yellows and craggy outcrops.

The Gare, or in English, railway station, at Marseille is a terminus. After discharging and picking up new passengers it reversed along the same route by which it arrived, before diverting towards the coast. There was nothing exciting to see from the tracks, but I'm aware it is a great city to visit, with a colourful maritime history. The next section of this journey offered gorgeous views of sun- drenched beaches and rocky, coastal glimpses that were a familiar backdrop in 1960's spy thrillers.

Antibes

Antibes followed Cannes, which looked tired and jaded from our windows. We alighted to a warm semi tropical sunshine and the gentle swaying of palm trees. Uncertain how long the walk would take us to our hotel we hailed a taxi. Three minutes later we arrived and were fleeced of our money by this modern-day highwayman. The receptionist inside the Chryshotel agreed that taxi drivers here are robbers. We are a little bit away from the beach and railway station, but we shall walk everywhere from now on.

We dumped our things and strode back into town, a 20-minute trek down the hill. At the railway station Joy complained of a sore heel. I nipped across to a nearby pharmacy to buy a sticking plaster and had only been gone 2 minutes, and already she was denying some slimy suitor the pleasure of her company for the night. Truly, some young wag had sidled up to her and invited his person upon hers for the duration, if she so fancied it.

I could stretch the truth here and say I challenged the fellow to a good horsewhipping and would show him what damage a set of biceps honed on chocolate macaroons could do to his perilously suntanned skin. Just the sight of me wading across the road in my baggy shorts, white socks and Jesus sandals, with my face smothered in factor 30 made him realise just what he was up against! He melted away quicker than card shark in a police raid.

Stopping for coffee we took in the surroundings. There were many British women wandering about who had obviously been living here for years. Probably after residing in some Chelsea mews throughout the swinging sixties. They all looked like dried apricots. Their skin resembling grainy images of the surface of Mars. They each had a neatly clipped and emaciated miniature poodle with them. Even the dogs looked about as happy as an in inmate on death row. This is the French Riviera, where the 60's beautiful people congregated, looking for James Bond or Leslie Philips to keep them in luxury. Well, I'm all that's left now, and it's too late, they've all passed their use by dates.

Antibes is a lovely town in every other respect. So many old buildings, street corners and squares. There are even contemporary shopping precincts so there should be plenty to occupy us for the next few days. We wandered around for a while until we got our bearings, then stocked up with a bag of food to enjoy later on our very own patio. The hotel had a small pool in which we could splash around and dangle our feet. For the first hour, there was no one else to invade our privacy. We then retired to dine on dates and figs, bread and orange juice and a bottle of Brouilly. (I'd brought our tasting glasses with us from Dijon). Tomorrow, we shall choose a beach to spread out on and eat out when evening comes.

The harbour in Antibes is like a playboy's dream. There were yachts the size of battle ships lining one wharf. Some were a gleaming silver or metallic grey. They looked like Teflon covered islands. The customary white hulls tended to be restricted to the small boats. Out beyond the harbour, even larger vessels were skulking in the glistening morning sunshine. Apparently, Antibes is the place where the biggest wallets bring their boats. We discovered that most owners rarely sail in them. A crew of dozens steer them to an appointed bay while the owner flies in to the nearest airport by Lear jet, and merely entertains guests on board before jetting off to meet the boat at their next playground.

One guy I met, from Northern Ireland, said he was there last year and Roman Abramovich's latest yacht was double parked. It was so large it acted as a breakwater so that the beaches were devoid of surf. Unimpressed by all this tawdry wealth, we watched idiot yuppies in the cafes drinking espressos and cackling frenetically into mouth pieces whilst glaring at their laptops. These are, I presume, timeshare sharks with branches in such exotic places. So successful they must be, that their office is actually any bar or café generous enough to lend them a power socket and Wi-Fi, in return for purchasing several espressos, while they struggle to attain impossible sales targets. Mixing these desperados with the aforementioned 'dried apricots,' you get a reasonable idea as to the incomers to this lovely, if fading resort. The old town area is gorgeous, with more side streets than a Hollywood car chase. The beach here in town is split into two. There are mounds of sand on one, and harder stuff for your feet and bottom on the other. Joy and I actually decided to walk away from both and spend the day sunbathing on a less populated pebble beach further along the coast.

We dumped our things a little way from an elderly couple who were squatting underneath a bumble bee striped umbrella. Joy was contemplating going topless. There were few others within sight capable of such a daring feat without the removal of several cardigans, surgical stockings and a tartan blanket. After a short while another couple plonked themselves close by. They were young, fit, agile and arrogant. The girl was soon down to a postage stamp sized bikini bottom (reminder, buy post cards) and just a layer of sun lotion which her excitable man spread almost entirely on her breasts. They did get hot and bothered several times and he spent much of his time on his stomach, hiding a tent peg. Brazen and shameless, but it whiled away the hour or two we spent enjoying the rest of the surroundings. The sea was calm and the sun blazing. We both dried quickly each time we emerged from the wet stuff lapping the shore.

Eventually, the clouds gathered and smothered the sun, even though it tried hard to escape each time. We decided to head back to the hotel and laze by the pool. Then, if the distant thunder became overhead thunder, we had shelter and a bottle of wine in our room. I suggested there might be an easier route back from this beach. A little further along is a tunnel that leads under the rail tracks, and joins the road taking us back to our hotel. Joy's lack of sense of direction is legendary and under no circumstances should she be trusted with deciding on which street the underpass might lead to. We would be in the Italian Alps by now if I'd taken her up on her suggested route home.

The weather cleared and despite the constant whistle of approaching aircraft heading towards Nice, it did not detract from the ambience of being in the beautiful warmth of the French Riviera. Joy tugged my arm. "Is this the French Riviera?" "Yes, darling it is." "Oh, my goodness, I never realised until now. How fantastic!"

I love Joy so very much. I hope they never find a cure for her.

In the evening we strolled into town for supper. Winding through the old streets it was a pure pleasure being in such a charming location. The shops were all busy with browsers. So were the bars, but nowhere was overly crowded. Youths were evident but not intimidating. We looked into and passed over a number of places. Some were too geared for tourists and others too expensive for the pocket. We found a restaurant which suited our mood and ate well. Snails and mullet for me, bruschetta and tagliatelle for Joy. The local wine is more than palatable. In fact, they produce fantastic wines here, particularly the rosé. I love the bottles they serve the table water in. They seem to prefer coloured antique designs with a stopper, or odd shaped carafes. Note to self. Visit bric-a-brac shop upon return to Britain.

Our day was all but wrapped up, but not before we strolled through the warm evening air to the viewing points overlooking the bay. We tarried, admiring the twinkling stars and listening to the swooshing waves just below us. An old church bell chimed the hour from an illuminated tower as we made the trek back up the hill to our hotel.

Unsurprisingly, beautiful sunshine greeted us once more as we laid breakfast on our little patio table the next morning. Another day in Antibes town awaits. Who knows what the day may bring! Though, we both consider today's exertions should be nothing more than a further reconnaissance of the town's alleyways and shops.

We stumbled upon a large flea market. I'd been told there was a daily market here by a woman I met in England a few weeks back. She lives and works here and bakes wedding cakes for a living. She jotted down a couple of recommended restaurants. We passed the street where her office (or café table) lies, but I never ventured to make further contact. The restaurants she mentioned were all pricey. We did peer through the windows. They were all very smart inside but the cost of a single seafood dish had me scuttling away like a startled crab.

This market however, appeared only the once during our trips into town. It was big and very busy. There were many people rummaging amongst piles of bras and other woman things. It seemed more like an open-air jumble sale.

All of a sudden, the heavens opened and it soaked everything and everyone. We made a beeline for cover and pretended to look interested in racks of horridly garish bikinis stretched on sticks.

The rain stopped after about 15 minutes so back we wandered through the alleyways. The lanes were part-shaded and cool as the shadows and sunshine threw contrasts across the walls. Windows adorned with hanging baskets and colourful flower pots were begging for an artist to arrive and capture the scene on canvas. It was all very appealing. The city has been in existence since the ancient Greeks arrived sometime around 400 B.C.E. The ramparts were built in the 16th century and the star shaped citadel on the hill was designed by our old friend Vauban. Indeed, the marina, where all the large vessels were berthed is named Port Vauban. One of the strangest shaped buildings however, is Grimaldi castle, which Pablo Picasso bought as a residence and is now a dedicated museum to his creations. Clever and imaginative as his work is, it's not my favourite style of art. I hope the portraits of the women he has painted are not representative of his past girlfriends. The museum is right next to the city's cathedral. The narrow road that runs along the front of these buildings is a delightful stroll. The rich blue of the sea is utterly beautiful here. No wonder generations of artists flock to the shores all along this Mediterranean coastline.

That was enough exploring for now. We did promise however, that after dinner we would check out the citadel up on the hill. In the fading light of the evening it looked very impressive under the glare of the spot lights. En-route we passed through Port Vauban and peeked inside the boats. The people on board looked bored. In one lounge, a couple of young women were slumped on a white leather sofa, resting their feet on Louis Vuitton handbags as they stared at a giant plasma screen. The high life. Row upon row of idle rich, being actively both.

It was 9pm yet still extremely warm. Joy and I were probably attracting the strangest looks as we prepared to scale the twisting footpath up to the fortress that looked no closer than it did from our hotel. We finally reached the entrance. It was a door the size of your domestic front door but the fortress was massive in circumference. There are turrets at each tip and the path around the perimeter undulated like a mountain biker's dirt track. There was no one about. Silence completed the scene as we stood near the edge and watched the last of the light disappear from view. The ocean, now a black blanket with the occasional flicker of a yacht's night light.

On the way down we faced a small bay. Joy was now fascinated by the fluorescent floats the shore fishermen were using. Some wore miners' hats, which, although practical in every way, looked out of place. We took the route home along the beach we had first visited when we arrived. Amongst the rocks we caught sight of rats the size of pit ponies. The underpass at the railway line was unlit. Rather than skip through at a pace, Joy spent a good five minutes fumbling in her bag for a torch. "It might be full of rats in the tunnel," she warned. She had no torch so she finally elected to switch on her mobile phone. I could not help laughing as she took off like an Olympic sprinter, with only the tip of her thumb illuminated as she ran through the short underpass.

Plan 'A' for tomorrow should be a visit to Tourrettes-sur-Loup. Don't ask me why, impulse I suppose. I'd read it was an irresistible ancient enclave, tucked high up in the Alpes Maritmes hills, with beautiful buildings to match the scenery. We'll check bus timetables and train connections in the morning. On the map it looked a great place to explore.

We visited the Tourist Information Bureau first thing, to enquire about getting to Tourrettes-sur-Loup. There are no buses, or trains and no taxi would take you for less than a king's ransom. No wonder it is still ancient and beautiful. You can't get anywhere near the place to destroy it. I'm not hiring a car. They drive like maniacs here and the 2 million scooter riders all have a death wish. That's Tourrettes off the list then. "F*k it."

Grasse

Plan 'B' was always in the back of our minds. Grasse is 20 miles away and can be reached by rail. After Joy did her usual trick of heading to the wrong platform, we jumped on a double decked, westward bound train. Straddling the coast for several miles, the scenery was breath taking. After Cannes, the train turned north towards the mountains and Grasse, mowing along valleys, cutting through trees and neatly trimming the borders of the little villages along the way. As we emerged from the station into the sunlight, the town loomed even higher above us, amongst a forest of trees and châteaux. There was a footpath marked on a billboard map, which would lead to the summit and the central square. We attempted one route and got to a dead end after a steep, lung bursting climb. Almost rolling back down to square one, we chose to wait for a bus. 20 minutes later and for €1 each we joined a throng of school children as the bus scampered noisily up the Z bends.

This place is fantastic. Twisting lanes, medieval buildings, cafes aplenty, all carved into the steep slopes of this utterly gorgeous retreat. The town began its industrial life specialising in tanning. Despite the high quality it produced its reputation was sullied by the smell of the fluids used in the production process. In the 16th century, one particular producer decided to experiment with fragrances, with the initial aim of masking the odour coming from the tannery. Then he came up with the idea of applying some of this fragrance to a pair of gloves, which he then sent to Catherine de Medici, the Queen consort of France. The fashion for scented gloves amongst nobility spread and Grasse evolved over the next 200 years to become one of the most famous perfume manufacturers in the world. Each August the town holds the fête du Jasmin, with decorated floats and the fire brigade spraying the crowds with fragrant jasmine water. There are tours open to the public at some of the perfumeries and several landmarks worth seeking out. For art lovers, Jean Honoré Fragonard was born here. His fine, delicate skills with the paintbrush earned him a statue, an art gallery and the name of a perfume company.

The views across to the Mediterranean are breath-taking and inside the city the architecture is so well maintained and photogenic. We had a fine lunch and a satisfying wander around the old streets before choosing to find that damned path to take us back to the station, way below. We crossed busy roads, over bridges, under bridges, everywhere we looked, nothing. Eventually, and by complete luck, we stopped at a narrow track that led past a massive pile of discarded beer crates. This was it. Descending like mountaineers into a steep jungle pass we followed the track, which became a path and then a steep straight decline, fortunately with a handrail, all the way down. It was very hot work. The exit of this path was within 5 metres of the wrong path we chose when we were looking for it this morning. We got home to Antibes safely and ended our day by dangling our aching feet in the hotel pool. Another train journey tomorrow perhaps? This exploring is addictive.

Juan-les-Pins

Let's start with a poser. You are swimming in the calm cobalt seas without a care in the world. You are oblivious to everything except the pacifying effects of rippling waves and the limitless expanse of the cooling water. Suddenly, something small and transparent floats right up to the tip of your nose. You can't quite make out what it is at first. What would be your lesser of two evils? The transparent object is either a condom or a jelly fish.

Skipping breakfast, we set off around mid-morning to the train station and the short hop to Juan-les-Pins. It has a long, curving beach, which can be seen from the train as it hugs the coastline at this point. The plan today was to laze about in the perfect heat of the Mediterranean sunshine. All of 5 minutes from departure to arrival and a further three minutes later we were ordering pancakes for breakfast in a small friendly café. The couple who own it had taken up the lease only last year and were working 7 days a week to establish the business, as much for the locals as the tourists. The home-made pies looked delicious and the Normandy flan she served me was more delectable.

The filling was made with apples and almonds, and topped with egg custard, which was slightly scorched on the top like a crème brûlée. The pie revealed the origins of this couple prior to their move to this delightful resort. They wanted to be in a warmer climate and hoped to make their living here, working throughout the year with a just a few weeks off during the closed season. We chatted about our journey and the places we were hoping to visit. They advised us that when we visit Menton, we should seek out a certain ice cream parlour.

Juan-les-Pins has attractions of its own. In fact, it has been a popular bolt hole for the rich and famous since 1926 when the railway station was completed. Charlie Chaplin was amongst the pioneering arrivals, and the town has been included in books and songs ever since. I should not have mentioned this to Joy. She sang Peter Sarsted's 'Where do you go to my Lovely' for the rest of the day. For book lovers, F. Scott Fitzgerald mentions the town in his classic 'Tender is the Night'. The word Pins comes from the Stone Pine trees that proliferated here before rail tracks and tarmac brought the millions of visitors.

The beach front here is a bit commercial. We kept walking until we could agree on a decent spot. Joy had bought 2 rush mats to go with our towels. Many parts of the beach front here have restaurants tucked against the promenade and a claim to a private section of sand. This means they charge for the use of plastic sun beds for the day. They were lined up in rows, like a field hospital. We kept walking.

The public sandy beach farther along however, was ideal, although it filled so quickly after we arrived it could have been mistaken for a refugee camp. I wondered if some of the aircraft flying overhead looking for Nice airport would drop red cross parcels for us all. It must have looked a sorry sight from the air.

People came and went during our stay. One dog was amusing everyone for a while as it yapped and bounced over the incoming waves, but then needed shooting with a tranquiliser dart as it became a bloody nuisance. The owners were told.

Joy and I dipped our sweltering bodies in the sea numerous times. It was lovely. Fish occasionally appeared around me as I gently ventured farther out towards a string of marker buoys. Joy headed back to sunbathe. There was almost silence, and I was perfectly relaxed, until my tranquillity was interrupted by the encroachment of an object, the transparent one mentioned earlier. It all but touched my nose.

Blowing out my breath profusely before sucking in I quickly managed to put some small distance between it and my face. Reeling clumsily in reverse, I managed to create an eddy which brought the object back to where I did not want it to be. A muffled cry emanated from my lips, probably infused with the term 'bastr't'. I finally managed to skoosh it far enough away to relax a little. Did I manage to avoid a mouth full of condom or a face full of stinging tentacles?

Seconds seemed like hours. I looked around to see if I'd swam into a shoal of them. Who knows? Condoms might gather together like eels do in the Sargasso Sea! I'm no expert.

It was a lone jellyfish. Tiny and probably harmless. I tried to relax as I swam to the shore. It was like trying to look cool when you've jammed your fingers in the photocopier. My limbs were no longer willing to make the lucid relaxed strokes to get me out of there. When I reached the shore, I must have looked like a giraffe on a skateboard as I hurriedly strained to avoid being knocked over by the breakers hitting the steep beach. Once Joy stopped laughing, she pointed to a couple of sticks, poking about a foot high out of the sand near the water's edge. Between them lay the carcass of a large jellyfish.

I love swimming in the sea. Fish swarming around me are fine but weed covered areas and floating things are a different matter. I did venture out again but not quite so far. It was a brilliantly relaxing day and as the afternoon threatened the onset of evening, we chose to walk home instead of taking the train. It took about an hour overall. There are beaches all around this peninsula. Bicycles or a car ride would open up an endless stream of beautiful views, deserted coves and peeks at billionaires' properties. Personally, I blame Charlie Chaplin.

Monaco

We bought fresh bread and some tiny buns called Bijoux, from the boulangerie close to the station. They had no change from €20 for my €3 purchase. I told them I'd return that evening as our train for Monaco was now approaching the platform. The girl spoke no English.

Not content to see how the ultra-wealthy live in the surrounds of Juan-le-Pins we decided to go for broke (pun) and head to Monaco, or Monte Carlo, for a wander about. The station there has been built inside the cliff. Already, the place looks exclusive. A large glass frontage at one of the exits led us down a dog-leg path overlooking the sea, to the bottom of the hill. The path opens out to a square, with a church. Joy noticed a display of flowers outside and folk gathering near the entrance. She thought it was a celebration about to begin and positioned herself amongst the flowers beckoning a photo call. I quietly tugged her arm and led her away as the hearse reversed up to the door.

The first thing you notice about Monaco is the narrow-ness of the main road. How F1 cars zip by without careering off at every bend is a mystery. No wonder it's often viewed as the most boring race of the season, there seem to be no passing places anywhere on this street circuit. Today however, was the turn of ordinary vehicles. The city was gridlocked. Nothing was moving and no one seemed bothered. Even pedestrians were in a tail back. Looking down over the wall, the marina stared right back at us in the glaring sun. It too is congested, with flashy boats.

We turned left and headed up the hill towards the big casino, a very famous landmark. Palm trees swayed over the stagnant traffic. Businessmen in sharp suits with mobile phones welded to their ears dashed by in every direction. Some guy was yapping down his phone "If....... could get to the helipad in time they would travel together to .... and fly out from that airport in time for the pm meeting in ...." It's certainly not the type of conversation I overhear in Starbucks in Wolverhampton. Others were reading through documents and looking worried, as if their stocks and shares were about to crash.

The rooftops of the hotels and casinos were now level with the inclining road. They all had garden walks, fountains and statues you don't expect to see on a rooftop. The Monte Carlo Casino was cordoned off at the front as there was a photography shoot in progress. The terraced café looked every bit the type of place where multi-billion-dollar deals are made. We snapped a few pictures of just us, not them. The views were lovely from the crest but it's all too Hollywood for me.

Many of the surrounding restaurants were plush inside and even the street-side cafes were uninviting, since they sported 'reserved' signs on all the tables. Lunch prices were ten times the cost of what we would normally expect. There was a convention being held in the Casino, for insurance companies. I had read that they were feeling the pinch this year and premiums were destined to rocket due to the latest natural disaster. Yet it hadn't occurred to them to hold their annual jamboree in Skegness to save on overheads!

I spotted some gawky, Rupert Murdoch lookalike, outside the Hotel Hermitage - probably the most famous hotel in the region. He was wearing brown loafers that held up his skinny bare legs, blue shorts, a dark blue, zipped up anorak, a coloured tie and white collared shirt. A fag was dangling from his lips and his bonce was shinier than a Christmas bauble. He was waiting for one of the chauffer driven limos that were queuing up at the front to whisk him away to a health farm that he probably owned. He looked so comical with all the shops along the road boasting names like LV and YSL.

In the park opposite, the fountains and pond attracted more Americans than Macey's on Sales Day. All snapping away furiously at a duck on the water. Maybe this little canard was seen as a cheaper lunch? What was more curious, was a big guy who looked as though he could have been a wrestling champion, walking a poodle. He sported a tee shirt with the logo 'Professional Dog Walker'. Full marks for his ingenuity. He looked bored senseless.

Monaco held our interest no more. It's probably a million quid a year just to park your Bentley, but since the traffic was still not going anywhere fast it's hardly worth it. I suspect most folk just wait until their fuel runs out and walk to the helipad.

After viewing a painting in a shop window showing the frontage of the Casino with characters from famous movies from a bygone era, we decided to head back to the station and take a short trip to another beach that we passed on the way here.

Villefranche sur-mer.

We arrived in time for lunch, which was taken at the first restaurant we came to, Carpaccio. We sat and ate plates of tagliatelle and risotto whilst looking across the Plage des Marinieres and out to sea from our pavement table. The bay here is one of the deepest in the whole of the Mediterranean and therefore became a military stronghold for naval ships. The town has a long history of battles, occupation and squabbling. There is a citadel that stands guard which was completed in 1556 by Italian architects to protect the harbour from smugglers and marauders. It has been cited as an inspiration by the French architect Sébastien le Pestre de Vauban, in the 17th century for the many fortresses he designed for the Louis XIV throughout France.

Today, the citadel houses 3 museums and an open-air theatre, it's a bit of a hike to the other end of the bay to get there, especially on this beautiful sunny day, so we wandered into the town instead. It was a nice surprise to stumble into a cloister of catacombs beneath buildings and between shop fronts. This is a lovely feature in this tiny town tucked neatly in this beautiful cove. We worked our way up the pathway that led to the church of St Michel. It's worth the scramble, not least for the views out to sea.

Outside the church entrance stood a rather large, older gentleman. He was standing under an olive tree, dressed in combat trousers, tucked inside military boots. A wide leather belt was wrapped around his ample midriff, well, most of it was actually south of his midriff. It was fastened by a bald eagle buckle, the size of a dinner plate. The well-worn tee shirt was emblazoned 'God Bless America'. He wore a leather biker's jacket. His portly face sported a (Yosemite Sam) drooping handlebar moustache topped by a baseball cap. He stood motionless, with a puzzled face. We left him staring at a pamphlet as we entered the church to have a look inside. It was cavernous, old, peaceful and ideal for a rest after that climb through several distracting alleyways. We stayed maybe ten minutes. As we exited the bloke whom I guess might be American, was still standing there staring at his pamphlet. I have no idea what had caused his stasis.

We headed back down to the beach to soak up the sun. The heat was on. It was another exhausting exercise for us both. We people watched some more but this next observation was just as remarkable as the others reported thus far. An old man in a pristine white suit and shirt walked onto the beach with a slinky Filipino girl on his arm. She was clothed in a green, flowing silk dress and stilettos. They teetered to the water's edge and she leaned precariously over and down to check the inside of one of his shoes and then the other. He hung on to her, like a pensioner to his Zimmer frame. Another man in a suit in front of us wandered back and forth, chattering loudly into his mobile phone. Everyone else on this soft, sandy beach were in bathing costumes.

After about 5 minutes the girl finished tending the old man's shoes and hemline of his trousers and they stuttered gingerly back to the road and solid ground. They hugged a bit and maybe displayed some other affection for each other. They stood there for another few minutes. The man on the mobile finally wheeled away, snapped the phone shut and the three of them wandered off. As the men assumed a deep conversation, she followed sulkily some metres behind. She looked over at the beach, longing to join us lazy gits and I'm certain I detected in her eye, the desire to exchange the old man for something less frail than an octogenarian with a bunion problem. Still, when she climbs out the limo back in Monaco an hour later today with that platinum credit card in her delicately manicured fingers, I'm sure she will have forgotten all about us.

Whilst waiting for the train home another train pulled in on the opposite platform. Shockingly all the doors opened on both sides of the train. The near side was a drop onto the tracks. Scary.

The open doors gave us a view of the passengers climbing off, onto the platform side thankfully. About 30 Saga holiday types were putting on cardigans and heavy coats. When the train departed, they were congregating together at the top of the stairs as if hoping the porter would appear to lug their cases for them. They were all grumbling and shivering in the tropical heat of the day. They must be English we agreed. Joy wandered off to find a drinks dispenser and returned to confound our presumptions. They were French. So, old folk are the same the world over. There's no escaping the onset of crabbit, freezing, old fogeyism of dotage, no matter your race. Damn. I'm closer to that than most.

Further passenger fun was witnessed on the train we boarded for Antibes. Two Hooray Henriettas, with matching high foreheads and swept fringes, had boarded at Monaco. Speaking loudly in Chelsea brogue they 'Yaah'd and Ok Yaah'd, all about getting 'sooooooooo hammered last night' and for their mixed lust for Tarquin, or was it Tudor?

Then, two ticket inspectors dropped by. They often don't. It's an offence not to have a valid ticket before you board a train in France. When asked to produce their tickets, Henrietta the first, claimed that, "the little man on the platform said we could buy our tickets once we boarded." The inspector replied that she would have been told, she must buy a ticket before travelling. She then admitted they don't speak French and therefore they weren't really sure what the little man had said. They then asked if the inspector could now sell them a ticket to wherever they were going!

"Of course," he said in English "But you must also pay a €50 fine each, for not buying it at the station before you boarded the train." Henrietta the second, deflected that her 'understanding of French too, was very poor.' In reply, the inspector admitted his English was perfect, so they could still converse clearly with him.

After a few retorts of "Absolutely terrible, outrageous. This is just not croquet," out came the American Express card and off came €100 plus the fare. If ticket inspectors in Britain could demand a fine on the spot, the commission from the proceeds would afford them one of the boats currently lounging about in the harbour in Monaco. When the inspectors moved on, I turned to Joy and said "It seems the Henriettas were soooooooo hammered for a second time."

Passing a beach slowly as we approached Antibes, I spotted a male sun worshipper, the size of a grizzly bear, loping along wearing only a thong. Oh, how we giggled. The young French girl opposite us had tears in her eyes as she shared in our mischief.

I returned to the bread shop where I purchased snacks this morning. There was a new crew working the evening shift. The first person I asked, reached behind the shelf at the back of the counter and handed me my change.

Dressing up for dinner (not in a thong) we headed out for supper. We dined at a sloping table in a street side café. Next door was a bar with tables outside. It was a bit noisy but the bustle gave atmosphere to the occasion.

A chap was sitting at a table in the pub with half a dozen others. He was one of those types who was not as 'in' with the 'in' crowd as he thinks he ought to be. He spent most of the time lighting up weedy looking roll-ups and trying to impress an un-impressionable girl. The rest of the group also ignored him. He resorted to leaning back in his chair and dialling numbers on his mobile in the hope that someone would answer. When they occasionally did the conversation was obviously stilted and cut short as the person at the other end was obviously busier than him. He resolved to sup more ale and suck on more fags. He tried so hard not to look utterly dejected as the evening wore on.

A large and loud stag party trouped by and headed for the same bar, but they staggered off before ordering any drinks. Phew, that was close. A girl in next to nothing with her thong clearly visible through a chiffon mini skirt, struggled to keep upright as her stilettos refused to negotiate the cobbled slope. It was a slapstick episode, until she finally edged her way to a table where her floppy haired beau was evidently waiting. He already had one girl in attendance and loudly ordered 'more champagne' as she joined them.

The waiter in our restaurant was terrific. He made such a fuss of everyone but particularly an elderly lady who came to dine here with her grandchildren. Nothing was too much trouble with her and despite the restaurant being extremely busy, he spoiled the children as well. When they got up to leave, he actually walked with his arm in hers down the road to a waiting car. Every day is a 'summer fruits' day.

Wednesday, our final day in Antibes. We made the most of it by doing very little overall. We lived it up by sharing breakfast in a café just off the town's main square before strolling round the shops. Gifts were expensive. The indoor market, which morphs into a strip of restaurants in the evening, had a massive stall with so many different spices it looked like a giant paint box. There were other foodstuffs on display too. I caught a stall holder eating slivers of cheese and not harassing customers to buy. She shared several with me and one that I finally tried was added to the picnic lunch we were planning.

Filling up our bag for the beach with other goodies, we headed off to grab the sunshine. Women on the beach here were dripping with expensive jewellery, including watches large enough to use as a capstan on a yacht. We reposed on gritty sand until finally choosing to do one more circuit of the old part of town before heading back to the hotel to pack.

Our next location on our exploration of the Côte d Azur is not too far away. Is Nice worthy of more than just a day trip?

Nice

Nice has been a magnet for sun worshippers to the French Riviera for more than a century. Its beaches and hotels first attracted the elites of Victorian Society, but human habitation (hominids) can be traced back 400,000 years. The city as a whole is now home to more than 1 million people. It looked good today as we arrived from Antibes. We had pre-booked into a bijou hotel, about a 20-minute walk from the water front. It didn't take us long to dump our things and head straight back out to explore the hotspots. The long Avenue of Jean Medecin is a retail focal point and trams run all the way down to the main square and then to the beach. It was such a pleasant walk, and reminded us of Miami's Ocean Drive, but Miami lacked the eye-catching architecture surrounding us here. Today, in the main square, lamp posts were topped with life sized, human figures, which were illuminated by ever changing colours at night. To the right, at the edge of Albert Garden, a stage had been erected, with large screens. A major international event was due to be transmitted, with live entertainment during the evenings. The park itself is a lovely area and curves right down to the sea front. There is an open-air theatre where concerts are regularly staged and during the high season there always seems to be some event or festival on the go. We walked on through a street market, admired the Fontaine du Soleil and trotted down the steps onto a very rocky beach that contained as many people as it had pebbles.

We shared an ice cream or two, and as the sun slipped below melting point on its arc towards sunset, we slipped above sea level and wandered towards the old town. It's a ten-minute stroll and a fabulous district. No wonder the Victorians flocked here. Buskers were scattered in strategic formation to capture and entertain the tourists. One duet, with violin and guitar, had folk waltzing on the pavements. Their musical talent deserving a better theatre than a street corner.

We found a tiny side street restaurant to suit our needs. It was a difficult choice as there are countless places that reach out to grab you. No one from these restaurants hassled us to enter and dine. We were left to choose without a prompt. The staff were friendly and patient and we spent more than an hour trying to empty a large bowlful each of mussels. The young waitress marvelled at my arrangement of empty shells. Unlike Joy and the rest of the world's mollusc eaters, I am the only one she had ever witnessed who lined the empty shells up by slotting them together in a big coil. Joy says I have O.C.D. I just like to be neat and tidy! I polished the evening meal off with a fabulous, tangy, lemon tart.

We strolled in the dusk through the labyrinth of alleyways and began the journey back to the hotel. We stopped outside a jazz bar as a scantily clad individual, in high heels and very tight shorts and a spangly jacket, was loudly showing off among a group of friends. Joy thought it was fancy dress night, but when the guy turned around and we could now hear him clearly, he just wanted to be known as Martine this evening.

At the top of the steps by the tram tracks, I stopped Joy and indicated she should peer towards the open window of a first-floor apartment not 10 metres away. Inside, a couple were making a fuss of each other up against the far wall. We giggled and walked on. Two doors along is the entrance to an adult only cinema. That's probably where all this inspiration comes from.

There were better dressed and less 'freestyle' street entertainers along the route in Rue Jean Medecin. We stopped off for a glass of local wine in a modern bar before returning to the quiet comfort of our hotel room. Our curtains well and truly drawn together!

The street outside was surprisingly quiet all night though we did wake very early as the man in the room next door to us was shaving. We could distinctly hear him swishing his razor in the water. The basin must have been right behind our heads. Joy found the remote control for the noisy air conditioning unit and we filled the room with cool air before opening the curtains to release glorious sunshine into the gloom.

Breakfast was sought from a large deli and we spent most of this particular Sunday lazing on the beach and supping litres of water and cola while grazing on bags of fresh fruit. The beach we'd chosen was further west than the one close to the Albert Gardens. The boulders on this stretch are bigger and less 'shifting,' so we could make a comfortable niche. It soon got too crowded as landing spots were at a premium. Speed boats whooshed passed every few minutes, with a parachute ascending to the skies revealing pairs of legs dangling below. The adrenaline filled trips lasted about five minutes before the next couple in the queue were strapped up and fleeced of a wad of Euros.

We splashed in the sea once or twice and let the world get on with whatever it wanted to do. Towards late afternoon folk began to drift away inland and we did the same. After tidying ourselves up, we walked to the port area. The boats bobbed and made for a photo opportunity, but the quayside restaurants offering Chinese, Indian and Italian cuisine didn't look as attractive as one would have hoped. However, the ferries to Corsica and Sardinia set off from here, which is something worth knowing. The clouds had gathered and were looking a little angry. We needed to move on with our exploration of this little corner of Nice.

Heading up the hill back and around towards the beach area, we stopped at the Monuments Aux Morts de Rauba-Capeu, a memorial to those fallen in wars. It was very tasteful and showed obvious respect to those who made our present peace on this continent possible. Behind the monument is the hill that divides the port from the city centre. It's a fair climb to the top. The summit is an afternoon's exploration in itself. The Castle Park leads to the cathedral, which in turn leads to the balcony overlooking the city, while a waterfall under your feet cascades into a pool below. There is a cemetery for past residents and a separate one for victims of the Holocaust. Walking amongst the trees and gardens, with the Provence mountains embracing the urban sprawl, is the perfect stress buster. In the fading light it seemed the most beautiful place in the whole of France.

As the road wound its way down towards the market stalls the heavens opened, and we had to quickly dash for cover. But not so quickly as to make the rushed mistake of choosing a rubbish restaurant in which to dine. We actually found a table at an outdoor restaurant in the market area. We sat outside but under cover, with linen cloths and smartly dressed waiters.

As the thunder claps rolled above our heads and the lightning flashed across the distant hills we ordered scallops with prawns for myself and a veal dish with a superb sauce for Joy. The accompanying bottle of Provence's finest rosé attracted the attention of two American ladies sitting at the next table. They admitted to being extremely reserved about what would be safe to order in France. A glass of white table wine was their tipple as they piled into pizza and lasagne. Looking ruefully at my masterpiece of French cuisine and at Joy's mouth-watering veal dish they suggested we must be a little more knowledgeable and adventurous about such matters. They also expected the rosé here would be as homogenised and trite as California's, massed produced, pink stuff. How wrong they were. I offered them a sample from our bottle.

They immediately ordered a bottle for themselves, and promised to be more relaxed about the French menu in future. We chatted amiably throughout the meal and learned that they were medical doctors on a rare vacation. They were very pleasant company. Tomorrow, they were heading for Lourdes. That's about 500 miles away. I could only think about all the beautiful places the real France has to offer in between the hotspots of Nice and Lourdes. Such a whistle stop tour will leave them without any real flavour of what this country is truly like. Americans are funny: they arrive in France fearing the food might be a bit dodgy, when a salad in the USA, often consists solely of an ugly chunk of iceberg lettuce smothered in thousand island dressing. They must look at the artistry on a plate here and wonder if it has come from Picasso's palette.

The storm had passed, the American ladies departed with big smiles and we managed to walk back to the hotel in the stuffy heat without ribald distractions like last night, or a drenching.

After a whole day at the beach the following day, we took a walk into the city itself to find the Acropolis. Joy expected an ancient ruin with statues and pillars, I had no idea what to expect.

At the Art Centre we watched a group of hip hop dancers practising their craft, close to the dragon statue, then we turned left and up the main street to be confronted by a modern, boring conference centre named the Acropolis. Nothing to see here folks, just move on. The city map describes it as a place of distinct interest. Even dinner disappointed, as the restaurant we chose failed to deliver in every respect. Oh, well, we can't pick a winner at every raffle. We wandered more and squeezed in our last hours in this gorgeous city before heading slowly back towards the hotel. In Rue Jean Medecin, we watched street dancers cavorting and spinning on their heads and, like the rest of the large crowd, left swiftly when the collection bucket came out.

Nice is more than just nice, but it was a bit heavy handed with my wallet. There are more modest places we could have found to spend our Euros but in general, it still attracts a more affluent clientele. Our conclusion is that the smaller towns along the coast have far more appeal by way of personal service, cosy enclaves and less populated beaches. We will try our luck with Menton. It was recommended to us as markedly better than the big-name places like Nice or Lourdes.

Menton

Menton is the final town along this coastline before we reach Italy. I had been enquiring about various places in Provence that could interest us, long before we left England. There are lovely harbours and bays dotted along the French Riviera which are very enticing, but Menton received the best plaudits.

As we alighted from the train, the sky was blue, and the sun was blazing. That's about the best opening gambit for any holiday resort for new arrivals. The streets were cluttered with people at kerbside cafes. The palm trees along the boulevard added to the balmy backdrop and set the mood completely.

Menton is a picture paradise, as it has just about every conceivable 'wow' factor for the casual tourist. Habitation dates back to the Palaeolithic age. Archaeologists have discovered graffiti from that era in nearby caves, as well as fossilised remnants in the surrounding hills. The Italian (Genoan) border has been moved several times to one side or other of this frontier town, until 1860 when the final whistle blew in favour of the French.

It's a tucked away haven favoured by winter tourists due to a less severe drop in temperature than elsewhere along the coast. A famous resident who took advantage of the sub-tropical climate was an Englishman, William Webb Ellis, the creator of rugby football. The poet and playwright, Jean Cocteau, was a son of the town. A modern built museum is dedicated to his works. Each year the town holds the fête du citron festival which attracts more than 150,000 visitors. The floats and streets are decked out with the most original and attractive displays, celebrating the famous lemons (and oranges) that grow here. Chefs the world over covet this particular type of lemon for their culinary creations. The event is reputed to be spectacular and hotel bookings during the time of the festival are usually snapped up well in advance.

Even without the 'Orange and Lemon Festival,' the old town is still a delight to stroll through. The narrow streets were filled with artisan shops, which easily distracted attention and extracted Euros. We made our way up through the honeycomb facings where every building deserved to be captured on camera. The plaza in front of the cathedral is often rigged up with seating for open air concerts that would be a highlight of any visitor's stay. The view across the bay reaches the hills beyond the Italian border. Stepped passageways lead to tucked away residential properties that invite exploration. When we were done with wandering back and forth up here, there's a nice climb down the other side to the port area. As we walked the long way back to our hotel, we noticed a lot of colonial style chateaux that are now employed as hotels. We saw no tower block accommodation.

We were staying at the Quality Hotel Mediterranean. I opened the first-floor patio doors to a balcony overlooking a courtyard, with lemon trees that I could almost reach. The surrounding buildings were painted in pastel colours, with louvered shutters and wrought iron railings dividing the properties. It all looked so restful and quiet.

I returned from a visit to a nearby supermarket with essentials for a picnic on the beach, comprising bananas, rolls, cheese, ham, wine and water. We hid the wine in the fridge, made a packed lunch of meat and cheese rolls and placed the water in the beach bag with our togs but I could not find the bananas. I see them listed on the receipt but they were not amongst the goods I unpacked on my return. I've no idea how I lost my bananas. Back on the street, Joy soon found the tourist information office. Her sense of direction might be questionable but she'd find a tourist office in Helmand Province. This one was located in a lovely looking chateau. We grabbed the freebie map to consult in more detail as we explored further.

From the sea front you can see Italy. There's even a sign pointing to the place. The harbour was full of proper boats. Sailing boats and fishing boats, there was not an oligarch's star fleet cruiser in sight. There are streets aplenty, with cafes and other attractions all along the way. One beach is sandy and has a sheltered bay for children to splash about safely. The other is pebbled and more suited for doing nothing except applying sun-block lotions. There's a small food market which was very popular amongst the locals. Fresh fish, fruit and other staples on sale. Note to self. Next time book self-catering apartment.

The beach we settled on was the one with pebbles. It was not overly busy. We found a spot amongst the parasols and picnic blankets, which were randomly strewn as far as the eye could see. The shingle may be less appealing aesthetically than soft sand, but at least it doesn't creep in your crevices. We needed stone resistant footwear to walk anywhere however. Joy had bought a tube of roll-on sun barrier cream. We smeared it on various body parts, before settling back to people watch.

Particularly evident were the ageing queens of the Côte d' Azur. These overly made up women would wade out into the sea up to their shoulders. Their heads held aloft stiffly as they treaded water, taking care not to damage their perfectly coiffured hairstyle and full-on rouge, eye-liner, mascara, caked foundation and ruby lipstick. I shudder at the thought of the oil pollution it would cause if it got mixed with water. They looked like a department store had dumped a pile of old shop window mannequins into the briny.

We spoke to one of them. A woman originally from Ayrshire who now lives in Cheshire. Through collagen puffed lips and Botox shot cheeks she told us they come here often but always drive. She revealed that it costs £1,200 for the round trip because they insist on bringing the dog. A bucket airline return flight can be a tenth of that.

Our afternoon passed as gently as the waves rolled onto the shingled shoreline.

In the evening the town was still buzzing. Street side cafes were doing a more than brisk trade and market stalls in the squares were surrounded with tourists, like ants on spilt sugar. We found the ice cream shop we'd been recommended to visit by the lady who owned the café in Juan le Pins. A peach flavoured mini mountain coated my tongue and was as delicious as I was promised it would be. I offered to help Joy with hers as she was evidently struggling. We strolled along the harbour walls and watched a fisherman pull sprats from the water with irritating ease. We took the precaution of reserving a table at a restaurant in the square by a church.

We returned to our hotel to freshen up for the evening. When we disrobed, we could see what effects the sun had on our bodies. More artistically, we could now see what the roll-on barrier cream did to protect our skin. The strips we'd smeared held so true that it looked for all the world like we had stripes. Where the lines did not meet, the sun had coloured my skin bright red. My shoulders and back resembled an Andy Warhol impression of a tiger. This sun block 50 did more than its job. But our application of the crème was so bad it acted like masking tape in a car body shop.

It was all Joy's fault. I had meticulously applied the lotion to her. There was little evidence of stripes on her perfectly browning torso. I was livid. Well, the red stripes were livid. We need to buy a better lotion for tomorrow. One that coats evenly and without the need for the steady hand of an expert sun cream applier like myself.

The restaurant was all but full when we arrived. It had been wise to book. We sat next to and spoke with, a fascinating Swiss couple. She, a teacher who writes books for children and he, a piano tuner of some note (ha, ha). They had cycled from Switzerland's dark interior just to sit with us at dinner. That's over 300 miles. I asked if they were heading straight back after the meal or will wait until the morning! They were very good company.

On the other side of us two little old dears, who I presumed had skateboarded down from the surrounding hills to sit with us, were adorable. They spoke no English but chuckled away and wished us 'bon appetite' with every course. It was a really lovely laid-back evening and the chink of glasses and mellow chatter all around made us feel like we were residents and not interlopers. I could see why William Webb Ellis felt so at home here.

In the morning Joy reminded me that our Swiss dining companions had informed us there would be go-kart racing all day on the sandy beach. "Will we be attending?" "Great idea" we harmonised.

No, we did not attend. We headed back to the beach and fulfilled our promise to laze out the whole weekend together. The sun was up earlier than us, warming the pebbles. We breakfasted well on croissants and cheeses and packed more water and goodies to nibble during the day. Armed with a bottle of very pricey sun barrier spray we were better prepared for the day's rays. I had the task of finding ways of getting the sun to fill in the stripes on my shoulders and back. This sun bathing lark is harder work than people think.

We swam together out to the boom perimeter and just floated in the placid water as it lapped very gently around our ears. When we sank below the surface a clearly audible crackling sound could be heard, like bacon frying in a pan. Most weird. We watched small fish swim about below our bodies and marvelled at the mountains and scenery as far as the eye could see. This was a moment of pure pleasure. Right now, we owned the world.

When the afternoon began to ebb, we strolled back to our hotel. As Joy walked on, I volunteered to nip into a shop and buy more water and fruit. I'll remember bananas this time. For my diligence, I awarded myself a rare treat of a few pieces of Turkish Delight. As I walked home with my heavy load, I had hardly put the first piece into my mouth when a small boy tugged at me from behind. When I turned around, he held up my sun glasses case. It must have dropped from my back pocket. His proud mother stood a little away while the boy spoke to me in French, smiled and handed me my property.

I thanked them both heartily in the best French I could muster, the little boy turned and headed back to join his mum, deservedly pleased with himself for his good deed. I looked at my bag of Turkish Delight and then to the boy, his proud mum hugged him and they both stepped back into the crowd. What a wonderful example of community spirit! I had secreted €100 inside that sunglasses case. It was still there. I felt more guilty each time I reached and ate another piece of Turkish Delight all the way back to the hotel!

When I told Joy the story, she was relieved to learn I did, in fact, give the little boy the bag of Turkish Delight. See? I rarely get treats!

After smartening ourselves up for the evening we sat on the balcony once again to enjoy the cooling air as the sun slipped below the rooftops. A petite pigeon landed on the balcony rail and ate peanuts from our finger tips. Actually, he dropped most of them over the edge to the gravel below. A family with a tiny baby ate al fresco in their own garden behind the lemon trees. A man on a balcony along the way ruined this scene by clipping his toenails and dropping the remnants onto the gravel below. No wonder the pigeon did not try to rescue the peanuts down there.

After supper we explored the old town again. It was quiet now and almost deserted. In front of the cathedral entrance, a stage had been erected. A concert here would be an amazing experience, high above the beach and in the shadow of the mountains. Sadly, we shall be gone before the first show starts.

Back at sea level market stalls abounded, all the way around and down to the beach. It was now dark and after 10pm. The stalls were crammed with jewellery, crafted items and paintings of all subjects. The coloured lights, strewn across the street above our heads, beneath this inky black sky created a real Mardi Gras atmosphere; family groups with children on dad's shoulders and smaller ones dozing in pushchairs. You couldn't buy a care in the world right now.

On the rocky spit at the edge of the beach stood a large tented pavilion. The sides open to the cooling breezes. On the stage, a six-piece reggae band were strutting about while the crowd before them jostled and jiggled. I love reggae. I can't keep my toes from tapping. One little boy, standing a metre away from me had a small guitar and was mimicking the guys on stage. He was lost in the moment. A photographic treasure. An old guy started up a conga and others joined in.

Joy slipped away in search of treasure amongst the stalls in the market. I had found my treasure in the rhythm of the night. For half an hour I was lost in music, lost in a paradise that many people only get to dream of.

When the band finally ended their set, I crept away along with the crowd to find Joy. She had been listening too and had found a necklace that needed only my consent to style. With her booty and my hedonistic state of mind we strolled slowly and waywardly all the way back to the hotel and slept until morning.

After a good breakfast we collected our packed cases and ambled to the railway station in good time for the connection to Monaco, and then another train to Toulon. The beach hugging journey is breath taking, no matter how many times we have seen it. If there's a chance to take a train anywhere between Marseilles and Menton, do it. It's a pleasure in itself. The glittering waters reach the horizon, and the cliffs that drop down into tiny coves are a joy to behold.

Toulon

Toulon is the final city we visited on the French Riviera. It has a name that makes it synonymous with Toulouse but the history, architecture and comparisons don't fit the perception. It's located by the sea for a start. It came to prominence in the late 15th century when a naval base was constructed.

There is still a very large military influence on the waters today. During the Napoleonic wars the port was blockaded for 2 years by the British fleet commanded by Admiral Nelson. It is rich in character as well as culture, with less emphasis on attracting beach seeking tourists than the last few towns we have explored. Though we still hoped to grab some sunshine whilst here. After a short walk to our hotel in Rue Berthelot we ordered lunch and cool drinks next to the Fountain of the 3 Dauphins.

The streets of the old town, that are locked within the busy ring roads are narrow, irregular and dusty. Many of the buildings would have fallen down long ago if this were a harsher climate. Soft ochre facades, blend and contrast between the cracks on the poorly maintained buildings. The retail shops offer unnecessary reassurance against the adjoining dismal, dark wooden doorways that lead to private apartments and store rooms. There is a distinctly Moorish element to some of the heavily shadowed alleyways. The sun's rays barely penetrate them for longer than the midday hours. However, there are plenty of people about and everyone just gets on with their business. We had no set plan to depart Toulon on a particular day. Armed with information that Joy gleaned from the Tourist Information office we had plenty to occupy our attention.

We made our way towards the quayside, taking random diversions through the lanes, passing the Notre Dame Cathedral and circled back through a street market that snakes towards the centre of the old town. The chances of being run over are limited to the ebb and flow of pedestrians only. There were no mad cyclists or silent electric vehicles in these passageways.

The street market that runs through the old quarter has an African feel to it. It caters more for locals than it does for tourists, which is no bad thing. There were more stalls selling fabrics, fruit and furnishings for the home than the usual tat fobbed off on holidaymakers. By the time we returned to our hotel we had pretty much worked out where everything was. Dinner was taken down on the quayside for the sole reason we wanted to dine overlooking the bay. Witnessing the sunset across the water was a bonus. The prices here are more expensive than we had expected but a quayside restaurant has a wealthy clientele, arriving outside their front doors on their expensive modes of transport, so we shouldn't complain. We noted that the restaurants all served very much the same dishes and there was far less choice than we expected.

Close to the open market is a large Carrefour supermarket, which dominates the shopping centre. This came in handy when we wanted snacks to eat in the room or out on an excursion. Today, we wanted an excursion We stocked up with a picnic and took the bus to a beach that had been recommended, called Plage de la Mitre. It's less than 2 miles away and we could have walked it but we soon got the hang of the public transport system here. The waterfront comprises three small coves tucked into the cliff. The first beach came as a bit of a surprise as everyone on it was naked. The second had a few families and some topless men and women and the third, just us. The view out to sea was beautiful, which is more than I can say for the nudists. I've seen less crinkly, discarded crisp packets.

We settled down for a few hours of serious sunbathing, but shortly after arriving a wind picked up and tiny tornadoes of sand, grit and dried seaweed, that resembled tagliatelle, swirled around and then dumped their contents over our bodies and belongings. The exfoliating benefits of the grit was lost on us. I dread to think of the damage it caused the nudists. The tagliatelle must have made the menfolk look like a plate of meatballs and dehydrated pasta.

It was time to leave. We headed back into the city and the old town, and paid a visit to the Art Gallery until the wind died away. The building itself is a masterpiece of architecture. The emphasis in some of the rooms was on paintings from around Provence but I particularly enjoyed the works of a local boy, Louis Auguste Laurent Aiguier. Naturally, coming from Toulon, his subject was specifically 19th century maritime scenes, which demand more than just a cursory glance. There's a large collection of work by modern artists and photographers too which gave food for thought.

Whilst taking refreshment on a bench in an esplanade Joy was entranced by a small Scotty dog that chased a large plastic lemonade bottle up and down the tarmac. It would stamp on the crushed container causing it to spring up in the air and the dog would leap to catch it before pushing it along by its nose until it hit a perimeter wall. She tried in vain to capture the antics on video but the dog always paused for breath at that moment, only to resume its game when she put the camera away.

The city has a citadel. It began in the Middle Ages as a fortified wall. As the military impact grew, so did the wall, adding an arsenal, towers, forts and an entrenched camp. It seems Joy and I have been joined on this trip by a third person. Monsieur Vauban, who arrived in Toulon in 1678 to further enhance the fortifications. As trade expanded to handle the demands of the military, the city began to spread further inland and along the coast into what we are about to explore for ourselves.

There are several buses per hour out to Mourillon where the better sandy beaches are. It takes about thirty minutes to get there and although we didn't take our beach gear with us, it's a very lovely area to stroll along the coastal path and stop at any number of cafes that line the pavements.

The following day we did take our swimwear as there is another superb beach that can be reached by the water-bus that crosses the bay to Les Sablettes. Joy did her best to get us shot by photographing French and foreign naval ships and submarines that were docked at the military base as we passed by. She did this in St Petersburg, not a good idea. She scares the life out of me. We reached the jetty at Les Sablettes without the ferry being strafed by gunfire. The land mass narrows to just a few hundred metres here, and on the other side from the jetty, we found such pleasures as to make any beach bum salivate. Lots of sand, cafes, walks, rocky outcrops and hazy sunshine. And no swirling tagliatelle.

Back on the mainland, after a wonderfully laid-back afternoon, we were promised an evening of upmarket entertainment at the Opera de Toulon for the down-market price of €10 each. A musical performance by the Toulon Symphony Orchestra, with guest, virtuoso pianist Yulianna Adveena. The interior of the theatre is beautifully ornate and well preserved. The performance simply amazing, as we were treated to the music of Wojciech Kilar, Tchaikovsky and Beethoven, played by a forty-five-piece orchestra. Yulianna Adveena had everyone captivated by her stunning abilities. It was worthy of any concert anywhere in the world. She truly is a maestro. For our miniscule entrance fee, we were sat up with the gods where it was excruciatingly uncomfortable. We were perched along a row of bench seats with less leg room than the RSPCA would allow for battery hens. It was worth it to the very last shouts of 'encore' and 'bravo'. During the intermission we could stretch our legs on the grand and delightful roof top terrace, and take in the views of the streets below. It was an absolutely brilliant evening. We just love these little surprises whenever we visit anywhere.

We set out bright and early the next morning to take the cable car up Mont Faron. The journey required a bus ride through streets built for anything but road traffic. We then squeezed into a swaying cable car that whirred up into the hills, opening the panorama of the whole of Toulon. The seascape includes the naval port and beyond. Across the peninsula is the popular holiday resort of Six-Fours-les-Plages. There are hiker trails up here, a zoo and even a military outpost that has a tank and several other shooty things amongst the trees. These weapons are a stark reminder that it has not always been tourists that this strategic location attracted. The zoo specialises in big cats and it's in a nice spot, well away from the bustle of the city. The views to the surrounding mountains and the walks available are ideal for the hiking fraternity. I personally belong firmly in the motorbiking fraternity. The Paul Ricard racing circuit is just 20 miles away. I can understand why race weekend at the track is preceded or followed by a few days down here in Toulon.

The port here provides ferry services to Corsica and Sardinia. This is a good alternative to similar services to those islands from Nice.

We were uplifted by the lovely laid-back way of life that Toulon has to offer. The African feel and ethnic ambience the market and cafes offer were so very different from Menton and Nice. The only intimidating moment I experienced, was the sight of a dog wearing a hoody in a queue in a bakery shop. It looked so menacing as it tried to stare me out, I decided to go and buy some fruit instead. We enjoyed the local breads, cheeses, and a grossly overpriced apple from one market stall.

Whilst standing at a Zebra crossing in the busy thoroughfare, we watched in shock, as a man driving a large car, cut across in front of a bus as both emerged from a side street. The car stopped dead in front of the bus on the zebra crossing, then did a three-point turn, on the crossing itself. Not finished with his display of sheer stupidity, instead of driving off in the direction he was now facing, the man put the handbrake on to consult a map. Another bus, now coming up from behind him slewed to a screeching, horn blaring halt in a blind panic. The guy ignored everyone and slowly found the accelerator pedal and drove off. He must hate bus drivers.

With the Toulon rugby stadium situated so close to the quayside, matchday must make for a fantastic atmosphere here. Joy's rugby leanings, based on her Welsh heritage got her thinking of doing just that one day. I agreed, if there's a motorcycling event on around the same time. But for now, it's time for us to say 'so long, to Toulon.

OCCITANIE

Occitanie is the most southern region of mainland France and covers a vast area, including the sub regions of Languedoc, Roussillon and the Pyrenees Orientales. The most central point is Toulouse. The western border is just beyond Lourdes. Our journey stretched across this gloriously varied and beautiful region. It began at the coastline and occasionally extended inland before we finally made our way to more northern territories. There are so many towns and cities to choose from, this book would resemble a Michelin Guide if we dared visit them all. Instead, we have been a little more selective, seeking out some lesser known locations promising much history, enlightenment and entertainment.

Sète

It's the height of the holiday season in France, so it was no wonder we only just managed to book the last available room, in a downmarket hotel in the centre of Sète. We chose this location because a family friend came here during a regatta and fell in love with the place. Less bourgeois, but equally enlightening was a film Joy and I watched, starring Audrey Tatou, called Beautiful Lies which was filmed in Sète. Everything about this place grabbed my attention for what should be a relaxed and memorable visit.

We arrived by train around 8pm and dragged our cases along the picturesque banks of the canals in beautifully warm, late evening sunshine, to our hotel in Boulevard Danielle Casanova. Despite the rather delightful street name we checked into a dismal looking dungeon that was however, clean and adequate. After a quick freshen up, we strolled 200 metres to a tree-lined square where several cafes were buzzing with diners. Sète is known as the Venice of Languedoc and has the reputation for being the ideal place away from the tacky tourist trappings that travel companies force upon us. The old town is all narrow streets and naturally evolved plazas. The canal system that leads to the open sea is as picturesque as a bouncing baby in a bonny bonnet. We were seduced by all this the moment we stepped from the train.

Let's start by getting our friend Vauban out of the way. The port here was silting up badly in 1686. The renowned architect came along, probably the week after completing his work in Toulon and upgraded the whole site. In 1934 FC Sète were the first French club ever to do the double by winning the league and the cup. You might say, they're the Preston North End of French football. For music lovers, Manitas de Plata, the virtuoso flamenco guitarist was born here, in a gypsy caravan in 1921.

Our first night in the hotel wasn't as peaceful as the ambience was in the city however. The noises from outside our door, through the walls and even from the reception area downstairs kept us awake. Telephones rang, door bells jingled and dogs whined. This ruined any chance of the hotel getting in our good books. We accept that a 2-star hotel would not quite match some of the wonderful luxuries we often enjoy when on vacation, and despite consoling ourselves each day that towels and bedding were changed, and the floors cleaned, night time was purgatory. I used earplugs most nights and Joy even switched on her MP3 player to garner some sleep, but we rose each morning, ruffled, discontented and towards the end of the holiday, pretty much exhausted. The house dog; a doleful and smelly mutt spent most days lying across the bottom of the stairs, filling the area with the bitter smell some dog lovers don't seem able to detect. He was often joined by a cat or two. We had several incidents with one cat. It seemed convinced that opening the window to our room was an invitation for it to creep in. At least the air conditioning and Wi-Fi worked. It was our compromise to go down market for the sake of being in the old city quarter and not the high-density resorts further out of town. The cleaning staff began work at 6am, slamming doors and scraping buckets. Thank goodness we could sleep on the beaches during the day.

On the first morning we ate breakfast in the hotel. It was spartan in that dining room. Apart from the dog that skulked about, no one else joined us. A croissant or bread roll with jam or honey were the only options. After this, we knew we'd be dining elsewhere.

Undaunted, we headed out as soon as we'd packed our necessities for the day into our shoulder bags and set off to explore the old streets and passageways. We soon forgot the disappointment of the hotel and it shall never be mentioned again. Walking up the hill away from the canals and town centre, we came upon the Parc Simone Veil. It's on a steep incline, surrounded by lovely terraced houses in a quiet corner. There are monuments and flower beds brimming with blooms. Paths weave through the trees that snake to a grotto. It's constructed with natural gnarled rock and stands next to a pond surrounded by shrubs and lawns. Giant dragon flies were zooming by and nobody else was about.

The sun was warming up nicely and sunglasses and a hat became necessary. As we walked back down towards the centre, I was photographing some of the local architecture when Joy shot off like a lioness after a gazelle. The gazelle turned out to be a little elderly lady pulling a shopping trolley. When I caught up with her, she said the woman was walking with purpose and that suggested she was heading for the shops and maybe the local market. Sure enough, we watched her duck into a side door of the Halles. We followed. It's just like so many market halls in France and the rest of mainland Europe; an oasis of splendour, noise, colour and choice. Discerning housewives and mothers and several of the male species were queueing at the most popular stalls. Fish counters competed with butchers' slabs along two or three galleys, and just about every other fresh food supply you could wish for. I love visiting these places. We stopped for coffee at a stall that had seating and tables along a raised platform. There is no need to queue, it's waiter service. Piping hot, excellent coffee and other treats were available at very acceptable prices. The waiter was impressively busy because he also delivers orders to many of the folk working behind the stalls throughout the market.

There are bars here too, so we need not leave at all, save for the beckoning sunshine outside. I cannot help comparing these markets to those in the UK. Birmingham indoor market has its virtues but I can't see them delivering the quality of product, service or surroundings that pervades here.

We wandered down to the waters' edge and followed the narrow roads through to the harbour. It's a working town, tourism is an add-on, not the other way around. We carried on towards the amphitheatre which overlooks the sea and from a high vantage point on the rocks, took in the view of the blinding blues and shimmering silver of the Mediterranean. To our right the Languedoc coastline arcs towards Narbonne. A corniche divides the Etang de Thau (lagoon) from the many beaches between here and Marseillan. It's in that direction that we plan to take a bus and grab some sand covered real estate for a few hours each day but today, we want to explore this delightful city.

The buildings are very old and the lanes narrow. Around every corner there is something to catch the eye. Along the front, scores of restaurants vie for your custom. The through traffic is almost gridlocked all day, but that just adds to the natural elements of a French port with a job beyond sucking the last Euro out of visitors' pockets.

There are artisan shops here too, and only a few tacky gift emporia were spotted near to the harbour itself. The main streets are wide enough for strolling and the shops are small enough to grab your attention every few metres. We had covered most of the old town by now and stocked up with groceries for our picnic tomorrow. The peaches were the size of footballs and there was wine we could draw directly from a barrel, if only we had an empty milk carton! There were plenty of sad looking individuals with empty milk cartons in the queue.

We stashed the produce in our room and headed out to choose somewhere to dine. We crossed to the other side of the canal where there happens to be more restaurants than shops. It's a little quieter too and we can watch the bustle back on the busy side and admire the boats puttering up and down between the two banks. On a small stage on the pavement a duet arrived and performed for the punters. They rattled off quite a few well-known numbers, in English and French, as locals and tourists sang along. We tapped a toe or two and felt good in the evening's warmth.

We finally dragged ourselves away and sought a bar for a nightcap back on 'our' side of the canal. Outside a bar next to the Halles a good crowd had gathered, as a quartet of Spanish guitarists rattled out their repertoire of upbeat bouncy tunes that made our senses tingle. They had tremendous skill and perfect harmonies. The father of the troupe, a whale of a man with a voice that commanded your attention when he sang, held it all together. His two sons inter-changing some rather snappy chords and rhythms. This was fabulous.

We sat for a while and soaked it all up. Everyone around us enjoyed it immensely too, until a drunk stumbled into view pushing a bicycle. He danced in front of them. Well, staggered as he held on to his bike and became a complete pain in the backside as he wound us all up. Finally, a lad in a large family group had a word and after a bit of finger pointing and the removal of a baby in a push chair from imminent harm, the cretin staggered off. A blind man who was sitting alone on a stone bench nearby looked relieved when the music started up again.

It almost ruined the evening for upwards of 30 people. Just for one individual. Actually, he was not the only one in such a state. There were several of these parasites wandering around the town day and night. Many of them have dogs that defecate down the boulevards and pathways like runaway muck spreaders. A small blot on this otherwise, wonderful landscape. We watched the musicians finish their set before slowly making our way back to the hotel to settle down. Our first full day here has been fantastic. Tomorrow, we will find a beach.

Marseillan Plage

Saturday brought more brilliant sunshine and we headed out to find the bus stop by the side of the canal. A very handy boulangerie had placed itself right next to the bus shelter and we enjoyed a light breakfast of pastries and bottled water before the bus arrived to take us in the direction of Marseillan Plage. There are plenty of buses that serve the whole community. They are cheap and more frequent than in some regions we have been to. I tore up the note I'd written out for bicycle hire.

The route today took us passed the family orientated resorts which we avoided booking when planning this stage of our journey. Once free of the urban boundaries, the bus turned onto the 8km long corniche, which separates the Mediterranean from the Étang de Thau. It's a large, shallow lagoon, cultivating many different species of shellfish. Finned fish are also found in the lagoons, forced here by the sea running through man made channels. It's a profitable business for the fishermen. The excellent quality of the water means that the mussels and oysters cultivated here supply around 10% of the demand in France. The western end of the étang is the entreport of the Canal du Midi.

It was very pleasant looking out at the water on both sides of the bus as we sped along. About 5 km into the journey the bus stopped at Le Castellas. We were hoping to alight here instead of taking the whole journey to Marseillan Plage but the doors at the rear of the bus would not open. I went to press the doors in the middle section but they would not budge either. A few passengers boarded at the front but no one got off. The driver could see me frantically trying to open the doors in his rear-view mirror, but he just closed the front doors and pulled away. Some English-speaking passengers suggested this was a pick-up only and not a drop-off. Damn, Le Castellas was where we had actually planned to spend the day. Marseillan Plage is more Blackpool than backwater. The bus didn't stop again until we arrived at our worst nightmare.

I'm in purgatory, why did the bus not stop at any of the named beaches along the route? There is not another bus for at least two hours.

This place is my idea of hell. Tacky is the term I use for the glue on floor tiles before sticking them down. I rate this place in the super glue bracket of tackiness. We walked for at least 3 hundred metres, between rows of wooden shacks, stuffed like a Chinese laundry with racks of beach wear and brightly coloured plastic nonsense. We made our way through this obstacle course that is strikingly devoid of any good taste, before finally stepping onto the sandy stuff that leads to the shore. It was now blazing hot and we decided to make a day of it and get in some hard graft, keeping the damaging sun's rays off the beach towels by spreading ourselves over them protectively.

Many of the folk here are not French. I could tell that by the fat slob family who draped Charlton Athletic paraphernalia over a tent, blocking any view we had of the sea, less than 2 metres in front of our towels when we went for a paddle. The father tossed me a smug grin of "I'm an antagonist, me, what yah gonna do abaht it?" I gestured as to why, on a vast beach he would want to do that? His wife looked towards me and then away apologetically, anticipating what for her would likely be a regular event. Her man faced me with the body language of a thug who thrives on conflict.

I counted to ten, then another ten, staring at him with contempt. He furrowed his brow and threw another snide glance, knowing that he lives for moments like this. I'm 6 stones lighter than him.

It only took a moment for Joy and I to collect our things and move well away. I know it is not the behaviour peculiar to only the British, but these people are the reason I am so utterly embarrassed to admit I'm from the same country as them. Too many of my countrymen and women seem to prefer being a pain in the neck, to just getting along with everyone. It is not that rare to hear our reputation referred to as a scourge when British holiday makers are mentioned.

It did not spoil my day but that's the second time in 24 hours that an individual has set about wrecking the party by selfish ignorance.

By 4pm we had soaked up the best of the sun and our picnic had all but disappeared. We headed back towards the bus stop between the wretched stalls. We did stop for a cola but only to get dressed properly and clean up in the café's toilet. Joy decided she may take advantage of these cheap costume stalls and found a bikini to suit. Unless you want one that dissolves in water, they are not cheap. She paid handsomely for something that looks pretty good on her. No, there's no photograph available, just take my word for it.

We had to wait another hour for the bus to take us back to Sète. Instead of waiting in the open sunshine, we found a chicken and chips bar with parasols. The Dutch couple who ran it opened up ten minutes early just for us and cooked up some leathery product that definitely looked like chicken under the coating of gravel you would expect to find at the bottom of tropical fish tanks. They are on a get rich quick programme, selling this deep-fried muck to the hundreds of punters who waddle back and forth all day from apartment to bar, with pushchairs and inflatable swans. I think I'd rather spend ten years in Barlinnie and save my earnings from sewing mail bags than this lark, but then the Dutch do have a funny way of doing things don't they!

We boarded an empty bus that became severely packed on the way back. It stopped at Le Castellas. Drat. Each beach it reached just drew another band of blistered and bothered bathers. Before we got to the last few pick up points, we beat the world record in human sardine packing.

We did not need to find a restaurant tonight. If the chicken supper we ate digested properly we only need a few drinks and a wander about to round off our day. Sadly, there was no live music to be had this evening. Friday was the last day of a music festival week that the town had put on. Even the bar where the Spanish guitarists wowed us was closed for business. We went to a hippy bar. It has a history of some flavour for being the 'in place' once upon a time. The restaurant was the least busy of all along this canal side street. At the back, small tables begged for occupancy. We asked if we could stay for a glass or two of wine and the waiter said, of course. We sat at a table only to be ushered to two high stools at the bar. The tables are for diners only.

Err, no thanks. I want to relax and drink my wine, not sit perched like a pet parrot above the bar. We left. How stupid. It was long after 9pm and the restaurants elsewhere were beginning to thin out and this place has less custom than the Marie Celeste on a foggy night. There are plenty of other places but it all ran a bit flat at this point. Since we were not eating, the restaurants are off the radar and the tiny bars were all too seedy for our tastes. Whiskered men and women sat like vagrants over ashtrays with TV's blinking and music blaring. It is definitely not what we want right now.

It was a beautiful evening and all the outdoor tables were occupied. Sitting inside was not an option. We kept searching. Our determination eventually paid off as we found a small café in a passageway that served wine and coffee. We sat outside and watched children racing small pushbikes up and down the alley as a proud Dad took photographs with a big fancy camera. The architecture here is so typically French. The family atmosphere was lovely as folk around chatted with us. No one came by to bother us at all. We had found the relaxed peace we had been searching for at last.

The following morning, we had to hunt for a different bus stop, as we planned to head as early as possible up to Mont St Clair before the crowds beat us to it. This is the high point that looks over the city offering a panorama of the ocean and surrounding hills. A chapel, a memorial and a large cross, make it a magnet for everyone who visits Sète. Breakfast was bagged from an upmarket boulangerie and enjoyed as soon as we reached the summit. The place was all but deserted. We snapped away with our cameras in every direction.

Joy wandered away a little and came back to see why I was kneeling and facing the stepped decking. I had my camera on 'video record' and my mobile phone playing a tune called Bob the Snail, by Bryant Oden. I was recording a very large snail making its way across the slats towards my camera. Joy shook her head. I think she has lost all hope for me. The snail moved so fast I had to move the camera back three times or he would have been sliming up the lens. David Attenborough would be so proud of me. Now, I can play the video and the song at the same time. I may even be up for some wildlife film award one day and get invited to the most exciting parties.

The 360-degree panorama is amazing and with the binoculars Joy remembered to bring, we could clearly see the oyster beds on the étang and bring the distant hills and towns a little closer. A stroll inside the tiny chapel revealed arched walls, like a wine cellar, painted with frescoes, (the type you'd expect to see in cave dwellings). Angels on horseback brandishing spears covered one wall and alabaster statues looked down at the lit candles in a side room. By the time a coach load of tourists began to file in through the doors, we had fulfilled our curiosity. The sun was beginning to put out some heat now so we explored some more of the area until a bus came. The private properties here are very desirable. Some are in a state of disrepair while most are well-maintained amongst lots of foliage and behind high walls. It's quite a unique location and I expect prices and availability to purchase are astronomic and rare.

Late in the afternoon I was idling and ogling passers-by, as we sat in the shade of a large tree supping a long cool refreshment. Joy was busy dealing with several texts, Facebook messages and then phone calls on my phone. I had no idea what was going on until she had finished a call. We have friends who live in Mus not 40 miles away. They insisted we should get in touch with them if we were ever in the area, and Joy had sent Olwyn an email before we arrived but had not received a reply. She thought they had perhaps gone away themselves but it turned out it was a misunderstanding of detail. Joy did not have the phone number to hand for our French based friends so she called her Italian friend and workmate, Jo, to get it. Jo had answered the phone in hushed tones and said she was in a doctor's waiting room with her brother in law and was happy to pass Olwyn's number on to Joy.

It was only after the call ended that Joy realised that Jo's brother in law does not live in England but Italy. She had used my phone to ring around half of Europe for a number just 40 miles up the road. The next phone bill is hers.

We were now invited, no, we were commanded, to visit Olwyn and Clive, as soon as possible and stay the night. They would even come here and collect us if needed. Well, that won't be necessary as there is a rail service that stops at a station near to their home.

We took great pleasure in checking out of our hotel a day earlier then we had planned. At last, we may get one decent night's sleep and also the opportunity to explore a little of the Occitanie interior.

We celebrated our good fortune of our final night in this hotel by looking for a restaurant on the far side of the canal. Sadly, the wind had picked up and sitting outside at the Alexandra restaurant was ill-advised as napkins, then menus, then topiary trees went scuttling into the canal. We moved ourselves to the relative shelter inside the restaurant entrance and watched as the waiters used bill hooks to grab the topiary trees from the water. The meal was delicious but we probably over did it on the desserts. During the night, our tummies were still full to bursting. I think Joy tried to sleep sitting up. The noise abatement society would be on a loser in this hotel as the comings and goings just never ceased. We were just relieved it was our last.

Mus

We sailed out of our room early the next morning, stepped over the dog, around the cat and waved farewell to the receptionist, who wanted us to pay again. I made her read the invoice receipt I received from her the day before.

Walking towards the station we took a different route, across the canal and down the street towards the port area. It's less antiquated and the streets are much wider. Several cafés with tables outside offered breakfast but we chose to get to the station in plenty of time to grab a croissant and eat once we were on board the Nimes bound train. Away to our right as we negotiated another canal, a swing bridge was being raised to allow a tall yacht to pass through. I could see at least three other operational swing bridges in this busy working district.

The walk to the station was through a leafy boulevard with classy restaurants and the very smart Molière theatre. It's certainly a quieter part of the city and has a touch of sophistication about it. The Victor Hugo restaurant looks particularly appealing.

The local train arrived around ten minutes late and spat us off at Vergèze-Codognan, dead on time. Olwyn and Clive were waiting to load our cases into the back of their car and within five minutes we were outside their stunning home in the centre of the gorgeously remote village of Mus.

They have owned this property for almost 20 years now and have built it up from a dingy shell to a beautiful home, with unbelievable patience and immeasurable sweat, blood and yes, several tears. The walls are a metre thick, and from the photographs they showed us, every centimetre has been renovated to make this a haven of rustic comfort and tranquillity. I felt at home the minute I crossed the threshold. We were made so welcome that they had better be careful. We might not leave.

As we sat and chatted in the parlour the arched ceiling kept the room cool. The now dormant fireplace, big enough in which to hang a hammock suggested this room alone would be absolutely perfect all year round. They showed us a tin box they had found hidden on a ledge inside the chimney when they were renovating. The box contained German military papers, a staff list, stamps, authorisation to travel passes and a roster for guard duties. The contents suggested that this house was commandeered during the German occupation in WWII and it explains perhaps why a side room as you enter the house could only be locked from the outside.

After lunch we tore ourselves away to explore the village. The chapel just behind the house has a named side road that is impossible to walk down. It's 70cm wide and the angled stone supports for the chapel's wall block access anyway. We stopped at a hillside where grapevines lined up in almost military order all across the valley. The blue-black fruit, well on the way to full maturity. A motorway now takes all the busy traffic away from the village, where once it clogged the streets. The dirt paths seemed to lead everywhere that I wanted to go. I could wander these lanes every day and not get bored. The road that used to be the main route for traffic revealed its history. Faded direction signs and old advertising slogans, that are usually seen only in old photographs, were visible on the walls of buildings. Clive pointed out a back yard, with open gates, cluttered with scrapped HGV axles and other metal parts. Even a rusting Citroen Diane just sat there, camouflaged under a growth of brambles. There were giant, heavy cog wheels all lined up, like biscuits leaning out of a fallen packet, and articulated trailers just left to rust. Wrought iron gates and awnings were scattered amongst nettles, weeds and shrapnel.

Some of the buildings are crying out for some TLC and there are barns that could become fabulous restaurants or gîte apartments. It all had that pleading look for a renovation project. The place was not a shambles by any means. Like most French villages, it has charm, with lovely cottages draped in greenery and long abandoned rose bushes growing above garden walls. The neglected parts are never obvious until you focus hard. There's a café/tabac shop, a post office and the mayor's house and apart from a small protestant church, that's about it for Mus. It's as brief as its name. I loved it. What a wonderfully tranquil haven in this beautiful part of southern France!

Le Grau du Roi

As the sun began to set, we climbed into the car and headed for the coast, some 40 minutes away. I think it is usually quicker than that to get there, but it seems today that everyone else in the region had the same idea. We found a parking space in the very popular resort of Le Grau du Roi. It was already full to bursting as we made our way to the quayside. Olwyn got us seated right by the waters' edge and we enjoyed an excellent meal which included more than ample portions of tapas, fries, side dishes, fried chicken and kebabs.

Joy noticed amongst the tightly packed rows of tables, that some people were being asked to stand up to allow a woman to wheel a pushchair through so she and a whole family could all sit at a vacant table. What made Joy's eyes pop, was that either the two babies being lifted from the pushchair were really dog ugly, or, they were really dogs.

Sure enough, two simpering mutts were lifted out and placed on laps. During the meal they were handed across the table to swap places with various members of the family. Their real children, with dirty faces, helped hand feed these dogs chips and other scraps from their plates. Actually, I think the children ate the scraps while the dogs got the choice cuts. The whole family stunk like skunks in a tramp's overcoat. Fortunately, we were almost upwind of them but I felt sorry for the folk seated closer. It did not mar our evening one bit. It was a great finale to our day. The portions we were served were so big I could not manage dessert.

We are on the very cusp of the Camargue here. There are wetlands, étangs, holiday resorts, ancient cities with bullrings and citadels and it's also a paradise for landscape artists. Coming here to stay for more than a night should be compulsory. We strolled along the prom for a bit, bought some prints as a keepsake from a gallery and watched pretty young things being courted by hopeful lads before making our own way home.

Chatting until the early hours we finally plopped into bed. Our only regret is that we did not make this meeting several days ago. It's good to have familiar company at times. Our bedroom window overlooked the village square and all the way down the valley to the hills in the distance. We slept in complete silence, with the window wide open (with mosquito screen in place).

In the morning the sky blazed blue from across the valley and up to the village square, right outside our window. What a stunning welcome we received to the new day. Sadly, we travel onwards today. Our destination is further inland, but we will be returning to complete our run along the Mediterranean coastline very soon.

Rodez

On a previous visit to France, I travelled alone to Rodez on a short flight from Stansted airport. At the time, I had hoped to take my motorcycle on a trip to the Moselle and dice with the German border for a few days, visiting castles and landmarks. As I was about to set off, Europe became deluged with rain which lasted for weeks. Joy had already arranged to visit family in Wales so I jumped on a very cheap and convenient flight to kick my heels in this little-known city. It lies within the perimeter of Occitanie in the western hills of the Massif Central and dates back to the 5th century B.C.E.

I took a taxi from the airport and stayed in a boutique hotel tucked down a lane close to the cathedral. The sun shone and shirt sleeves were the order of the day so I was pleased to have avoided the awful weather in northern France.

It's a beautifully tranquil city. The lanes lead to courtyards and the bars get busy at night when the tables outside fill with revellers of the passive kind. I spent my days of solitude doing much as I would if Joy were with me. Except maybe spending a little longer in a motorcycle showroom, staring goggle eyed at a sparkling Moto Guzzi that had a price tag I dared not look at. The guy behind the counter actually brought me the keys to take it for a test ride. I resisted but that was a 'Satan! Get thee behind me moment.'

The street market that appeared on the Saturday morning flooded the courtyards and squares with happy stallholders and customers in waiting. I spent most of the day stuffing my face with treats from every available stall. There's enough about this city to make for a great weekend break. The architecture is crumbling but eminently habitable. There are alleyways and passages everywhere. The half-timbered shop frontages line cobbled streets and artisan artefacts fill the shelves inside. There are several churches, a big cathedral and a modern art gallery (that looks like it was built from a rusting oil tanker), that all crave inspection. Parks, scenic views from the top of the town and more bars than one could frequent in a weekend, all add up to great value for money, if the cheap flights continue. I even strolled around a funfair one afternoon that looks to be a permanent feature during the high season.

I really enjoyed my visit. I dug up more historical tit-bits for my collection. My key discovery here was that Rodez was the central point for establishing the exact measurement of the metre. This was attempted in 1792 by measuring the distance between Dunkirk and Rodez, while at the same time, the distance was measured from Barcelona to Rodez. The combined results would determine the value of metre, which is one ten millionth of the distance between the north pole and the equator. It must have been some walk. The project was not concluded until 1799! The man responsible for this ground-breaking achievement, Jean Delambre, was rewarded by having his name inscribed on the Eifel tower in Paris and also a crater on the moon named after him.

Figeac

The railway station on the edge of town is where the buses congregate. Public transport reaches into the rural areas, which offers some nice surprises. I took a train to Figeac, which is 40 miles to the north. The walk from Gare de Figeac took me across the River Célé where the buildings instantly appealed. Passageways that seem too narrow for vehicles threaded their way through to the centre. I felt transported back in time by the medieval brickwork and balconies. It is another classic old town in this remote part of the countryside. A major draw for visitors is the Champollion museum, named after the man who first deciphered the hieroglyphic symbols of the ancient Egyptians, in 1822. Born in Figeac, Jean François Champollion began his interest in antiquity at a very early age and went on to unlock the scriptures of the Pharaohs. The museum is dedicated to his work and the displays, layout and educational activities were fascinating. It also traces the history of writing and is a terrific place for scholars, and families with inquisitive minds.

There is another museum in Figeac, devoted to aircraft propellers and aeronautical products. It's called the Paulin Ratiers Museum, after the name of the aircraft components manufacturer in the town. I ogled the motorcycle in the front window but couldn't quite convince myself to venture inside. I was very taken by the town itself, which has retained more of its medieval heritage than many of the larger towns we've been to. It might be more beneficial to visit here by car, or at least, check-in to a hotel and pack hiking boots. The Célé valley has much more to explore than just these cobbled streets; cliff side villages and deep gorges can be explored on foot, by car or boat. I had only time to absorb the attractions of Figeac for the day.

It appears that no matter where I go in France, I find that there's something else of interest just around the corner. I took my leave on the last train back to Rodez, my notebook had gained another entry with the suffix "Must return."

LANGUEDOC/ROUSILLON

Le Somail

Our next destination is less than 90 miles away from Sète and takes us inland, into the Aude department of South-West France. The Canal du Midi runs through Le Somail, stretching from the Étang de Thau at Marseillan to Toulouse. We arrived in Narbonne by train and hired a car to take us the rest of the way to this picturesque hamlet. There is plenty to explore in the area on foot, by bicycle and car. We had booked a gité for this stay, owned by a retired English couple who live in a house attached to the site. It should be decent enough as they are from Middle England and both had professional occupations. The slight 'plum in the mouth accent' I detected from our telephone conversations, suggested a lot of comfort will be built into the furnishings. Bicycles were available for a small fee (to pay for maintenance costs, he said) and are locked in a shed under our balcony.

It is not often we do a self-catering excursion but the glorious arrays of fresh foods in French markets always make me salivate and I wanted to have a go at preparing some meals myself for a change. Once we check out the kitchen in this apartment, I shall set about stocking up on all the ingredients.

It's not a long drive from Narbonne and the roads were clear and well signposted. As we left the main road, we had to take a very narrow lane to get to the centre of the village. I thought I had taken the wrong choice as it resembled a farm track. As the first bend took us to the right, we were now driving alongside the canal itself. Boats were moored along the bank, underneath an avenue of plane trees on both sides. It was an idyllic setting from that moment. Le Somail itself, looked as pretty as the photographs in the on-line brochures. Actually, it is prettier.

We found the block of buildings that were to be our home for the week, less than 200 metres from the canal side. Several other guests were milling about as we climbed the stairs to the balcony where each gité was situated. We greeted each other with gracious smiles and tentative handshakes. Of the three gités, we had been allocated the central one. Our neighbours were all English. On the left an elderly couple, who seemed quite well to do, and on the right, a chap from Nottingham who was very pleasant. The rest of our welcome party it appeared were the woman who cleans the place and some of her friends.

She plastered us with advice as we were shown around our gité. Let's stop calling it a gité from now on, it is not a gité in the true sense, but a couple of first floor rooms in a converted garage. It contained the cheapest furniture Ikea could legally stock. It is merely a holiday apartment. Our cleaning lady/host pointed out things in the room that worked and things that didn't.

Eventually she left and we dumped our stuff and headed to the canal to find the barge that operates as a grocery store for the whole village. We added a few essentials to the items we brought with us. I'm very doubtful there is enough of a hob, let alone a kitchen suitable for much more than boiling an euf.

There are cafes and restaurants in the village and on the first evening, there was no argument as to which we would choose. It's right next to the canal. The village also boasts a couple of small art galleries, a well-known book shop, and a wine outlet, offering degustation every day. Erm, that's it. Brilliant. Visitors often arrive by boat as they make their way along the canal but there are also quite a few tucked away B&B's and hotels around. This promises to be a lovely relaxed stay. We have the whole region to explore.

We sat at a table under an enormous horse chestnut tree outside the restaurant and ordered a carafe of wine and a plate of local olives (lucques). The sun glinted over the tiled rooftops, the ducks played follow their leader on the glistening water and all the world's troubles floated away beyond the avenue of trees that line the banks in the languorous current.

Supper was sublime. Steak for Joy and fish for me. Simple, superbly cooked and not a morsel wasted. As we wallowed in the pleasure of the encroaching sunset, I spotted an otter in midstream paddling away, with its nose just above the surface. I bounced up and captured the wee fellow on video, just in time. Others around the restaurant were less quick off the mark. Maybe it was a normal event for them. I told the friendly waitress she got our bill wrong. She had omitted charging for the second carafe of wine. Tomorrow, we shall tread new ground, well the wheels of a pushbike will. If we're up to it.

In the morning we opened the shutters of our bedroom to reveal vineyards as far as the eye could see. Grey clouds failed to darken our mood as we prepared breakfast, using chipped plates and cheap cutlery for our fresh bread, honey and jam. The kitchen equipment was restricted to a tiny fridge, a single hotplate, microwave, toaster and a kettle. We needed a trip to a supermarket, to stock up on washing up liquid, cloths and other cleaning stuff. Toilet tissue was almost at the rationing stage, so we had no time Toulouse.

Sallèlas-d'-Aude

I inspected the 6 pushbikes in the shed. None of the other guests were likely to use them so we had the pick of the crop. Sadly, the crop has failed. Several had flat tyres and others looked un-road worthy. I managed to find two that did work but as we rode off, they squeaked louder than train wheels on rusty rails. Neither bike had comfortable seats. Our postures during riding was more hunchback than straight back. Gear changing was random as the mechanism kept slipping. We never really got the right gear for any length of time as the bike would whirr and clunk with each rotation. It was so noisy and cumbersome as we rode along, flocks of birds took off in fright.

At least Joy's bike sported a basket on the handlebars. I had to tip my seat right down at the front and sit right back on the rear edge to avoid self-castration. But the brakes worked. We kept to the back roads and dirt paths. The land around was flat as we cycled in between vines and almond trees. There was hardly a soul about. The upside of this being, we were never spotted using such preposterous vehicles, but the downside was that if we did fall off and injure ourselves, we might not be found for days.

About three miles away is the village of Salèllas-d'Aude, which has a supermarket. We locked the bikes up, as if they were worth stealing, and were the only customers as we wandered around inside. I depressed myself by checking the prices of the wines. I would have to pay three times more for some of these lovely brands back home. At the petrol pump, fuel was more expensive here than in Britain, so maybe it balanced out a little.

There's a deep-water lock in the centre of the village and there are a number of seating areas where folk can come and while away an hour, watching the boats slowly making their way through, from both directions. We watched one giant river boat approach and agreed, that hiring one of these, at up to €2,000 a week in high season, was not for us. Progress seemed so slow and the fact that you are actually trapped inside the bi-directional waterway is a bit restrictive for our desires. With a car or motorcycle we can branch off and head up into the beckoning hills and explore a Château or two. I suppose it can be done on a pushbike that is stowed on the barge but it still doesn't appeal. I can't help feeling that the master of the ship just likes dressing up in epaulettes and peaked cap, and make believe he is high on the ocean wave. We certainly spotted a few Captain Birdseye's, holding on to the helm, his spouse and friends spread out on deck, with a glass of wine and cucumber sandwiches. They waved at us like royalty as they passed. Most even had a ship's dog.

Back at the apartment, the neighbours warned us that the heap of lentils on the floor under the kitchen units was poison for the mice. I joked that I had already scooped our pile up and made soup! They told us they too, were unhappy about the poor quality of the kitchen facilities and awful crockery. The lady complained bitterly about the 'sheer obscenity of it all.' The gardens were nice enough, with blooms and shrubs, plenty of trees and shade, and there were BBQ fireplaces scattered around. We took advantage of the outdoor pool making the most of the afternoon. We never saw the owners, even when we knocked on their door. It was disappointing that they were not enthusiastic about delivering what they advertised.

I spent an hour trying to cobble a couple of working bicycles together from the scrap in the shed. I found a few tools and began salvaging and swapping bits. We want to explore along the canal and see whatever there is in both directions.

I managed to tighten the gearing system and changed the seat on my bike. Joy said she might be able to cope with the seat on hers, if we had any Novocain. All I could find was a packet of frozen peas. We're hardy souls, if a little stupid. We set off and ambled along the path on the right bank in the direction of Toulouse. Young and fit cyclists on machines built for this terrain shot passed. Some took to the rugged track behind the line of trees to get around us. We kept to the hardened mud along the edge. The tree roots and debris on the rutted, lumpy path higher up the bank was a nut cracker.

We admired a pair of black swans and waved back at the passing boats. We stopped on a bridge to admire the gorge below where a shallow river headed down through the forest. A tiny cottage by the water's edge with all the hallmarks of antiquity was picture postcard stuff. Crossing a viaduct, picnickers sat way below us by another river. We finally came to Port du Robine. The junction here is very pretty, with boats moored all around a confluence but unfortunately, the area beyond has a large factory and a scrapyard appearance.

The bicycles were far from suitable to travel for very long. It was time to turn back. We crossed over the canal at the road bridge and headed back on the other side. A café appeared in a gravel clearing by the bank. We considered stopping but it was only a converted shed with an ice cream hoarding outside and several cheap aluminium chairs and tables.

As we reached a junction where a narrow road led through meadows, two very ancient cars trundled to a halt in front of us. They were both powered by steam. In one vehicle, the occupants wore bent, stove pipe hats. The other car was driven by a fellow who was probably born the same year these cars were made, 1908.

I have no idea about cars or their means of perambulation but these were very different from anything I had seen before. They were both open topped vehicles, with levers and pulleys sticking up like something out of Chitty, Chitty Bang, Bang. One front grill plate stated White, and another plaque said Lucy. It was odd hearing the engines whistling like an asthmatic with a tooth missing. The occupiers/owners of these lovely contraptions had come to enjoy a picnic. They rejected my offer of a straight trade for our 'modern cycles' so we mounted up and peddled away.

The track on this side was not, as the local map told us, navigable by bicycle. There are tree roots in abundance and stumps sticking up in the middle of tightrope thin trails. This was trials riding country. I need a 125cc scrambler. We found it best, if tiresome, to walk the bikes the next few hundred metres until we were adjacent to an open vineyard and a more rideable surface. Until that ended. Progress was slow and we were relieved to see the outskirts of Le Somail come into view. We'd been on this safari for about 3 hours. The bikes were locked away in the shed, although the bottom of the canal was probably more appropriate. I don't think we shall be making any further use of these abominations while we are here. It's either the car or Shank's pony from now on.

The sun was blazing nicely so we made our own lunch and spent the afternoon in the back garden by the deserted pool. Tiny lizards popped their heads out of cracks in the wall to see who had come to join them and the afternoon drifted towards evening in a delightful way.

Before supper, we walked along the canal, in the opposite direction to this morning. It was a lovely experience, so beautiful and so serene. The silver barked plane trees lined both sides as far as we could see. In the distance, the hills of Minervois began to draw shadows and to our left, the allotments were busy with gardeners, cheerfully pulling tomorrow's fresh vegetables from the ground. There were tall rows of tomato plants that looked more like an orchard of red apples. Long rows of lettuce plants, the size of wedding bouquets were being cut and stashed into wooden crates. More workers were loading them onto vans at the roadside. Between us and them, a field of vines ready for harvesting. Miles of open fields, dotted with church spires and terracotta rooftops filled in the rest of the landscape. We had the type of view where the whole world looked at peace with itself. If I was President, I'd make it a rule that everyone is given a place like this to visit and take in the moment. The glow of an autumn evening throwing so many colours on the trees behind us, the sky busy with restless birds and a landscape beyond imagination.

We left the ducks on the canal to settle down for the night and made our way back into the village just as the few street lights sparked into life. Joy began to worry that she could find nowhere that sold postage stamps. She accepted that not all shops would have stamps for sale but her collection of postcards was beginning to pile up. She had written out all her messages but without a stamp she could not post them. Several places sold postcards, none stocked stamps. A crisis loomed.

We closed the shutters, opened some wine and dined on home-made pasta with chorizo, crusty bread and salad. We ate off chipped plates and drank from odd shaped tumblers. The wine eased the aches and two comfy cushions helped with our sore bottoms from the bike riding. Sleep beckoned. Tomorrow, it's time to get the hired car to begin paying for its keep.

We got 'Gordon' the Garmin Sat Nav up and running, and off we went to the supermarket for more groceries. Joy had listed some places where street markets were held. Le Rodarte first. We drove right through it, nothing. Not even a shop was seen. The next village was Rioux Minervois. This is a much bigger place. We drove round it, Gordon telling us to take the next right, which did not exist. It was a brick wall. Then we shuffled up through tiny back streets so narrow they were barely wide enough for a wheelbarrow, our wing mirrors almost scraping window ledges as we edged along. Round and round we went. Behind fences and high walls, a school yard, twice, and a church. These streets were so narrow at one point, when we had to stop and wait for some old guy ahead to get his bicycle out of the way, a woman opened her front window and used our wing mirror to put her makeup on!

Eventually we found a wider road and a way to get out of town. Again, there was no street market. Joy's lip petted. No markets, no postage stamps. Her life was becoming unbearable.

We drove along fabulous little roads, past Châteaux, wineries and slowed to watch the automated machines strip the grapes from the vines in the fields. We were now up in the hills and driving into the Herault region. The scenery even lovelier than the area around our village. At Peyriac we could not find a market either, so we turned back and stopped at a cooperative winery where tractors were queuing to deliver their trailer loads of grapes. I poked my nose in to see how the process of winemaking was done. Joy came to join me as the proud and friendly staff were happy to let us watch. Overloaded trailers tipped piles of grapes, leaves and stems into a hopper that has a giant screw at the bottom. As it turned, the grapes were pulled into a hole and above our heads a chute burst into life as all the leaves and twigs were spat out into a waste container. Very few grapes got left to be disposed with the vines. There were various hoppers for the different variety of grapes that were being brought in.

Inside the shop I drooled over the prices of the wines direct from the producer. I could have bought a case of this stuff but I'm not that big a drinker. I bought two bottles of their finest red and left with a big smile. Stupidly, I also left my reading glasses on the counter. My only remaining pair being sunglasses.

Minerve

We looped back to stop in the village of Alises that had a street side café with tables outside. It was not very warm out here but the coffee was hot, good and cheap. The village of Minerve is the high point, literally, of this journey. It is built over a gorge and you have to park up and pay. It's quite a walk from car park to village. The drop down to the gorge is pretty cool as we wound down the slope towards the dwellings. These precarious structures defy the logic of building them in the first place. There are a few gift shops and a café here but besides the church and the views there is not much else. Joy did spot a little shop that doubled as a post office and she asked the woman behind the counter, who was eating a sandwich, if she could purchase some stamps. The woman shook her head and said she was closed for business until after 2pm. It was just after 12.30. Joy trudged out of there looking very disconsolate.

A causeway across the gorge, which was once the only road into the village, is still intact but not open to the public. The town was a refuge for the Cathars in the early 13th century, who escaped the massacre at Beziers. That nasty Simon de Montfort, the 5th Earl of Leicester, laid siege to Minerve, which finally succumbed after six weeks of onslaught. The bridge across that gorge must have taken a battering. A visit to the town is well worth the effort, as long as you don't arrive around midday and require a postage stamp.

We stayed a little while longer and then made our way back down the hill. The road twists and turns for about 10 miles and continues down to the main road leading to Olonzac and Homps. We were recommended to dine at a particular restaurant at Homps. A dessert they specialise in is not on the menu but if you ask, they will happily serve it. It was closed for the day! So, we left the car outside and walked through the village, looking for another place to eat.

The Canal du Midi runs through here too and the scenery is not unlike all the other villages en-route. It's not as pretty by any stretch as Le Somail but a pleasant watering hole all the same. Close to the waters' edge was another restaurant; En Bonne Compagnie. We stepped up to a canvas covered patio and sat at one of the few unoccupied tables that were laid out with cutlery. The boss woman was English. She nodded to Joy as we picked up a menu. It seems we were the last patrons they would serve this lunchtime. It was just after 2pm. As we waited for our food, they turned away several people who had sat at the tables missing a menu. Joy reckoned they declined at least €240 worth of business in about fifteen minutes. I have never witnessed French restaurateurs do that. They usually stay open until customers stop arriving.

The other patrons around had all come off the barges and boats that were moored along the bank. The menfolk wore jaunty caps and white trousers. Snippets of conversation we overheard included the cost of this, and prices of that, but all in the tone of bragging and not complaining. It was typical water borne boating talk, the kind you hear in the dining rooms of all the private marina restaurants across the UK. And a few golf clubs too I might add. The meal itself was very non-French, unless you include French Fries. We had a piece of chicken with our chips. But the local rosé wine, from Corbiéres, was gorgeous. I took only a small sip of it since I was driving, Joy popped the rest. The lemon tart for dessert was nice too, so the meal was not a let-down at all. It had rained heavily here overnight, which brought one or two lovely highlights with the noisy table of Brits nearby. At one point the canvas awning gave way and drenched one woman with captured rainwater. But to top that, a few minutes later a rather large lizard slipped from a branch that overhung the same table and landed with a daze in between the plates and glasses.

Well, everyone else laughed.

The boat people left to disembark to another café, probably all of 2km downstream and I poured Joy into the passenger seat of our car and off we set again. Hairpin bends and panoramic views kept the attention sharp and Joy awake all the way back to Le Somail. The sun had flickered into life so we could relax by the pool once more, whilst Joy slept off the effects of the wine.

Narbonne

The next morning, the sun blistered its way through the gaps in the shutters. It might not be a scorcher yet, but the smile on our faces as we left for the day suggested this might be the sunniest spell so far. We headed into Narbonne and parked up a little away from the centre and walked through the back streets to the market hall. As we wandered through the cathedral grounds, we stepped inside to take a look around. Many of the stone icons had been defaced long ago. The faces of the characters and saints had been chipped off deliberately. There are hundreds of stone effigies tucked into every nook and on every ledge. The cathedral has been destroyed and revived many times since the 4th century, but the blame for the defacements lie squarely on the shoulders of the 18th century's French revolutionaries. At least this cathedral is still fully operational, others that were desecrated never recovered.

We exited to even brighter sunshine than when we entered, and we crossed the Canal de la Robine that bisects the main avenues to join the bustling throngs in the market. To Joy's delight there was an outdoor and indoor market today. All she needs to do after this is find a place that sells postage stamps and her life will once more be complete.

The stalls outside had plenty of choices, not the same clothing items and reject rubbish you often see in British markets. We ambled up and down, admiring this and that and bought a couple of minor trophies and listened to excited folk trying on outfits over their current clothing and posing in front of mirrors. One girl with her utterly bored boyfriend was trying on every skimpy article she could lay her hands on. We wandered down an aisle and back again to find her merely at the next carousel pulling items off one by one and measuring them against her body. He looked completely catatonic as she begged his opinion on each. A family of Lancastrians seemed to be strolling in pace with us. They were harmless, if loud, but I caught a potential catchphrase from one as she opined, when picking up anything that caught her eye "I think I like this, but I'm not really sure. Oh, and I think I like this one too, but I'm not really sure."

Poor Joy had to listen to me parroting this phrase for virtually everything I ate, sampled or viewed for the rest of the day, in a sharp, Mancunian accent of course. "Eh, our kid"! At about this point something hit Joy in the eye. It almost floored her. It must have been a bug but it took several minutes and a bit of a panic to get her contact lens out and sorted. At times like these there is little I can do to help, Though I did spot a fancy dress stall a way back down the aisles and I could have bought her a pirate's eye patch if she needed it. I said this market had everything.

Handbags were very inexpensive and the styles were not just rip-off designer label stuff. It really was an interesting experience to see so many different stalls selling different goods. The indoor market is amazing. Not so different from the Mercado de La Boqueria in La Ramblas in Barcelona, but not nearly as big. The fruits, fish and other foods are so attractively displayed. Cafes offered pancakes, coffees, tapas, olives, cheeses, and all types of meats under this one roof.

It's this type of hall that I wanted to come to if we had the opportunity to take stuff home to cook for ourselves. But with only a single hotplate to work with, we were restricted to pasta pot meals. The seafood in this part of Europe always amazes me. I also tried olives, tiny pastries and cheeses. We finally selected some filled baguettes and other fancy stuff for our picnic lunch and tore ourselves away to wander through back streets to window shop, return to the car and then head off for part-two of our day. There are some nice alleyways with specialist shops in Narbonne. We stopped for coffee in a café and Joy finally found a Tabac that was happy to sell her a mountain of postage stamps. I even spotted a post box so she could, lick, stick and slip the cards to her fans worldwide who wait patiently each time she is away, for news of her antics.

Saint-Pierre-la-Mer

The sun was blazing and giving off heat as we followed the instructions from 'Gordon the Garmin' and the road signs towards St Pierre, one of the beaches on the Narbonne coastline. I'm not convinced about the efficacy of the Sat Nav system. It suggests you turn down a certain street that might not exist or worse still, ask you to take a left when it means drive straight on as the road merely bends slightly to the left. And Gordon cannot pronounce French names at all. It's hilarious as it comes out all disjointed and gobbledegook.

The road to the coast is fabulous, the surfaces are smooth and once you leave Narbonne proper it opens up to reveal gorges, forests, vineyards, wine producing Châteaux and stunning vistas as the road twists and curves up and over the hills. We finally opted for a spot on the beach that was almost deserted, yet a café and a few amenities were not far away. The sun was just perfect for stretching out and the surf whispered sweet nothings as I let the tranquillity transport me to another universe. The sand was soft too and at this moment all is well with the world.

Lunch from the picnic stash was terrific. More folk came and spread themselves out as the afternoon progressed, I fetched ice creams, paddled in the shallows and even wandered up towards the port area. This beach is miles long. Looking south-west we could just see the mountains of the Pyrenees which act as the backdrop to the resort of Argeles-sur-Mer, which I shall report on in a later chapter.

At one point, behind a high wall that separates the beach from the road, I noticed 3 palm trees in a row, moving slowly along. The trees were at least 10 metres high. It was a bizarre sight. It wasn't until there was a gap in the wall that I could see they had been loaded onto the back of a truck and were being taken away. I wasn't certain why they were being taken away and neither was Joy. I suggested, perhaps, they had been arrested for 'Tree-son'. I found it funny but Joy complained I might have spent too long in the sunshine.

We packed our things back in the car and wandered off for a little stroll. In a café, the proprietor, a wine producer himself, showed me his wares and invited me for degustation. It was Joy's turn to drive from now on anyway. A most delightful 45 minutes sped by. We returned to Narbonne to find a restaurant for dinner. The evening atmosphere was more sinister in this town than we'd experienced during the day. We spotted three youths throwing stones at a man who was minding his own business. A moment later the three recidivists, turned on their heels and ran off like fugitives. The man had stopped a police car to complain.

In the town we wandered for ages looking for a restaurant that would attract our attention enough to enjoy supper. The ones we saw were either, empty or poorly furnished. Cheap, alloy chairs and tables are not my idea of fine dining 'muebles'. Besides, the locals that were sitting about smoking and drinking coffee were all a bit roughneck looking. A couple of students were strolling about asking folk to swat one of them in the face with a custard pie; obviously some student fund raising wheeze. We spotted several broken raw eggs lying about and it did not take Sherlock long to surmise that certain recipients of these eggs were not altogether acquiescent to such antics.

We ended up wandering through some very shady districts, where youths gathered in clusters and stopped chattering as we passed. The streets narrowed and the alleyways began to look less well maintained. The little town map Joy picked up from the Tourist Information Centre earlier in the day however, depicted images of quaint houses and narrow, fun filled passageways. A couple of cafes up here were very tiny and more suited for just the locals. Methinks we'd better circle round and get back to more open spaces and perhaps the car and home. We can eat in the village restaurant instead.

The police we saw the man complain to earlier were now patrolling on foot. We picked up the pace and returned to the car, disappointed that Narbonne is never going to feature on our list of top ten French city breaks.

Inside the restaurant back at Le Somail it was busy with chattering diners and quiet, romancing in some corners too. To my left a table of British folk were celebrating Gran's birthday. Behind me a table of French folk just celebrating.

To my right, a 30's something couple, quietly dining and peering lovingly into each other's eyes. The ambience was terrific, until the Brits started on the next round of drinks. The laughter turned to cackling and the voices raised to the level that intrudes on everyone around them. One lad in the corner with them seemed a little embarrassed but the rest of the group cared not a jot. The couple next to us visibly winced more than once and nodded to us in agreement that it's not acceptable dining etiquette. When the group finally left, the whole place breathed a sigh of relief. The waitress said it's what Brits are known for. Joy noted that Granny had paid for the whole bill. Happy Birthday Granny indeed.

The French table behind me consisted of many more folk than at the British table, and yet, I did not even realise they were there until after we had eaten.

Sigean African Nature Reserve

Today is our last day here. We still have the car and there's more to explore. The beach was a target again but the clouds put paid to any ideas of lolling on the soft sands. In fact, it was raining here and there, so trips to picturesque spots in the region seemed the most sensible plan. We set off after breakfast for the district around Sigean. 'Gordon' attempted to force us on a toll road but we circled a roundabout twice to avoid it. The 'A' road runs parallel to the toll road and that suited us perfectly. South west of Narbonne is a nature reserve, comprising lakes and African wildlife. It's a popular park that provides safari tours and lots of educational activities. If we had arrived with children, our day would have been taken up here. There are also some pretty villages dotted around, but the roads are only vaguely included on the map. However, it was a treasure hunt of a journey, with surprises around every bend.

We did not venture into Sigean town, but toured until we found something that caught our attention. Our intentions today were to keep on the move and explore as much as we can of this tantalising area. At the edge of a village we stopped at a large graveyard that had a memorial dedicated to those fallen in war. Only the hum of bees (there was a beehive behind a wall) and the crack of a crow broke the early autumnal silence. An old 'soldier' carrying a posy of flowers, hobbled along the footpath as we were leaving. Greetings were exchanged before we took ourselves back to the car and off to explore some more.

Bages

We next parked outside the delightful village of Bages. Steep steps led up to houses in winding alleys; a church bell tolled the hour once we reached the village summit. Everywhere pristine clean. We wandered under low archways and through extremely narrow cloisters to reach viewing points that looked out across the lakes to the sea, or inland to distant hills. The place was almost deserted. The café where we stopped for refreshment is almost cave-like inside. Outside there's a fountain with a statue in the midst of a cluster of parasol protected tables. It is idyllic in the extreme. There are quite a few eating places here which suggests we had chosen the quieter moment to explore and enjoy this gorgeous find. One restaurant was preparing for lunchtime visitors. It looked more like a private cottage inside than a restaurant. Red napkins were stuffed into wine glasses on white linen covered tables. The sash windows looked out over the bay.

The lakes below are very Scottish at first glance, with their hilly surroundings. Only the flamingos, wading through the shallows told a different story. As we drove on, manual labourers in a vineyard had stopped for a mid-morning break. A police car was parked nearby, and 2 uniformed officers appeared to be sharing the respite with them.

Gruissan Plage

We drove all around the edge of a lake heading for the coastal resort of Gruissan. It's nothing like Bages. It's a crazy place. The village on the right looked to be little more than a few terracotta roofed buildings and a church. Gruissan Plage looked like a holiday resort from hell. Dozens of rows of wooden chalets on stilts. It's more like a housing scheme in a big town, than a holiday resort. The whole layout is a criss-cross pattern of streets lined with almost identical two-storey chalets. The beach and bay are enormous and can obviously cope with the multitudes of summertime visitors. The grass strewn sand dunes would be a pirate's perfect hiding place for plundered treasure for the children.

We lingered a while and toured some more before setting off homeward. The beaches along here in both directions, go on forever. Port-la-Nouvelle, south of the lakes appears better equipped for those not seeking barrack style accommodation. There's a little more sophistication about it than the funfairs and burger bars in Gruissan Plage. If it was a sunny day we would have liked to have settled there for a few hours. The roads and scenery are as variable as the resorts around this part of coastal France. It's got more choice than a tin of Quality Street.

We headed back to Le Somail via the back roads, passing gorgeous châteaux, pretty villages and crossing the Canal du Midi via a lovely arched bridge. We pootled through many hamlets, up twisting lanes and through vineyard lined avenues. It was a very pleasant day of exploration.

We parked the car by the apartment and wandered for the last time around the galleries and bookshop in the village. After our week of romping, it is still the prettiest hamlet in the district. It was a shame about the apartment. The couple next door had begun loading their car up for the long drive back to Blighty. They said they intended to head off extra early the next morning. I don't think they ventured very far this week at all. They were still complaining about the facilities. They told us they had to go and buy a casserole dish to make supper!

The guy on his own, said he was staying for another couple of weeks. His wife had died not long ago. We shared a glass of wine together. He seems pretty contented to just enjoy what life serves up for him and he had his own bicycle. No wonder he could still walk after every trip!

With the single ring and a microwave, we concocted a fine supper of all the scraps we had left in the fridge and packed our bags for our own getaway in the morning. The apartment was cleaned and everything put back in its place. I made no further effort to meet with the landlord who had promised to come and see us.

First thing in the morning we loaded the car and by 7.45am we were off. The couple who said they were leaving extra early had yet to stir, their car was still waiting on the street. At 8.25am precisely we dumped the car off with the pleasant girl at the car hire firm in Narbonne and went to find somewhere for breakfast. We had discovered so much about this part of Aude and the Herault region. You could almost stick a pin in any village and use it as a base for exploring, either on foot by car or, if you dare, a bicycle. Just make sure it's got a soft saddle and working gears before you set off.

Carcassonne

The train from Narbonne to Carcassonne takes around 35 minutes. From the vantage of the railway station Carcassonne is unremarkable. It could be a hundred other European outposts. We took a cab to the hotel we'd selected for the next few days and as we crossed the bridge towards the old part of the city the vista changed in an instant. It was like a giant curtain on the stage, lifting to reveal a beautiful scene in a ballet. The castle stood to our right on top of the hill. It's the largest and most stunning castle I have ever seen, like an Arthurian fairy tale.

Our hotel, the Demeure St Louis, is located at the foot of this hill, not 300 metres from the battlements. It's not quite a hotel we are staying in, but a guest house. Bernard, the proprietor came rushing out to greet us. From that moment he was the perfect host. Ever available and always happy to help and advise. He leaves no detail to chance. He insisted on carrying both our cases to our rooms. The old house has history and as much character as any château. The whole interior is a picture of everything gorgeously traditional and French. Our bedroom was massive, with 3 windows (with shutters and drapes and tangerine coloured calico netting), all of them offering a classic view of the castle. The sitting room for our own use was unbelievably chic. Antique furniture included a chaise longue, highly polished floor-boards and creaking doors with clunky keys. This room was bigger than the ground floor of our own house.

The breakfast room had only one table, like a banqueting suite. Glass fronted cases around the walls contained wine decanters, old plates and other appropriate items. At breakfast we would be dining with all the other guests around the same table. Another sitting room off to the left was strewn with sofas, armchairs and reading material. The gardens were ideal for relaxing and taking in the sunshine. A serpentine pond contained dozens of koi. A waterfall increased the ambience as we sat on wrought iron chairs around iron tables and watched the occasional conker drop from the branches of the many trees in this autumnal idyll.

Bernard recommended a restaurant or two up inside the castle walls for us to try as we headed out for supper. The sun was setting, but the warmth stayed with us as we made our way up through the winding, ancient streets towards the castle grounds. By now it was close to 8pm and few of the shops inside were still open. Tomorrow is scheduled for intensive exploration. Tonight's visit is for food and wine consumption only. We settled on a delightfully decorated restaurant in the sumptuous French style we love so much. There are Italian and even Japanese restaurants within the ramparts but for our first night here, it had to be French, surely?

The outside tables looked uncomfortably crowded, so we selected a quiet corner inside. It began to fill up with diners in here too, shortly after we arrived, but it was still pleasant and peaceful for all that. Joy chose fresh scallops for starters, a steak for her main course and a slice of chocolate cake that needed some assistance to devour. All was perfect she said. The scallops were stunning. I chose foie gras served with pink peppercorns and an odd, though perfectly complimentary, glass of Gaillac sweet wine. It worked. For my main course I chose roast piglet in honey which was as scrumptious as it sounds, and a slightly disappointing nougat ice cream to finish the meal off. Actually, I finished off Joy's chocolate cake for her and we washed it all down with a terrific white Corbiéres. What a great start to our stay! We slipped away after parting with just the right amount of Euros to match the quality of the meal and surroundings. On our way back, we peeked into an alleyway or two as a taster for tomorrow's excursion and left the floodlights to guard the castle, as we headed down the hill to our bed for the night.

We slept well enough but the floorboards creaked occasionally. We later realised the creaking was caused by Bernard as he routinely switched on hall lights and closed windows each night. As for ourselves, we crept about as quietly as we could to avoid disturbing others but could not avoid making the odd squeak here and there.

At 8am we opened the shutters to find the sun peeking over the eastern horizon, flooding the room with shafts of startling light. At breakfast we were joined by couples from Australia, Russia and a Canadian woman with her Lebanese husband. There was also a girl from the UK travelling alone, who joined in the conversation. It was so educational and friendly chatting almost like old friends. The Canadian lady was a fine-art dealer and the young English girl had just completed her master's degree in the same subject. It was a fascinating topic. Bernard meanwhile, flitted about, serving hot drinks and replenishing bowls as we helped ourselves to cereals, breads, honey, conserves and the freshest of fresh fruit salad. Joy slipped up by adding milk to her tea which was Earl Grey. She opted for coffee thereafter.

Everyone except Joy and I were 'passing through'. We were the only ones staying for more than one night. Breakfast lingered, until slowly, we all dispersed to head separate ways.

Armed with sun glasses and baseball caps we proceeded once again, through medieval streets towards this double-walled, fortified citadel. It took ten minutes, maybe twelve. It was not yet busy. The shops were opening for the day's trading and everywhere we looked gave a modern but not entirely inaccurate picture of what life inside these walls must have been like for the past 1,200 years. The castle site actually dates back to Roman times. The Visigoths and Cathars once held the upper hand in this region. I tried to absorb some of what it might have been like for those in whose footsteps we now tread.

The narrow alleyways reminded us of Dubrovnik old town but with a little less blatancy in its tourist appeal. The usual trinket shops abound and prices will fleece your wallet quicker than a nagging teenage offspring on a Saturday morning, if you are not too careful. The tourists falling into the traps that I could tell, appeared to be mostly Australian. Their distinctive brogue (or were they New Zealanders?) could be heard in all corners. The lanes lined with medieval buildings were only marred slightly by cafe signs, bars and souvenir shops. It's understandable. I did not expect to be transported entirely back into the mists of history when we crossed under the portcullis. We bought tickets to wander the ramparts. It wasn't cheap but the views across the countryside are stunning. People have settled in this area since 3,500 B.C.E. The Romans built a hilltop fortress around 100 C.E. and the fortifications have been constantly extended since then.

The Visigoths took it over when the Roman empire collapsed and the location became an important strategic centre all through the ages. Joy's intimate knowledge of history recounted that this castle was featured in the Hollywood blockbuster, Robin Hood, Prince of Thieves. My favourite trivial piece of history relates to the invasion by the Saracens who came from Barcelona and overwhelmed much of southern France in 725. However, they could not take the fortress here, due to the efforts of the Frankish King, Pepin the Short. What a humiliation for the vanquished Saracens! Maybe that's where the phrase 'to come up short' comes from.

We needed a coffee. The open plan decking of an Australian bar, oddly enough, appealed the most. It offered a good view of a dried moat between the castle, which was home to the plebs, and the inner Château Comtal, which would have been the abode of the protectors of the realm.

The place was beginning to fill up now (the castle that is, not the moat) and most of those arriving today were old folk who were none too steady on their feet. This time of the year I suppose the more agile and tender of years have all headed back to work or school, leaving the old codgers and us (cough) time and space to enjoy our own holiday.

Inside the château, we inspected the artefacts and museum pieces like disinterested royalty. I'm not one for peering at chipped pottery and faded tunics. We made our way surreptitiously through the clumps of guided tourists, who were being sandblasted with facts and anecdotes. In my view, all that detail will be forgotten before they even climb back on to the bus. Some were so old they'd be hard pressed to remember where they actually were, let alone that in 470 C.E. some bishop met his end whilst sitting on the toilet overhanging the ramparts when a Visigoth's arrow found its way up the 'U' bend.

We carried on around this enormous perimeter. The sun was gleaming across the rooftops and visibility went to infinity from this lofty perch. In all directions the views are fabulous. We lingered like romantics in all the best places until we ran out of wall and had to descend back to ground level and a coffee bar. Lunch menus were not enticing us yet but a delicious almond biscuit the size of a surf board was. It was barely 2pm and we felt we had seen the best parts of this castle. We chose to cross the river Aude and invade the 'new town' to pillage some lunch.

The modern side of the city is fine. It has many narrow streets set out in a squared-off grid, adorned with a plaza or two, but Place Carnot is obviously the most popular square in which to congregate. The giveaways were all the tables and parasols in front of all the restaurants and bars that surround it. We found a free table and sat to rest our feet. A large fountain and bandstand were ignored, except for a couple of energetic toddlers that dashed between the two in a game of make believe that only they knew the rules to. We watched the world come to a halt, as other folk arrived and slumped in the afternoon sun to enjoy company, coffee and cigarettes by the packet.

After a light lunch it was time to explore further into the surrounding streets. We ended up alongside the Canal du Midi. It is nowhere near as pretty here as it is in Le Somail. The city as a whole was not up to what we had perhaps hoped for. We'd all but finished what we would wish to see already, but no matter. Maybe the folk who arrive for just one night at Carcassonne had the better idea. It could be done in a day. We shall make the most of the rest of our time here. A fruit shop provided distraction with fresh and succulent Muscat grapes, figs and other intriguing delicacies. A bottle of Picpoul de Pinet was purchased and we made our way back to the hotel to take in the late afternoon rays in the gardens. A very good choice.

Bernard refused to allow us to open the wine until he'd chilled it and brought proper glasses. We insisted he take a glass with us. He did but only a small one. He is such a lovely guy. We read our Kindles, smiled like idiots at the luxury of our current circumstances and watched new guests arrive as Bernard fussed around them, just like he with did us.

Supper was enjoyed back in Place Carnot. The birds in the tree tops were shrieking as they bickered over their beds for the night. We settled to dine on a cold meat starter, followed by roast duck, sliced and doused in a very tasty gravy and a fine bundle of chips. The price, as we expected, was lower than that charged inside the castle grounds.

We people watched. I noted a girl in a short dress and a dimpled country smile standing by a large ice-cream dispenser in the square, being wooed by this slim, shady, sleazy, greasy guy in a leather jacket. They were accompanied by a Danny de-Vito look-alike. A strange ménage à trois. Sleazy guy was blowing smoke in her ear as he whispered. She seemed less than interested, but she never left his side. They then all sat down at a table and ordered wine. Cigarettes were being ignited with the rapidity of sticks of dynamite in a spaghetti Western. Sleazy guy was now all over her, like a rash, and the squat guy just sat by and smiled. When Mr Sleazy disappeared to get some cash from a nearby A.T.M., squat guy tried to grope the girl, she pushed him away with a half-hearted refusal. Ten minutes later the three of them left together. Sleazy began swinging a large bunch of keys in one hand and groping her bottom with the other, she leaned her head on his shoulder while the squat guy was trotting alongside, his little legs struggling to keep pace. We then played a game of "What happened next?" My guess was, they were heading off to prepare for a business presentation about a critical new I.T. firmware solution. I can't tell you what Joy suggested!

We were also surrounded by a group of louder than they should have been, Australians, who spent ages trying to divide the bill between the 10 of them! As the activities around us faded, so did our own energy. We drifted slowly back to the hotel in the warm darkness of the narrow streets. Sleep came easily and only the promise of a train ride and a trip to Limoux for more exploration got us up bright and early the next day. That and the anticipation of who we would be sharing breakfast with this time.

Limoux

Today's new guests included folk from California and what is becoming the obligatory Australian representation. It seems southern France for them is the current 'Shangri La' of holiday destinations. The Americans were heading off to Lourdes by car. Bernard advised that the toll road route would take three hours and the back roads almost six. Mrs California who had slightly better hearing than her pleasant husband decided the old codger was up to driving the back roads. They were both in their seventies. She secured the old fellow in the driver's seat, strapped herself in and Bernard waved them off from the gate. He turned to us and quipped, "He will need those healing waters of Lourdes by the time they get there."

We were on our own pilgrimage, to Limoux. An appellation for some of the finest wines in the whole of Languedoc/Roussillon. I've been sampling and enjoying the Crémant sparkling wines that many of the regions across France produce, which are every bit as good as any champagne, but for legal reasons they elect to call it crémant. Limoux produces its very own crémant, but Bernard advised us to try Blanquette de Limoux instead, or as well as! I take advice seriously when it is delivered with such a passionate tone. The hunt was on.

We strolled in the morning sun to the railway station and boarded a petit train (one coach) bound for Limoux. It trundled up into the foothills of the Pyrenees, stopping at several small villages, many without platforms. One or two station buildings have been converted into private dwellings, with sun loungers, washing lines and children's toys cluttering the platform. The scenery is lovely. We passed lots of streams threading their way through the primary forest. It was an enchanting image of France 'au naturel'. When the forest cleared, we passed acres and acres of vineyards. Some had already been stripped of their fruit, others waiting impatiently to be relieved of their burden. In several fields, labourers were working their way methodically along the rows of vines, stripping them bare.

Limoux is an outpost town. It has a reputation for colour and culture, with plants and flower baskets on display under street lamps and on window ledges. We arced towards the centre. The church steeple was our compass as we took a different route to the one the other passengers were taking. There are some beautiful views of the surrounding hills and along the river Aude, on which the town stands. It is as photogenic as the Cotswolds.

Joy followed signs for the Tourist Information office but they petered out at the next crossroads. We never did find it. We did find the Place de la République though, which was similar to all town squares in that it had several gift shops, a delightful fountain, and more importantly, several bars and cafes. We lounged and lazed for a while soaking up the pure pleasure this lifestyle offers. No rush, no rain and no worries. Absolutely no worries. The Aussies must be using that phrase here every minute. No wonder they all head for these shores.

The streets off the square are narrow but only a couple draw you more than a few metres away from this heartbeat centre. Shops with anything worth spending time peering in at the windows fizzled out and were replaced by offices, dry-cleaning outlets and hair dressers. It was very pleasant making our way up the alleyway, towards the main road. Once there a few restaurants dotted the wide pathway on one side and a supermarket on the other stocked a few bottles of Blanquette de Limoux. We had accomplished our mission.

Blanquette de Limoux is absolutely gorgeous. My history book on wines tells me it was the original sparkling wine, and Dom Pérignon allegedly stole the recipe from the monks of St Hillaire (a nearby monastery) when he was returning from a trip to Spain. I wondered if he finished the Cava, he bought in duty free by the time he reached here!

We stayed for lunch. I had a confused moment with the pretty, young waitress as she offered me something for which I had not a clue what she was talking about. She pressed her palms together and voiced something I might desire. I declined politely but when our food arrived, I realised I needed olive oil. Idiot that I am, it was this very condiment she was offering when she brought our carafe of water. I apologised profusely and she fetched it without losing her professional smile. My mistake was nothing compared to Joy's, as she looked up a French word in the dictionary, called the waitress back and proudly asked her for- a condom. The girl flushed, before Joy realised, she had meant to say, condiments. I was quite disappointed when the waitress returned with salt and pepper.

There was little else in Limoux to keep us here other than the tranquillity that seems as visible as the bricks that built the town. It's known to be a popular settlement for British migrants. It was now mid-afternoon and siesta had fallen onto the town like a magic spell. Everything now closed up, bar the bars and the supermarket. We strolled back to the railway station via a church that had been converted into a museum, (which was still open), had a quick look round and waited for the first train out of town. Sleepy hollow it was. The journey back down the hill was just as pleasant as on the way up. 40 minutes later we were back in Carcassonne. Bernard chilled the sparkling wine and shared a glass with us, as we basked once more, in the sunshine, in the gardens of the hotel. A little later, after Bernard had left the premises, a frantic old lady approached me waving a cordless telephone in her hand. She spoke no English and the caller evidently understood no French. I put the phone to my ear. An American couple, called Ferrari were due to stay here this evening and her (elderly) daughter was ringing from California to check if she had survived the journey. We eventually worked out which room the Ferraris were 'garaged' in, and since there was no answer when I knocked on their door, I pushed a note under and told the daughter to call back later. The French maid (Bernard's mother I believe) was most appreciative of our help.

The next morning when we met the Ferrari's, they said they had asked Bernard if they could move rooms. The note I'd written and shoved under the door was still inside the unoccupied room. These Ferrari's were not pleasant people. They seemed extremely picky and full of niggly complaints. We kept our distance.

Our last evening in Carcassonne however, was spent back in the castle grounds, enjoying a very nice meal out in one of the squares. Calzone and local cider for me and mussels and chips for Joy. Delicately she ate each succulent mussel from its shell by using another shell, like pincers. We thought this is how all people eat mussels. Well, we'd seen it often enough in our travels to feel we were following the correct etiquette. More of that later.

It was late, dark and very atmospheric wandering through the streets and around the inner grounds of the castle. Despite the fact that lots of other people were about, we could catch a sense of what this place was like in medieval times. I shudder to think how the hordes would defend it now if we came under attack. Many of those around me would struggle to climb the battlements without rolling back like a dropped cannon ball. Any nimble army would soon claim victory. Maybe that's what gave King Pepin the Short the distinct advantage.

The whole city of Carcassonne felt safe, peaceful and so relaxing. However, we have arrived after the high season. The car parks around the exterior of the walls look capable of taking hundreds of buses, so I guess in the summer this place *would* be under siege.

It was a good choice to come here. Maybe the three days we had booked were a day too many, at least for us, but there are museums and galleries we have omitted to visit. The river and the du Midi canal walks are reputed to be very popular. We packed our cases when we returned to our hotel and planned to take the 9.01am train back to Narbonne and change there for the service to Argeles-sur-Mer in the morning. Bernard would book a cab for us at 8.40am and we now looked forward to a complete change of scenery and pace. I'm not sure it's possible to reduce it even further.

We were up extra early in the morning. The sun was already warming the floorboards through the opened windows. We had packed most of our things into our cases the night before and this time we were the first to sit at the big dining table at breakfast, beating the Ferraris into third and fourth place, by a good few laps of the breakfast bar. They were not running as smoothly as us. Snooty, grunting and misfiring on a cylinder methinks. A quite unpleasant couple as I've already mentioned. They seemed to complain about every little thing; demanding a different type of butter or bread or tea, goodness they were difficult. Bernard attempted to appease but, in the end, he resolved to fuss over Joy and I all the more, filling our cups with coffee, adding jams and breads as he ignored them.

Bernard had phoned for a taxi to take us to the railway station and it arrived early, creating a good excuse to leave the Ferraris in their pits as we whizzed off through the streets ahead of the pack. Saying farewell to Bernard was emotional, he was an absolute gem.

PYRENEES ORIENTALES

The journey from Carcassonne was lovely. We had a little hiccup with the timetable and had to wait an hour longer for our connection at Narbonne, but that was the only set-back.

The vineyards on the way to Narbonne were a sight to store in the memory banks. Every hill and glen dedicated to viticulture. Closer to the city's boundaries the landscape altered very subtly to include citrus groves and occasional meadows where horses roamed. The fun inside our carriage was delivered by an Aussie couple who proved to be as ignorant outside the 'barbi and tinnys of 4X' lifestyle as you could satirise. They were studying a map, while he wrote his own notes about their stay in Paris. She scolded him for spelling Louvre correctly. "You're an idiot" she said "In that case it would be pronounced Loov-Ree." She also contradicted the pronunciation for Champs-Élysées. "It makes no sense," she bickered. "We walked along that big street with the arch at the top. Somewhere on this map it should have the spelling S-H-A-M-P-S." This charade carried on throughout the trip.

We left them to their petty family discord and alighted at Narbonne. Within minutes we were on another shiny, local train heading to Perpignan. We were now travelling directly south and the landscape became much more 'Mediterranean'. Unlike the road that we drove around the last time we were here the railway tracks cross right through the middle of the La Berre lakes. Gruissan Plage to our left and Bages and the African animal reserve at Sigean on the right. We were leaving Languedoc for Roussillon and seeing barren wasteland, inlets, lakes, storks, heron, flamingos, ponies, sand dunes and vineyards all competing to take our eyes from the languid and not intrusive wind turbines on the hilltops. A power station only served to prove heavy industry also lurked in these parts. The train slewed into Perpignan and we had time to grab a snack before completing the last leg of the journey to Argelés Sur Mer. A short, two stop stint dropped us close to the sortie at the station. A lady taxi driver kindly lifted our cases into her boot and we sped off to the middle of a highway and found the exact same frontage of our hotel as seen on Google earth. The price of the cab ride was reasonable compared to the rip-off drivers at the Côte d'Azur end of this coast line.

Argelés-sur-Mer

The Hotel du Golf is clean, nicely furnished and modern. Any marks on the freshly painted white walls in our room were not there until I'd smudged them myself, with the insides of several mosquitos. Oh, it was also me that left a small black mark on one side wall, as my suitcase scraped against it when I tried to squeeze between the bed and wall to get to the wardrobe. Sorry, Mr Golf Hotel owner.

Other than that, it was perfectly adequate. The view from our tiny balcony however was out of this world. That is if you ignore the main road, railway line and overhead power cables between the hotel grounds and the sea. Beyond these, the trees drop down to the Mediterranean, which was as sapphire blue as you could imagine. Little white yachts dotted the waters and to our left a cream streak of beach stretched and curved for miles and miles without interruption. In the near distance is the town of Argelés and beyond there, a dozen tiny beach resorts all the way to Narbonne. We had a private pool in the grounds and the view behind went up through folding hills and low topped mountains, all covered with vineyards and trees. Vines were sunbathing even at the entrance to this hotel as they awaited harvesting. The September heat was suitable for our own bit of sunbathing.

It was mid-afternoon now and we were told that once we crossed over the road a tunnel burrows under the railway line and a path from there leads down to a secluded beach. We could also walk from here into Argelés, "20 minutes tops," said the receptionist. So, we changed into appropriate clothing and headed out with hope in our hearts and a spring in our step.

The secluded beach was composed of brittle shingle and inhabited by a few souls but it did not crave our attention as much as the need for a long, cool drink. We decided to attempt to reach that enormous sandy beach around the cove. After 20 minutes hiking between bush and thorn we added another 90 minutes by wandering along gravel paths to a deserted housing estate. All the shops we passed were shut for the season and the bars were either boarded up or closed. We finally reached a fenced off harbour and saw life forms inside. It resembled an exercise yard in a high security prison. A glut of tourist shops for sailors interspersed with sea shanty bars did little to revive our fast depreciating enthusiasm.

It took another 10 minutes get around the harbour fences and find an entrance before we could slump in a bar for a rehydrating tumbler of something cool and grossly overpriced. This was a miserable exercise. We took a vote on whether to hire a car. We also considered other options: cancel the hotel and find a place at nearby Collioure, or Argelés itself (unless it too had closed down for the winter). The car hire option was elected. It certainly had the best manifesto.

We originally wanted to book a hotel in Collioure, but the best ones we found on the web were all full, hence the reason for the Hotel Golf. The Plage area in Argelés is dismal but the beach itself is amazing. A car would definitely give us the best of all worlds. We can enjoy the solitude and views at our hotel and then leap frog the built-up parts and sink our toes into the extensive and ankle tickling sand on this deserted beach.

We walked another mile to the very edge of town, until we saw a car hire firm next to a petrol station. Here, the kindest of businessmen in the car hire industry sorted us a hatchback for the duration of our stay. Stupidly, I had no idea I was compelled to traverse half the region of Roussillon to find a coffee bar let alone a car hire depot. So, it was no surprise that I did not have my driving licence on me. We had to walk back to our hotel, and in the morning, come all the way back again to collect the car. I'm having a toddler tantrum inside. Why I am ever allowed out without mittens on a string I never know.

Joy, ever optimistic and supportive against my growing self-deprecation turned the sojourn into a fun adventure. "How fit we shall be in this heat to have walked the equivalent of the Pennine way in just 18 hours," she exclaimed. "We can sing songs on the way back to keep our spirits up." I looked around for a heavy object and somewhere that was secluded enough to bury a body! We did find a few short cuts on the way back and a path that led behind some empty holiday homes and reached the hotel much sooner. Joy had discovered this shorter route, so digging a shallow grave was put on hold for another day. From our room, we watched the sun set across the bay, like the slow descent of a curtain after an exhilarating first act. Tomorrow, should be a lot less stressful.

The mosquitoes that visited their squashed cousins on the hotel wall had taken the hint and left us alone. The traffic noise outside on the main road was barely noticeable and only one train rumbled through the night air. Joy produced our breakfast from the stash we bought yesterday evening. Grapes, cheeses, cold meat, tomatoes and fruit juice. We sat on our balcony and watched other guests below us on a patio eating much the same from the hotel restaurant, except for a fistful of cash more than we had paid. Intrepidly, we set off to the car hire place. The journey this morning had direction and purpose. We found more short cuts and enjoyed the scenery along the summits as we stalked like veteran hikers. Speaking of which, at one point we had to wait at a gate while a long procession of around 50 ramblers filed by, some with sticks, others with walking frames. Many smiled and thanked us as they passed, but a few were too aloof to countenance our existence. One or two looked bored beyond recovery.

Our own mini crocodile, of two souls, marched onwards and we collected our car with alacrity. First stop was Lidl's. It was just up the road. Prices in here suited us perfectly. 6 litres of water, sandwiches, fruit, wine and paper plates. We shall recover the cost of the car hire with the bottled water alone.

Next stop the beach. It's a mile away. We set out our belongings in typical fashion. The sand was gravelly more than grainy, but it was perfectly agreeable. The vista to our left and right was nothing but beach. Very few people joined us. The holiday season has obviously passed. I don't think we had anyone closer than fifty metres distance at any time. The sun blazed safely and the sky was unblemished by cloud. The hills behind completed the whole scene in an enchanting package of solace and calm. Bathers that ventured into the water were mostly elderly but they too seemed happier to soak up the absolute quiet of the day. We read, dozed, drank, ate and smiled. By 4pm I was suitably satiated and toasted like a pink marshmallow over an open fire. Peace reigns on planet Earth.

Banyuls

We made use of the car in the evening by driving beyond Collioure, to Banyuls. This is almost the most western town on the southern French coast. It's a pretty place. Ideal for a short visit and supper. My only regret was that since I was driving, degustation at any of the many cavés was out of the question. Banyuls is famous for dessert wines, Collioure, for dry wines. I petted my lip several times.

It's a much-underrated town, somewhat overshadowed by the more famous landmarks of Collioure. The main road avoids Banyuls altogether so travellers probably miss it completely in their hurry to reach Spain. Yet it has a lovely craggy coastline as well as a nice harbour and not too much urban sprawl. The town has been around since the 4th century B.C.E. and the bay area is lovely for strolling and relaxing in at any time of year. It must be terrific for walkers as there are hikes up through the hills that lead to Andorra and the rest of the Pyrenees that end at the Atlantic.

Taking the coastal road to Llanca just over the border into Spain, is about 22 miles of brilliant twisty, steep, hairpin bends and viewing points. It was so worth hiring the car just to get the chance to explore this hemline of France's geographical wardrobe. Wandering around on foot back in Banyuls had us wondering if we should set up camp here another time and bring walking boots, sun cream and a detailed map. It's just lovely in every respect. Very different to its eastern counterpart of Menton. It's more rugged, rustic and rural. It was a pleasure to have been able to witness both extremities of the French Mediterranean coastline. It's not much of an achievement for some folk I'm sure, but we felt like we had explored both ends of the solar system.

Supper was taken under a thatched parasol, facing the sea. I had bream followed by something chocolate. Gorgeous. Joy, a lamb dish and a glass of wine. Entertainment came virtue of a foursome close by. They all ordered mussels. These were served in a big pot for each diner and the heavy lid being used for the discarded shells. Etiquette in such places usually calls for the mussel shell to be lifted by hand and an empty shell used as a pincer to manoeuvre the morsel of mussel from its mooring. Like I explained earlier, it's the method Joy used back in Carcassonne. Some people use a fork instead of a shell. The two oversized women in this quartet caught my eye by swirling the contents of their pan with their fists, pulling out a shell, ripping it open with their fingers and shoving each half in their mouths and sucking on the shell, like babies on a bottle. Slurping noises emanated, like the surf on a pebble beach. Both halves were sucked dry including, mollusc, juice and I guess, the occasional parasitic worm cast that often clamps to the outer side. They even ate the black stringy bits of whatever it is that hangs from the shell.

Both men in the group had eaten their fill as they chatted amiably together. Their pots were evidently not empty. The two women then thrust a fist into these pots too, swirled and shared out the spoils. They continued to suck noisily and gurgled while the menfolk sat with folded arms, quietly looking out to a black canvas of ocean. The upper arms of the 'bottom feeders' flapped and shuddered like great oaks in an earthquake as they slithered into the pots like an octopus trying to find the safety hatch on a submarine.

The drive home retraced the drive out and the twisting roads and hairpin bends made for a lot of fun and crunching of gears. Tomorrow we shall come this way again, but to supper at Port Vendres, which sits between Banyuls and Collioure. Another bottle of Blanquette de Limoux awaited us this night, in the fridge in the hotel room. We wish to look out at the black canvas of ocean without carnivorous distractions.

I found a burning cigarette on the roof of my hire car at the hotel in the morning. Because of some ignorant buffoon flicking their fag-end from the balcony, the indelible mark it left may well lose me my deposit when we return the car.

While we shopped in Lidl's for our daily bread, an English chap remarked to Joy that her absent minded singing brightened his day further. "What a treat it was," he said, "to find people so happy with life these days." He was a nice old chap but I could not convince him to take her off my hands for keeps. By the time we reached the near four-mile long stretch of deserted beach, with our purchases, the cigarette incident was all but forgotten.

On the sands, kite flyers arrived to add a little activity. The eastern-bloc style apartments in the background were all but abandoned ahead of the coming winter. We lazed in a silent, gentle sizzle until around 4pm when we retired to baste a little more at the hotel pool, and stayed there until it was time for a withdrawal back to barracks and a shower.

Port Vendres

We drove along the now familiar coast road and admired the prettier parts of Port Vendres. It's a bit commercially exploited so it didn't quite gain the same number of points as Banyuls, but it's still an appealing town. We wandered along the quayside, the tall masts of the boats filling the marina, looked like a tray of cocktail sausages on sticks. We got side tracked through side alleys and inspected the ancient cannons pointing across the bay. Having lived in Scotland for many years, I wanted to see if they had been made at the Carron Ironworks in Falkirk. The cunning company showed little favouritism in wars and was happy to sell to both the British and French Navies. I was still unable to sample the local wines but I did buy a bunch of grapes that were beautifully sweet and fragrant (Muscat), so I consoled myself to tasting them pre-fermented instead of the fully liquidised version. After running out of alleyways the sun had disappeared completely, so we headed back to the hotel to eat our supper from the leftovers in the fridge. We detoured through Collioure on the way home. It was very busy. Parking was at a premium but we vowed to return there on another evening to complete a hat-trick of resorts in this gorgeously attractive corner of France.

With the sun keeping true to its promise to return without a cloud since the day we arrived, we had yet another lazy day. Peppered only by a confusing tour of Argelés town. It's horrible, like an English seaside resort from the 1970's (Minehead perhaps). It is not full of penny arcades, but wooden shacks hosting bars and cafés that are designed merely to cater for large volumes of tourists rather than create any ambience of coastal charm. We were pleased we'd chosen a hotel far away from it all. At the beach we lay on our towels, read our Kindles and watched a flotilla of yachts float back and forth on the glittering diamond and lapis waters of the Med. The rolling hills behind once more reminding us that heaven on earth is not apocryphal.

I watched a young couple take to wind surfing, possibly as novices. Gingerly they wobbled slowly along until they became more accustomed to the pull in all directions of wind, surf, muscles and senses. After an hour I saw them still surfing but looking decidedly more adept. A cool hobby, which I must say appeals more to me than owning a yacht. I read in Warren Buffet's biography, one of the richest guy's in the world, that the two best days of being a yacht owner is the day one buys the thing and the day one sells it.

Another glorious day of perfect peace and sunshine. We picnicked and prostrated ourselves like we had not a care in the world. Perhaps we don't.

We also lazed and swam in the hotel pool again in the late afternoon. Back in our room Joy was shocked to find that someone had lifted her bikini top. Now, I get blamed for a lot of things but lifting a woman's bikini top is not on my rap sheet. She searched everywhere for it, recalled every step of her day from breakfast time to beach removal and could not for one second, think how she could have mislaid it. A mystery looms.

We headed back into Argelés town to find the best route to the railway station. We need to know this for our journey to Toulouse. The roads around the town are totally confusing. One-way systems hampered our reconnaissance and narrow streets that would scrape wing mirrors if you did not remain plumb centre. I jumped a red at a set of lights because the damned things were obscured by a shop awning. The non-tourists lurking in the streets in the town looked less than financially solvent, more likely under the influence of a solvent. Dark eyes in leathery tanned faces peered into the car, as we groped our way between the flimsy café tables lining the kerbs. After several attempts and circuits, we could not find any signpost for the Gare. However, we finally found it ourselves. I had hoped that on the day we leave Argelés I could drop Joy off at the station with the cases, return the hired car and walk from there in time for the departing train. I've no idea of the route I would need. We'll stick together and take a taxi from the car hire place.

We headed out for supper back at the beach-side complex in Argelés Plage. We looked around the market stalls. There were few attractions; a parrot squawking on a lady's shoulder, clothes racks of tat and unsexy apparel. I spotted a gay night club called Pot Chic and a cluster of low brow restaurants, sprinkled with miserable looking holiday makers mulling over beer glasses. Our luck changed when one restaurant did invite a closer inspection of the menu. It was busy on one side with smokers and noisy revellers, but on the other it was quieter and more in keeping with our desired dining atmosphere. It served its purpose and we did not leave disappointed.

Our last full day by the seaside. We breakfasted on the beach in order to get as much 'sun time' as we could. We delighted in spotting some antics of other bathers around us, although once more none got much closer than 50 metres. I noticed a girl doing a sort of drunken gymnastics routine. She was fully clothed and attempted a few postures from the Oriental book of stretching body parts that really should be left discretely tucked away. It was as funny as hell to witness as she kept falling over and then began writhing frantically in the sand like a flailing beetle. After a minute or so she would stand up and try another yoga type exercise only to topple over and then belly dance her way back up. I was in stitches. Her cartwheels never got half circle before her whole body crumpled like a badly stacked pile of logs. Once she had finished her routine, along came the second act. We were then entertained by what I can only suggest was a miracle.

A middle-aged couple hobbled down the beach. The chap was slowly assisting his female companion with each step as she was burdened by a pair of crutches. It was sad to watch her struggle across the sandy expanse to a spot 20 metres short of the shore. He helped her get comfortable by spreading a towel for her to repose on. He then arranged a windbreak, using her cotton shawl, draped over the two crutches that were now impaled a metre apart into the sand.
I thought this was a lovely way for a couple to spend a day together, despite her obvious infirmities. After she had sucked a cigarette to its end whilst taking in her surroundings, she made it to her feet unaided, and trotted down the final few metres and into the surf like an un-pegged, bouncy castle tumbling along in a tornado.

She swam with complete ease and composure for at least an hour. Her partner merely looked on, though at one point he did dabble his feet into the shallows to cool off. She reached the marker buoys that stretch parallel to the shore, dividing bathers from boats. She swam back and forth for some time and whistled and waved to the guy to go join her but for the most part, he just rolled over and read a book.

When she finally emerged from the water, I was dumb struck. She glided like Hattie Jacques on a Segway, in a graceful waltz back to her berth, slumped down on the towel and lay there like an abandoned sofa. She lit several more cigarettes and drank about half a litre of vodka straight from the bottle, before heading back into the water for another Olympian swimming session.

I'll never refuse a request for alms again. Witnessing miracles like this, changes you for life you know! Several onlookers had the same opinion as me and were quietly clicking away with their cameras. At one point, the shawl had slipped away from one crutch leaving the appliance standing all free and forlorn while the other flapped like a national flag at an Olympic medal awards ceremony. Forget going to Lourdes. The real miracles are here on the beach at Argelés Sur Mer.

Collioure

In the evening we drove to Collioure for our final night out. I managed to park up in a very busy corner and was advised by a nice American chap that this late in the day parking is free. Others were queuing up to feed the hungry slot machine at the pay station.

This town is very pretty, probably the jewel in the coastal crown. It has so much charm you could hang it from a bracelet, but today it's teeming with folk. Joy noted a few hotels about the place. These hotels look wonderful and chic in photographs, but in reality, they were plonked in between shops and over restaurants and bars. Some she spotted were down creepy alleyways. Many looked decidedly less attractive than the brochures suggested. We concluded that we had made the correct choice with the Hotel Golf and hiring a car. Collioure is beautiful. It has a tiny shingle beach, which evidently, becomes extremely overcrowded. The prices everywhere reflect how popular this place is, and we must have saved quite a few Euros by staying elsewhere.

Another American couple asked us if we could help them find their hotel which was marked on the map but nowhere to be seen. Joy jogged up and down and I pointed to where I thought it should be. Joy headed into a shop to ask and came out with that usual grin of a person who has the answer. She took them a few metres to a gap between two shops and pointed up an alleyway. Their hotel was there. It was one of the places we had tried to book when we first decided to come to this region. It was not as nice as the one we had finally ended up staying in. Smug mode all round.

We popped into the Bar le Templiers. It is a shrine for artists and has been a frequent watering hole for them since the 1950's. Picasso himself endorsed the patronage and the walls on all floors of this bar, restaurant and hotel are covered with more than 2,000 paintings. It is known that some struggling artists paid their bar bill with paintings instead of hard currency. It was also used by the novelist Patrick O'Brien who wrote maritime novels, often about the Napoleonic wars. He lived in the town and was considered part of the furniture. It's a fantastic place. The bar itself is shaped like a boat so the theme is arty, maritime and classically authentic. I felt rather pleased to have found this bar. It meets with the distant cousin, La Coupole in Montparnasse, Paris for connections to the art world. We could not get a table here to eat however, and will have to find somewhere less auspicious for our supper. Joy was quite upset as she had brought a finished colouring book for payment!

It's not the Bar les Templiers that attracted artists to the region. This area is known as the Côte Vermeille. The light along this 12-miles of coast casts magical hues on the architecture, the skies and the sea. The artist Matisse went a little crazy for the light which is reflected in his garish colour choices when he painted here. In later decades, Sir Winston Churchill himself was often seen leaning over an easel along these shores. We snapped a lot of memorable views as we took a stroll around the tight bay. Guarding the town is the Château Royal de Collioure. It's said to be located on a fortified site that was under siege in 673, when the Visigoth King Wamba, was called upon to subdue a rebellion. The Château came in handy again in 1642 when 10,000 Bourbon troops, including Musketeer d'Artagnan ousted the Spanish

Hapsburgs, who had controlled the town since the 12th century. The Catalan dynasty might have ended, but the infusion of Catalan culture remained and is positively celebrated here to this day.

There is a famous hydrographic polytechnic here where Jean Nicolas Pierre Hatchette, a genius mathematician became professor at the academy at the tender age of 23. His works and developments in geometry and hydrography helped Napoleon Bonaparte in many of his campaigns. His brilliant mathematical mind laid the template for geometric influences for the generations that followed. The building itself looks over the sea from the edge of the bay. Today, Collioure is flush with American tourists. All the Aussies it seems, congregate around Carcassonne and Marseille, and all the Yanks stop off here.

While dining, we had little choice but to listen in to a wonderful piece of self-promotion at the next table. An elderly man and his wife had been joined by a British couple who had nipped across land from Biarritz, "to check out this town," they admitted. The woman was boasting that Biarritz is far better than this place; the sea is warmer there, the light better and probably, even the toilet paper softer. But she admitted they had just decided to come for a day or so since living as they do in their winter home in Biarritz can be so tiresome. The husband was regaling them all with tales of how they so enjoy the fact that the wine museum in Biarritz is so superior to any place of similar ilk in this neighbourhood. He even claimed that the King of France (Louis the Drunkard probably), gave the building to the people of Biarritz to open a museum of wine, which obviously made it all the more impressive.

The ageing couple they were talking to were Norwegian. Upon learning their nationality our English boaster had to tell them, that since he was a senior member of the Royal Society of Ocean Racing, he often travelled to London on business and stayed for free in the rooms within the grand H.Q. of the R.S.O.R. He only mentioned this because the King of Norway offered the building to the British for free, following WWII. Since the building is on prime land and therefore worth a 'bloody fortune,' he himself remains ever grateful to the Norwegians for their generosity.

At this point the Norwegian couple swallowed two cyanide capsules and jumped off the balcony into the water below.

We strolled away quietly with mirth in our minds and took a long slow drive home. Collioure is a lovely place. I can see why it is famous for artists and pompous gits alike. But for us, we were pleased we needed only to drop-in to check it out.

We were up early next morning. Each day on the holiday seemed to take a little longer for us to get out of bed. We needed to get the car back to the hire firm and then a cab to the railway station. We ate in our room from the store we'd purchased the day before. We heard the clatter of plates from the dining room below us but felt more than happy with what we'd laid out on the last of the paper plates before us.

We packed the final few things into our cases and Joy found her lost bikini top sitting snugly under her suitcase. Mystery solved and accusations about my cross-dressing interests were once more allayed. We said our goodbyes to the staff. The hotel was comfortable, quiet and we slept well each night.

There was no fuss when we returned the keys to the car hire company either. We'd scarcely covered 300 kilometres, the lovely countryside and adjacent towns are all very close together. A taxi arrived and got us safely to the station on time. The route the driver took was even trickier than the one we had plotted the day before. I think he drove through someone's back yard and nipped down the fruit and vegetable aisle in a supermarket as well. Thirty minutes later and we were on our way. At Narbonne there were delays for trains to Toulouse but this worked in our favour.

Toulouse

A delayed train heading ultimately for Bordeaux was just arriving and although we had no seat reservation for this 'earlier service,' the Train Manager looked at our International travel vouchers and said we'd could board. We had to stand all the way though. The train was packed. Two bottles of water later and with stiff limbs, we arrived in Toulouse nice and early. We grabbed a cab from the station because in my excitement I'd forgotten completely where I'd put the sheet of paper with details of how to find our hotel on foot. It was only a short haul, but the cost of the journey reminded us we were back in the sort of city where taxi drivers should wear a mask and carry pistols.

We walked into the courtyard and up to the reception entrance of the Hotel Grand Opera. It's palatial. Alphonse the bell hop, took our cases with a smile and led us to the reception desk. I'd written an email when we first booked, to request that they put a posy of flowers into the room for Joy's pleasure. As soon as I mentioned my name the receptionist smiled broadly and without hesitation, reached for a tassel fobbed key and beckoned Alphonse to lead us to our room.

The lift was tiny, very cramped and as we pressed against Alphonse's shiny buttons Joy remarked how she hoped the room would be as nice as the hotel seemed, but perhaps larger than this vertical chariot.

Alphonse nodded and said "Your room Madame is verwy Niiiice." We were guided along a corridor with polished panels on dark red walls. The heavy door to our room at the very end of the corridor opened into a suite that had Joy's jaw gaping. We entered a hallway with two built-in mahogany double-door wardrobes on one side and a half-round table against the wall on the other. The hall led first to the bathroom, a separate toilet and bidet room, and a right turn into a mammoth bedroom. Opulent just about describes it. The beamed ceiling with subtle lighting also hosted a large brass tipped, wooden fan right in the centre. The headboard of the bed comprised a 2 metre tall, post-impressionist portrait of a woman in period French costume and a bonnet. I was to spend the next three nights lying in this bed with my head resting against her (clothed) left breast. We had a private balcony, complete with pot plants and a view of the courtyard. I thanked Alphonse and tipped him a centime, explaining that Euros these days are worthless! I hoped the upgrade was a courtesy, as it would otherwise cost me a fortune. I noticed they had omitted to place the posy of flowers I had asked for, but not being one to complain, I chose to let it lie.

We unpacked as calmly as we could, placing all our things in the right places. I removed the resident champagne from the fridge and replaced it with a bottle of our Blanquette de Limoux. We urgently needed some lunch. Joy had spotted a Flunch café just a street or two away. Once inside we filled our plates and glasses from the shelves of this quick and convenient eatery.

Back near the main square there are little alleyways and streets leading off in all directions. Which to choose first? It did not matter. The whole city was buzzing and we felt we had struck gold by way of a fabulous place to explore on this leg of our French journey. There are lots of little shops down all these narrow streets that lead away from the Place du Capitole. They all seem to end up in a square peppered with bars and cafés and occasionally, lovely restaurants too. Toulouse is a vibrant university city, with more than 100,000 seats for learning so it was no surprise to see the bars crowded with students. The university was founded in the 13th century in a bid to quell the heretic uprisings. I'm guessing it worked as we witnessed no drunkenness or raucous behaviour anywhere. We drank in the view of the Garonne river as it meandered around the next bend towards its eventual confluence with the River Dordogne in Bordeaux. The churches, buildings and features all around are ageing, photogenic examples of exactly what you hope to encounter in such an ancient city. We probably missed more gems than we captured.

We have actually arrived back in the region of Occitanie, in the Haute Garonne district. Toulouse is known as the pink city and was the capital of the Visigoth empire back in the 5ᵗʰ century. Frankish authority reigned in the 8ᵗʰ century under the tutelage of King Pepin III the Short. He fought off all contenders for control of Toulouse and the region of Aquitaine, finally defeating the thorn in his side who went by the name of Duke Waifer, in 768. Pepin died that same year and was succeeded by his son Charlemagne. Subsequent rulers of Toulouse included Charles the Bald, and his son Louis the Stammerer, who in 866, went on to become King of France. The history of Toulouse may be amusing if the names of past rulers are listed but it undoubtedly played a crucial part in the creation of a single nation.

The Canal du Midi terminates here which adds a nice touch to our encounters with this most famous French waterway that began at the entreport in Sète. In the art world, several famous painters hail from Toulouse, (Lautrec not being one of them, he was born in Albi, 40 miles north of here). I'm particularly drawn to the work of Paul-Jean-Louis-Gervais. My guess is, he could never paint clothing very well! Other sons and daughters include Didier Pouget, Paul Pascal and the current living sensation, the actress, painter and sculptor Marine Delterme. There are art galleries and museums all over the city. The cheekiest being Les Abattoir which displays modern art in a converted slaughterhouse. Our pick for a culture fix was the galleries at the Hotel d'Assezat which was less than a ten-minute walk from the Place du Capitole.

Whilst stopping for cool refreshments in a street side café we overheard 2 pompous American girls boasting to each other about their absolute wonderfulness. It was amusing to hear their 'simply uncompromising' generosity to others, which they agreed was their uppermost character fault. We strolled away with a raised eyebrow and sardonic smirk. Public self-effacement for their unbridled charity is possibly the only way they can reveal to the world such obvious, uncontrollable traits. They also made sure we could hear just how many countries Daddy had paid for them to visit whilst they continued with their intensive studies. I think only a few countries are left in this world before they head-off to bore another planet.

Looping north and to the Basilique St Sernin brought more proof of the tranquillity and pure pleasure it is to be in this city. It's a lovely building inside and out. Originally built in the 4th century the Basilica is a feature in the pilgrimage route of the Santiago de la Compostela.

Our somewhat shorter pilgrimage took us along the Rue du Tour and back into the Place du Capitole. This street is fabulous. Little cafés and shops all the way down and a delightful distraction in every window. Violets are the feature of this city. It's not mine nor Joy's favourite scent but it made for a colourful display in many of the gift shops. A giant citron' cake did however, tingle all my senses and left a sticky mess on my fingers which was a pleasure to clean up 'feline style' afterwards. Joy just looks on with the resignation of a mother who has yet to impose table manners to her three-year old.

Back in the hotel room we found a bottle of pillow mist spray. It is a delicate air freshener, containing no violets, that lightened the fragrance in the room, but only if you spray it once. I used it like a fly killer and we had to evacuate for half an hour before it dissipated! We took refuge on the balcony outside, supped the bubbly and watched the sun slowly set over the pinkish, terracotta roofs. Life does not get better than this. Looking back through our years of work and study, with all the pitfalls and hurdles that is thrust upon almost all of us, we take none of this good fortune for granted. We still compromise and will shop for budget food and eat in our hotel room, or stay in a budget guest house when it's feasible. This rare luxury here in Toulouse is a moment to feel rewarded for past years of effort. In mitigation for our indulgence, the sparkling wine came to a tenth of the cost of the bottle of champagne we hid behind the TV.

We showered and dressed up smartly for the first time in quite a while. Wandering through the streets at dusk we searched in vain to find a restaurant that appealed to both of us. In the end, we returned to the Place du Capitole, not 100 metres from our hotel. We sat outside Le Florida restaurant. The waiters were sharp, polite and helpful, which was a relief as our French was messy, crude and useless. Everywhere I've ever been in

France the answer is the same. If you try your best but fail, they will forgive you. If you snap your fingers, speak loudly in your own language, you will be struggle.

Several other patrons in this restaurant had dressed similar to us, apart from a few. One loud American woman in a West Ham United shirt (what?) was the loudest of all the chatterers. She was picky about everything and droned like a twin propellered aircraft throughout the evening. Actually, the Americans won first prize for excessive volume and tiresome discourse on every occasion during our stay in Toulouse.

We opened our dining account with a Pastis for me, and a white wine for Joy. Her starter of risotto was stunning and as tasty as you could hope for. Yet her steak was fatty and fell short of expectations. My foie Gras was amazing yet my sliced duck failed to impress. Flower sellers bothered us as they glide between the tables shoving cellophane covered bunches up your hooter as you are about to stick a fork in your mouth. But it was a good evening all told. The ambience and lighting fitted perfectly with the grand buildings that enclose this popular square.

We wandered in another direction after supper and found bars and cafés about every 100 metres. We have more to explore tomorrow. Back in our room, the pillow-mist had reduced to just a mellow fragrance. We retired in a beautiful bed and slept throughout the night, as the overhead fan twirled gently and silently.

We slept-in later than we had planned. The curtains had blacked out the world completely and the sun burst in like a scud missile when they were finally opened. We skipped breakfast to explore the many market stalls that now filled the square outside. Traders with African products were mixed amongst locally produced wares. It was mostly leather goods and clothing but there were some interesting stalls selling jewellery, artisan items and curios. There were book stalls too. If only I could read in French, I'm sure I would have spent all my pocket money before we had breakfast.

We stopped at a bench, devoured a baguette between us and then headed to Bvd. de Strasbourg. There is a street market there as well, selling only farmed products. It lines the pavement down one side of this main thoroughfare. The range of products is breath-taking. Several varieties of grape vie for your pennies as well as more exotic items like figs and different types of chestnuts. Among the vegetable stalls we could easily get dizzy trying to determine which type of lettuce or tomato to add to a salad.

After all the fruit purveyors, of which there must have been 100, we stopped at two vans opposite each other. One selling breads and cakes, the other, cheeses. Joy flirted with the handsome bread seller and I the pretty cheese purveyor. We were seduced into buying more than was strictly necessary. Joy's purchases included a dozen tiny cakes which I did manage to finish off in quick succession. Comte and Mimolette cheeses were amongst my swag.

We continued along this street until we reached the Japanese Gardens, which are situated within the landscaped Compans Caffarelli Park. It's really peaceful and beautifully maintained. We were fortunate to be here when the early autumn colours around the ornate ponds were at their best. Strolling between manicured shrubs, we came upon a pagoda next to a traditional Japanese bridge. Ducks floated silently on the placid water while art students squatted, sketching and drawing every aspect of the surroundings. The scene was a living painting itself. We found a more secluded spot and tucked into our picnic lunch of breads, cheese and cakes, whilst watching others stroll by with toddlers, or carrying brief cases as they headed without due purpose from one meeting to the next. In one corner a guy was practising juggling with skittles while a group of students gathered together on the grass and sang happy birthday to a slightly embarrassed girl. The sun proved less able today, and in the shadows, the coolness brought goose-bumps to join the goose-bumps we had already cultivated due to the idyllic surroundings.

The south side of Place du Capitole is where the designer shops cluster. We preferred to seek out the tiny privately owned outlets that are scattered in between and around these monsters of capitalism. I found shirts galore to add to my dwindling collection. Many other places kept distracting us as we aimed for somewhere else. Kitchenware, specialist tea suppliers, artefacts, antiques and wine shops. We could not hurry. The narrow streets curve and merge with other narrow streets yet we were always still close to the centre.

We stopped at a specialist tea room and I ordered a pot of a rare white tea, accompanied by a lovely ice cream dessert. A woman at the next table, chain smoked no less than 4 cigarettes over one espresso. She was looking ever more distressed each time she received another text. An elderly couple hobbled as gracefully as they could to a table and sat with their tea whilst staring like newlyweds into each other's eyes as they chatted quietly. He occasionally brushed her hand with affection as he reached for the tea pot for a refill. It made me tearful just witnessing them.

Joy had caught the shopping bug. She spent a lifetime inspecting scarves of every shade, fabric and style to match whatever she could recall in her wardrobe back home. She does this only when I've been subdued into a state of total harmony with the world.

We found the St Stephen's Cathedral in Place St Etienne. It's another delightful landmark. It boasts some wonderful architecture inside. There is even better architecture outside, though it's not actually a church. The offices and apartments along the left-hand side of the street have rows of blue shutters at the windows on every floor. The effect of the simple lines has immense charm. Close by, a wine merchant had presented his wares in a unique style, as each bottle stood like a soldier, holding a spear, with a description at the foot. Behind, a cleverly angled façade hid the stock of each label. I had little opportunity to buy any but I hung around anyway. I should have sent Joy back to the scarf shop. We wound up the day by accepting a carrier bag full of samples from a young girl promoting a shop down a side street. It had creams and potions at extravagant prices inside. We had to promise we would visit the shop in return.

Another tea supplier close to the hotel had some fabulous products for sale. I did promise to return here as well, and I did, the next day. I bought a couple of gorgeously blended teas to stuff into our suitcase. We needed a little rest before preparing for the evening and after an hour sitting on the balcony of our hotel, watching delegates from a conference mingling at a bar, we togged up once more for supper at a different quarter in this wonderful city.

We had no luck finding a suitable venue near Place Wilson, or along Blvd. Lazare-Carnot, and ended up near the Victor Hugo courtyard. The restaurant that caught our attention is called Entrecôte. Inside we were confronted by bright yellow paper table cloths and no menu. The choice comprised entrecôte steak, cooked to your liking, an endless replenishment of fries and copious refills of water. The place was very busy. We were shown to a table at the back of the room, next to an English guy and an American. I'm guessing they were work colleagues, attending a business meeting in the city. Now, I have mentioned the loud boastings of Americans already on this trip. If the others were merely loud and distracting, this guy was capable of breaking the sound barrier. A young French couple on my left ended up seething at this guy. The lad said he wanted to shoot the American after just five minutes.

The conversation went something like this. Full volume:

American, to quiet Brit: "WHAT AIRLINES DO YOU LIKE TO FLY ON?"

Brit: "Mumbled" reply.

American: "WELL, RYAN AIR ARE AS BAD AS SOUTHWEST IN THE STATES YOU SHOULD KNOW." And he proceeded to tell everyone about several experiences of absolutely no interest whatsoever. He then went on to boast that he'd been to Vietnam whilst studying for his MBA. He talked about Marks & Spencer's bad practices in food production.

Then he continued to inform everyone present: "IT WAS A TRIP TO THE EASTERN ASIAN COUNTRY FOR THE SOLE PURPOSE OF MY RESEARCH FOR MY MBA."

He also told us that he, "ONCE CYCLED FROM PETERBROUGH TO IPSWICH. WHICH WAS 100 MILES. WHY I DID THAT I NEVER KNOW BUT HEY BUDDY, YOU GOTTA TRY IT. YEAH?"

The British man looked like he would rather choke to death on a piece of steak, than put up with any more of this chuntering prat. The restaurant staff kept trying to diffuse the situation by hovering nervously but to no avail.

He also told everyone what Singapore was like, what he thought of the Russian people, and that German food was awful because it comprised merely of meat and two veg. There was no cessation to this moron's world knowledge.

When he was presented with the bill he shouted: "I SUPPOSE YOU DON'T ACCEPT AMERICAN EXPRESS HERE EH? WELL I HAVE 5 OTHER CREDIT CARDS I CAN PAY WITH."

Everyone in the restaurant stood up and offered to pay if only he would leave the building immediately. It was torture. Why is it that the friendliest and most cheerful people in the world include Americans when on their home ground, but stick them on foreign soil they are either shooting at you or shouting at you?

The young French couple, wearing baseball caps and piercings next to us may have looked a little rough around the edges but were both quiet, respectful and friendly. A family where a dad and fellow guests took it in turns to try and placate a crying toddler, because he also wanted to kill the loudmouth! The mood throughout changed palpably when the American guy left, followed by a sheepish and visibly destroyed colleague.

The Place du Capitole square was crowded in the corner next to the Grand Opera House. It must have been the interlude during this evening's performance of Tosca. We had considered going ourselves but it had been sold out long before. Smart suited men and evening gowned women mingled, taking in the cool night air, many with a wine glass in hand. We made our way slowly through the crowd and back into the hotel for much needed sleep.

Our last full day here. The sun once more, was blazing like an exploding ball of gas in the sky, which of course is exactly what it is! The market stalls were again in evidence but there were much fewer today than yesterday. We had petit-déjeuner in a small café and bought more goodies before dumping them back in the hotel. We had a good look around while we were here. It's very opulent all over and is perfect in every way, save for the creaky floorboards. Thank goodness we were on the uppermost floor. Even tip-toeing from the bathroom resembled a forest of dead trees cracking and falling onto rock-hard ground.

Out in the city we stomped towards the Grand Park where several couples strolled, hand in hand. A fountain sprayed high into the sky and next to that, a statue of a young man with something tucked under his arm. "That's Bacchus" suggested Joy. "It's a wine jug he's holding, he's the God of wine." I was not convinced. I approached it and snapped a picture. "That is not a jug Joy. That's a chicken under his arm!" I later learned that it's called the Winner of the Cockfight by Falguiére, a son of Toulouse (1864). The original sculpture can be found in the Musee d'Orsay in Paris.

In the Royal Gardens a family of picnickers were feeding ducks by hand as cameras clicked away. There is supposed to be a maze here, but we never found it to get in, let alone find a way out. The Jardin les Plantes is the largest garden area. A waterfall and deserted twisty paths lead to streams through well-kept gardens. Despite the encroachment of winters' destructive inclemency, it was still lovely in here. We snapped quite a few pictures of cottages, a wicker windmill and real chickens, with beautiful plumage.

We walked alongside the canal to the port area. The main centre of Toulouse is surrounded by water, be it the Garonne or a series of canals. At a juncture where barges were moored, we stopped for lunch in a lovely pub. The Italian styled burgers and onions were too plentiful to finish. A pug dog that was lazing on a settee came and snuffled for leftovers. Three rough looking lads, as polite and friendly as Andy Pandy and his friends, had sat next to us. Not one person in here besides us spoke any English. It made for a very pleasant hour. We all shook hands when we departed.

Walking past one of the shops where I had purchased a couple of shirts earlier in the week, I noticed some guy inside ranting and raving at the proprietor. It got violent as I quietly peeked through the window, from a safe distance. The guy then started flinging shirts all over the place as the shop assistant and boss man waded in to stop him. Two passing armed police officers had not noticed this fracas and I felt compelled to point it out to them. They burst into the shop to confront the miscreant only to calm down instantly and leave the shop with a nonchalance of disinterested window shoppers. They said it was no longer a problem and wandered on their way. Maybe they just didn't stock his collar size!

Back at the hotel we collected our cases and thanked the staff for looking after us, leaving the building for the last time. We had only one regret, there is a rugby match scheduled at the Stadt Toulouse stadium the following day. We would both have loved to witness a game here. Especially, if it a was two-legged affair with Toulon.

AQUITAINE

Bordeaux

Bordeaux is one of the top three places anyone would name if asked about the famous wines of France. It's often used as the benchmark for wines of quality produced anywhere in the world. For me, being a wine enthusiast, it's like the holy grail. But this region is not all about wine.

We arrived by train in the early evening at the Gare St Jean. Directly outside is a terminal for trams and buses. We were staying at the Apartment Hotel Victoria Garden, at Place de la Victoire, a very short bus ride, and an even shorter walk down the Course del la Somme to get there. The street itself has a number of bars and restaurants near the square but was quietly residential by the time we reached the security gates of the complex.

After checking into the hotel, we were soon back out in the Place de la Victoire searching for somewhere for dinner. The old city streets begin right here. It was lively with revellers as there is a university faculty right on the doorstep. The atmosphere was good and the glass of wine with our meal sealed the feeling that this was going to be an excellent base for our visit.

This city has few inclines, buses and trams are frequent, inexpensive and cover every area we expect to visit. In the morning with the sun shining brightly, we were not idle in getting ourselves back in the square. After photographing everything around us, including the giant turtle (with offspring), we headed under Le Porte d' Aquitaine and aimlessly along the streets and passage ways. Buildings of architectural interest abound and beckon you down side alleys and between shops and bars. There's a square or recess around every corner and a very relaxed bustle is created by the many students, locals and tourists. There's every kind of shop, café, bar and tourist attraction squeezed into these enclaves. Beyond are tree-lined avenues, parks and monuments, with plenty of seating available for when we wanted to just stop and watch the world go by.

The beautiful river Garonne that we last saw in Toulouse, is impressively wide as it flows through the city, and as we reached the esplanade, we had two lovely surprises facing us. The first was a flotilla of tall ships and timber-built yachts lining the Quai that had sailed in the day before from Liverpool. They looked extremely grand, with all the rigging and beams adjoining the very high masts. The second surprise was the staging of the major wine tasting event, the Bordeaux Fete du vin, which is held only once every two years.

We queued and purchased tickets from the onsite kiosk for the following day. The event stretches the whole way down the quayside from Ponte de' Pierre to the Quinconces Fleuve tram stop. The price of our ticket included day long travel on the trams and buses. This is to alleviate the awkward circumstances of drinking and driving. The fact that it is merely a wine tasting festival, does not underestimate how much is actually swallowed during the event. Spittoons are optional.

For the rest of our first day we walked for miles yet never seemed to stray very far from the narrow lanes. The half-timbered buildings make Bordeaux one of the largest 18th century urban areas in Europe containing over 350 historical monuments. The bars and bistros are often small enough for only a couple of large families or a band of touring motorcyclists to squeeze in. The gardens and parks are so well maintained, the only caution needed is to pay attention to the tramlines that run through the centre of some parks and around blind corners.

We had a fantastic day. A heady mixture of smart precincts, churches, secret passageways, delicatessens and wine merchants. After strolling through downtown and having to stop so many times to take in the pure pleasure of all the buildings, we didn't even get as far as the ultra-modern construction of the Cite du Vin museum. Now that we have tickets for the wine tasting festival, we put a hold on visiting this auspicious venue this time round.

The history of the city began around 300 B.C.E. In the 3rd century C.E. the Vandals arrived, followed by the Visigoths and the Franks. The Aquitanians came along next and things only settled in the middle of the 8th century when Duke Waifer sparred with our friend, King Pepin the Short, which resulted in Bordeaux being named capital city for the region.

In the 12th century, a certain Count Henry Plantagenet married Eléonore, Duchess of Bordeaux and very shortly afterwards ascended to the throne of England. This gave the city great sea trading opportunities, which lends credence to the immense status and rich history of this Atlantic Ocean port. Bordeaux has leapt into my top 5 of the best cities in France for anyone to visit. It's not just the wine. It has an amazing amount of charm and the history that can occupy any visitor for days. It helps that the landscape is flat and everything is close at hand. It's just aching on the legs because there is so much of it.

We must have stopped for snacks and coffee more times than on any visit we've made in France so far. There's so much to soak up. Speaking of which, I need a large supper this evening; I've a lot of wine to soak up tomorrow. We chose a small bistro close to the hotel, declining to join the student patrons of the Bad Mother F*cker bar. I didn't fancy a hot dog at lunchtime either from the take away named Doggy Style! Fortunately, there are more than enough options for the discerning visitor who would want to avoid making grandparents blush when they show the holiday snaps back home. I did say I love this city.

By mid-morning we were on the tram and expecting a large queue for the grand opening of the wine festival. It was a bit overcast and since all the stands are out in the open, we have to keep an eye on the sky. I don't want water getting into the wine! We alighted at Quinconces and strolled back through the park. Joy pointed to a statue and asked who Michel Montaigne was. Big mistake. I spent the next half an hour, as we queued to get our first glass of wine, enlightening her to the brilliance of this great man, who was Mayor of Bordeaux. He inherited many hectares of vineyards back in the 16th century. His first admission was that he could not tell a grapevine from a cabbage. His real achievement was his genius in philosophical awareness and intellectual guile. I promised to lend her my collection of his books 'The Essays of Montaigne' when we get home. Poor Joy, she should have asked me about tall ships.

The ticketing system of the wine tasting had been carefully thought out by the organisers. Each card we held allowed for 12 samples, plus a dessert wine, from any of the stalls along the quayside. Fortunately, with thirty different stands, each offering a fair choice, there was little chance of me having any credits left over. However, Joy didn't think she would get through anywhere near her allocated quota. I'm sure we will work something out! We had a plan already. Joy will select white wines, I'll select reds. We can sample each other's choices as we see fit. We were armed with a handy pouch that held a tasting glass and a leaflet, wipes, and of course, the all-important 'credit' card.

We fared extremely well, there was no rush. We had snacks along the way, bottled water and a little notebook for our tasting notes. It was not overly busy, so queuing up to point at a bottle and handing over our tasting glass was not restricted by time. After each glass was emptied, we rinsed it out at one of the water stations and headed for the next stall. I don't think we poured many samples away. The tall ships docked along the Quai were enticing folk to pay to go on board and do some more tasting. I'm not so sure that some of the enticers weren't press gangs. After three glasses of Haut Medoc and suddenly you've signed on as a galley slave for the next race to Freemantle! We had more than enough distraction on dry land, getting to all these famous wine producers.

We did stop for lunch, leaving the quayside and crossing the road to squeeze into a corner of the grand and beautifully maintained Le Belle Epoque restaurant. The ceiling inside is magnificent. Whilst enjoying my tray of oysters we got talking to a group of men from Sunderland. They said they had booked their trip a year ago and had travelled especially for this event. When we admitted we had just stumbled on it by coincidence, one guy wanted me to write down the lottery numbers for the coming weekend. We were then joined by a German couple and our lunchtime discourse became more of a soiree than a quick bite. The conversation was anything but snobbish comments about various wines. It was just lovely banter.

We all eventually realised there were more wines to be tasted, so we left and blended in with the growing crowd to point our tasting glasses at other bottles on the stands.

When we had completed our intensive research, we compared notes and came to the conclusion that first prize went to a white Bordeaux, from the Appellation Pessac-Leognan. When we return to the UK, I shall search out a supplier and see if we can obtain a bottle or six.

The final hour was spent watching children and adults splashing between the spouting fountains of the large Reflecting Pool. A shrilling bag pipe player added to the scene, with the Place de la Bourse being the back drop for a thousand photographs. The sun held sway in the sky and I began to sway on the ground! We had cleared the credit cards and could queue at the kiosk to purchase another round of tickets for tomorrow. Joy promised to listen to more about the wonders of Michel Montaigne on the tram back to the hotel if I didn't buy more tickets.

The wine festival, in a small way, restricted what we had intended to achieve with our first visit to Bordeaux, in that we had lost a day of geographical exploration. However, my wine knowledge had greatly improved and I think Joy has applied to appear on Mastermind with her chosen specialist subject of the Mayor of Bordeaux in the 1500's. This cannot be our last visit. We both agreed it has so much more to offer. The very reputation as a world-renowned producer of fermented grape juice has possibly hindered its attraction of being a fantastic city whatever your interests.

We are pushing on. There's more to this region beyond the banks of the Garonne. We are going to hire a car and head even further west. It holds some delightful surprises, beyond degustation.

Arcachon

We took the D1250 road out of Bordeaux instead of the quicker A63, as dual carriageways and streams of HGV's didn't seem so appealing. Both roads are very straight and run almost parallel. The quieter route should offer more time to enjoy the surroundings along the way. It's only about 40 miles to the bottom lip of Arcachon bay so the slower average speed on this road is not going to make a lot of difference in the end. The first village we came to was Croix d' Hins which is not featured on many maps. It is a few miles short of the town of Marcheprime. You pass it before you know it. There's a railway station here and little else except for a few houses. What is intriguing about this hamlet is that it was once home to the biggest airfield in the world. In the early 1900's, three thousand hectares of this flat expanse was owned by aircraft builders Louis Bleriot and Gabriel Voisin. The land is right next to the current railway station and the two aviator pioneers trialled a number of their prototype aircraft here. The work they did here eventually led them to accomplishing the feat of being the first to cross the English Channel by powered flight. There's absolutely nothing to be seen of their existence or the airfield now, except for a column that was erected in 2010 to commemorate the death of another pioneering pilot by the name of Leon Delagrange. He took off in a prototype aircraft with a bigger engine, which caused the bodywork to break away and Leon plummeted to his death at that very spot.

It wasn't until we passed Biganos that the horizon changed. We were now driving through the bay side villages along the southern shores of Arcachon

Bay. It's all very interesting, neat and modest. There's lots of forestry despite the buildings and we arrived at our booked apartment in a tiny estate at the top of a country lane, just outside Arcachon. The apartment was superb. A ground floor flat with our own garden and picture windows that overlooked a forested valley. The estate was once part of a Government scheme for military telecommunications. There are war time bunkers and a derelict site comprising several buildings along the footpaths that are now used by dog walkers and joggers. A tall radio mast stands on a hill top. There's a giant golf ball construction behind security fencing suggesting a listening post that reached way beyond the horizon of the Atlantic Ocean. We walked around the base once or twice during our stay. Wildlife and flora were in abundance and the forest cover made for a delightful if unexpected scenario.

Dunes du Pilat

We took the car a few miles down the road, driving through a forest and arriving at the largest sand dune in Europe. This didn't sound much like a boast to us. Even when we parked up amongst the trees and had to cough up a fee, we were still not convinced. We were greeted by a couple of wooden shacks selling beach guff and a café with low grade facilities and supplies. Still we were not convinced, but the Sunderland guys back in Bordeaux said that we should not miss checking this place out. We followed a trail through the woods as the muddy soil underfoot turned to sand. Deep sand. Soft, deep sand, that began to spread in a wide radius through the surrounding trees. Then the sand became a steep slope. Like a dune. We are still deep inside the forest. We had to remove our shoes to cope with the climb. Children were running about in front of us, older folk began to wheeze and slow their progress. As we climbed, we broke away from the forest and saw in front of us, what was unarguably, the biggest sand dune in Europe. It was a very long and arduous climb to the top. Once we reached it the slope down to the beach was even steeper, and a very long way down. Looking around as far away as we could see, the dune had woven itself into the very fabric of the forest floor. Across the outlet of Cap Ferret Basin, we could see the lighthouse and the peninsula some 3 miles away. To the south, this yellow/white dune stretches and dominates the land. Whilst the Atlantic was a sheet of royal blue, scarred with exposed sandbanks and the white swale from tiny yachts twinkling in the bright sunshine. The reason behind this fabulous, natural marvel lies in the way the winds and tides force more sand every year to pile up along this particular shoreline. The dune expands constantly and is still pushing into the forest that does its best to protect inland vegetation. Houses are slowly being engulfed by the encroachment of this 'living' phenomenon, and conservationists are forever making efforts to keep the sand at bay.

It was worth the hamstring pulls and muscle aches to reach this point. I feel ashamed, I had no idea until now that this place existed. The beach below was somewhat busy but it looked deserted further south, so we made our way back down to the car to explore some more.

Biscarrosse Plage

There are long beaches all the way along this coastline. Some are easier to reach than others. As we drove south, we checked out several narrow roads that led us to a parking strip and then a duckboard walkway to a deserted stretch of sand. Some were occupied by surfers and camper vans and little else. Any one of these remote beaches would be ideal for a hideaway day as long as you packed enough food, snacks, a wind break and a Portaloo. For a more sociable escape we chose to follow the duckboard path to the beach at Biscarrosse Plage. It's busy, but big enough for everyone. There's an estate or two of chalet holiday homes and bars, without giving it that Torquay look. It's very peaceful, as if the developers have yet to add a funfair, casino and a hundred gift shops. I won't tell them.

We had a lovely relaxing day here. Lunch was easy to find because we brought it in a Lidl's bag. But there are restaurants to be found if you nip into the main centre of Biscarrosse Plage or even Biscarrosse town itself, which is a few miles inland. If you are really adventurous, the beach just keeps going south to Biarritz and beyond to Spain.

This is an amazing part of France that I had no idea existed. I was under the impression that the land west and south of Bordeaux would be either vineyards or marsh. I would have regretted going to Bordeaux on my exploration of France and missed any of what Joy and I had seen so far. And tomorrow, we have much more in store as we aim to circumnavigate the Bay of Arcachon and go try the oysters for which this basin is famous.

We ended our day back in the town of Arcachon itself. It has a lovely quayside and port. It's ideal for an evening stroll and we found the perfect restaurant in which to stuff our faces with mussels, crusty bread and white wine. Back at our apartment we were fit to burst, with elation, fulfilment and of course, joy. If we have overdosed, it didn't matter, just two doors up from our super quiet apartment was an ambulance station.

Cap Ferret

It was slightly overcast when we set off at about the same time that commuters were heading to work. We had a light breakfast on the balcony of the apartment and hoped to reach our intended destination before hunger pangs set in. It's about a 45-mile road trip to reach the south western point of Cap Ferret peninsula. If we took a ferry, it would be 3 miles. We chose the road around the bay which on the map, appears to hug the shoreline. It might give us some great views across the water. It didn't quite work out that way. Taking a left at Biganos, instead of the Sat Nav insistence that we take a wider but quicker arc, we ended up negotiating several villages with speed reducing bumps, tailbacks queuing to park in Aldi's and more traffic lights than Blackpool has illuminations. We never saw any coastline.

Once we reached Lège-Cap-Ferret, at the very northern point of the bay, the vista changed and things were looking up. Even the sun began to shine. The road now hugs both shorelines of the peninsula. We passed through much prettier villages that reminded us of Cornwall, with brightly painted wooden shacks, sheds and boats. It's lovely. At Belisaire, the tourist trappings begin to take over which makes it an ideal place for families and gatherings. There are plenty of bars, shops and cafes, many with wooden fasciae and it's difficult not to give in to temptation and take a walk around the town. A narrow-gauge railway nips alongside numerous small beaches. Not surprisingly, fishing is the main industry here and Arcachon Bay is ideal for shell fish cultivation. It's all very idyllic and has more of a village community feel than the bigger town of Sète and the Étang de Thau.

We wandered a little down the pathways that take you in between clusters of wooden lock-ups and dilapidated holiday cabins. Many are festooned with hanging strings of shells and other maritime objects. We were searching for a beach front café that served exactly what we were looking for; my second breakfast. There are a number of these cafes along this coastline that serve only oysters or langoustines, with wine or tea. It's 10am! We found a nice looking place and sat out on a patio looking across a small sandbank to the bay beyond. My wine and oysters were fabulous, Joy chose the langoustines. They were plucked from the tanks that lined the wall by the kitchen and prepared immediately. Crusty bread and garlic mayonnaise (aioli) completed the accompaniments as the sun climbed in the sky, varnishing the water with a golden sheen. Several wooden boats were moored around the sandbank while others pottered back and forth across the expanse. I could eat breakfast all day here.

Sadly, one glass of wine was the limit as we have more exploring to do. We kept driving south until there was no more road. The tip of the peninsula is called **Plage Mirador**. To get to the beach proper is a bit of a walk. Much of the area is fenced off for conservation purposes but a pathway leads up, over, around and down many grass strewn dunes until a beach is reached. It's an enormous beach. It stretches northwards for around 12 miles. From this point we can see south across the bay, to the sand dune at **Dunes du Pilat**. It looks as if a giant JCB has shovelled the whole of the Sahara Desert over the forests. By mid-afternoon, we walked back to the car and pottered through the lanes to find a café and followed up with a search along the coastline for other beaches and viewing points. We then made our way home to Arcachon before it got dark.

On our final day we headed back towards Biscarrosse Plage and stopped short at a beach that had a wooden 'Caribbean' cabin café next to a car park. There's a public toilet close by too. I had the unfortunate need to utilise the closet. It was a hole in the ground, with a foot shaped plate on either side to step on. The only way to steady myself was to squat and rest my upper back against the wall for balance. I leant my rucksack against the door and held my shorts in my hand. How do I get out of this position when I'm done? There is a flush, like a firehose nozzle protruding from the wall between my legs. I pressed the lever. The jet shot out, almost hitting the door of the cubicle. It flooded the whole floor. I had an instant high force bidet experience and a cold wash cycle for my nut-sack, rucksack and shorts. It almost took my legs from under me. The water gushed out under the door and flooded the rest of the toilet area. There was no toilet paper, and my beach towel was in Joy's backpack. Drenched through I pulled my soaked shorts on and waddled back outside and across to the table in the café where Joy was waiting. She was worried for me. I'd been gone a long time. Oh, yes, I can laugh now.

It was another lengthy walk up the wooden duckboards and steps to yet another deserted beach. At least I dried off very quickly in the sunshine, before wading into the sea. The whole day, beyond that point was uneventful. Except for Joy's random outbursts of mirth. She just kept saying sorry, but it was just so funny seeing you emerge from that toilet looking like you had fallen in a lake. Thoughts of digging a shallow grave in a forest clearing began to return.

We finished up the trip with a superb supper. A drive along yet another section of coastline and a peaceful final night in our apartment. The fresh air working wonders on our sleep patterns. In the morning we dropped the car off back in Bordeaux and boarded a train, direct for Paris, and home from there. We are coming back to France very soon. Next time, with our own car.

BRITTANY

This trip was planned with the intention to explore the area in Brittany around the town of Huelgoat. There are quicker routes than the one we chose to cross the English Channel. When I go to western France, I would normally seek a crossing from Portsmouth to Caen, or from Plymouth to Roscoff. This latter route is the most direct as it is takes less than an hour to drive from the ferry terminal to Huelgoat. On this trip, Joy and I took our own car and crossed the channel at Newhaven to Dieppe. The journey from there to Huelgoat is more than 300 miles, but we wanted to explore more of France along the way. The journey proved to be every bit as entertaining as we had hoped.

Before late autumn gave way to winter, we set off for East Sussex. This was Joy's first trip to Brittany and I was eager to show her some of the very special places I had encountered when I toured on my motorcycle the year before. First, we have to get to the ferry port and cross the channel. That's always less exciting than it really should be, what with the busy English traffic, ubiquitous roadworks and the various concerns about border security, luggage checks and potential delays. Once on foreign soil however, we just know all the stress melts away as the holiday feeling kicks in for real.

We had booked an early evening sailing from Newhaven, therefore we planned to reach the town around 2pm. The journey down was uneventful and my diesel driven car was put through its paces, to see if it really was more economical and reliable than my old Alpha Romeo. The gauge certainly showed promise, with hardly a dent in the fuel used by the time the 190 miles were covered.

We looked for somewhere to eat in the town. This must be the most godforsaken place since Sodom lost to Gomorrah in a play-off for worst ever city. The barman in the pub we found by the quayside looked at us askance when we tried to order food. "It's gone 2pm" he said. "We don't do food after 2pm."

We drove back into the centre of town and parked up in a square that looked like it could be used as a feature for a 1960's 'Desolate Town's' documentary. The precinct was so uninviting we felt sympathy for the sad looking weirdo begging for money as he sat on the steps of this concrete ghetto. He looked like he was waiting to be removed from his mortal coil. If I lived in this town, I would feel exactly the same.

We did find a café that was empty, apart for a couple of mums with pushchairs. It resembled one of those tatty hairdressers you occasionally see in run down town centres, but in this case a few tables were spread about and to our delight, food was still being served. We ordered a meal from the menu listed above the counter. We were the only customers ordering anything. The guy still got the order wrong. It was cheap without cheerful, but it filled a gap until we could eat properly on the ferry during the crossing.

The port is small and the ship that took us to more attractive surroundings and better cafés, was not busy. However, any idea of a pleasant voyage was ruined by a brat of a toddler in a play pen behind the rows of seating. It was left to scream and run about like a demented farm animal. His moron of a father just kept whispering to the child without effect. I had respite to hand as my MP3 player was in full working order. Joy, who was canonised for her extreme tolerance was struggling with it today and had omitted to charge her MP3 adequately before we left home. We tried to find other seating but the crossing was choppy and the upper deck areas were not going to do me any favours in the sea sickness avoidance plans. In the cafeteria, the chairs were hardly comfortable enough to sit on and eat a meal from, let alone settling back to relax.

During the journey I telephoned the B&B where we were due to spend the night to tell them what time we hoped to arrive. I only got an answer machine. However, a few minutes later I received a polite text. It advised that the reception would not be manned when we arrived but the door would be unlocked for us and there would be full instructions on how to find our room.

We alighted the ferry at around 10.30pm, and within 20 minutes made our way through the empty back streets of Dieppe to the Chambres d' Hôtes Villa Mon Repos in St Aubin-sur-Scie. We easily found the gated entrance, parked up on the gravel forecourt and grabbed our suitcases. The porch light helped in the darkness and when we entered the building I switched on the hall light to find a blackboard at the bottom of the stairs that read 'Welcome Mr Smyth,' followed by the name of our room (le Frére), breakfast arrangements and how to log on to Wi-Fi. Our boudoir was beautiful. Very individually designed and decorated with a lot of attention to detail. This was no mancave and certainly not Newhaven.

Sleep came easily. In the morning we were greeted in the communal kitchen by James who prepared our breakfast. We were the only guests last night (and I had crept about like a burglar as well). We chatted for quite some time before we headed off to cover the 300 or more miles to get to Huelgoat. The hotel grounds are lovely too, we made no haste to depart, we should make it by sunset. There's a relatively direct route from this little village to Brittany that can be completed almost all the way by motorway. There are also several routes available that will get you hopelessly lost and confused without accessing a motorway at all. We chose something in between. We were in no hurry and can enjoy a little exploration along the way.

We headed south, but instead of taking a right turn onto the D929 at Tôtes we continued onwards until we reached Duclair. The reason for this was a desire to cross the Seine and drive for a distance along the bank before turning west just after La Bouille. The first bonus appeared at Duclair. Instead of the anticipated bridge across the Seine, a car ferry was waiting. We were waved on board just before the barriers came down and the ferry shoved off. Fumbling for euros in our pockets turned out to be futile; there was no charge.

It was only a few minutes before we were back on the road and to our left the River Seine was making its way majestically north as we continued upstream. Already we were aware of the lack of traffic around us. The sun was shining too and everything was going fabulously well. Except the GPS (Gordon the Garmin). We had programmed it to show the way to our final destination and because we kept heading south, it was going apoplectic by constantly telling us to turn back and start again. We ignored its postulations. We switched the GPS voice off because 'he' cannot pronounce a single French name without sounding ridiculous. We eventually had to turn right, climbed a hillside that hugged the shoreline and after several very challenging hairpins, not to mention first gear shuffling, we headed down the other side and found Bourgtheroulde. This is a typically French laid out town that has several cafés, ideal for a lunch stop. It had turned out to be a very pleasant detour, we even kept away from the ring roads of Rouen.

We were heading west now and passed through, or close to, Brionne, Bernay, Orbec, Livarot, Vire and Villedieu-les-Poéles, before finally joining the motorway to Avranches and on to Huelgoat in Brittany.

It took us several hours longer than the motorway route would have served up, but 55 extra miles to the 300 anticipated were worth it. The Renault was sipping juice more sparingly than a lost Legionnaire in the Kalahari. Our base for the next couple of nights was the hotel in the centre of Huelgoat overlooking the lake.

Huelgoat

In the morning we filled the tank with fuel and the boot with groceries. The weather today was not conducive for anyone but ducks. Being on higher ground, this part of Brittany gets more than its fair share of high winds and rain. But at least the forests and vegetation are verdant. We took a wander through the local market which was fascinating for the array of produce and various artisan stalls, but it was agreed we should head north away from the squally showers and make for the coastline for lunch. We first stopped off at Guerlesquin, close to the foothills of the Arrée mountains in Finistère. It is the type of town I would love to live in if I resided in France. It is small enough to have charm yet big enough to sustain a thriving community, and with a 17th century prison plonked right in the centre it has some unique attractions. It is free to take a look inside. It's like a mini castle. In August each year the town plays host to the "World Standing Stone, Throwing" championship. The whole town has character and lives up to its self-proclaimed title of 'Quirky'.

Locquirec

We reached Locquirec by the time the sun had chased the rain clouds away and although it was too cold to sit outside, we enjoyed lunch in a gorgeous fish restaurant right by the quayside. This craggy coastline is littered with coves, bays, cliff top views and so many villages that it would be advisable to arrive with hiking boots and a thermos flask. We resorted to wandering about the streets and the easily accessible hillside after lunch. There are plenty of art and craft galleries here. Local artists and jewellers thrive on the tourists that seek such eclectic trinkets. Several buildings in the vicinity have thatched roofs and plenty of natural distractions for the more laid-back visitor. The sun made a special appearance just as we felt like sitting on a bench to watch the world go about its business, which happily, wasn't very much. The tide was ebbing and the wind had dropped completely. Down on the beach, dads and mums with small children pottered among the rock pools. Small boats emerged from the estuary, some heading out for leisure, others rigged up for more serious fishing.

When we could finally pull ourselves away, we took a circuitous route back to Huelgoat via a very twisty and beautiful coastal road through Poul Guioch, which then hugs the amazing bay en-route to Saint Michael-en-Grieve. We then turned inland to Ploumilliac and finally southward to Lanvellec and home. The whole day was a living art gallery of landscapes and seascapes, through pretty towns, coastal havens and beautiful forests. The skies stayed clear when it was most beneficial so we could linger at will.

After a good breakfast in the hotel du Lac, a clear, dry sky meant Huelgoat could now be explored. It's a mecca for walkers and traipsers, as it has enough attractions within the town's boundaries as well as the surrounding woods, to keep visitors occupied for more than just a day. The centre piece of the town is the man-made lake, a fortunate legacy of old silver and lead mines that have long since closed. We are now in the heart of the Arrée forest and beyond the weir at the edge of the lake, the water hurries into a wooded valley between and under boulders big enough to sink an oil tanker, let alone the proverbial battleship. Legend has it they arrived here as a result of mythical giants having a tizzy fit. It certainly could look that way. Clambering over them was fun and next to the rough-hewn path, the deep, aptly named La Grotte du Diable (Devil's Throat), that you can climb down into is certainly fun, if a little unnerving. The water can be heard below as it rushes through in a great hurry to get back into daylight. Joy didn't dawdle either, as she returned to the surface after rapidly clicking off several photographs in the semi darkness.

It's a very pleasant walk through these woods. We had to weave between and under several boulders to reach a clearing. Hiking paths criss-cross the hillside, and on the edge of a downward slope, stands a single rock about the size of a family caravan. It's known as the Trembling Stone. Press your hand in a strategic place and it will rock. The owners of the chalet at the bottom of the hill don't seem to be worried. A little further away in the woods, which can be reached by road, is a white house covered with ivy that doubles as a café and bookshop. It's very busy on a good day. Hikers and bikers flock here. It's deep in the forest, and a great idea to put a bookshop and café here. We arrived in the car but today it was closed. The rolling gardens at the back have semi sunken boulders and a variety of sculptured metal flamingos and other creatures, which should keep the children occupied while you relax with a coffee and a good book. We decided to head further afield once more.

Morlaix

We travelled north again but a bit further west than yesterday, through the Amorique Natural Regional Park. Morlaix is 30-minutes away. The roads were just fabulous; void of traffic, with inclines, declines, hairpins and long straights. The town itself may be limited for beauty spots and landmarks but there is still more than enough to demand some exploration down the winding, cobbled streets. The viaduct that crosses east/west is particularly noteworthy, especially with the boulevard underneath replete with bandstand, street side shops and cafes.

We enjoyed a casserole lunch in a small café and wandered round to another square that has restaurants aplenty. Folk were sitting outside, enjoying the gentle sunshine and the languid ambience. The half-timbered buildings hereabouts are wonderful examples of how ports and cities looked 200 years ago.

We ended up back at the car and set off further north for Plougasnou and the rugged, sea bashed coastline. We stopped and wandered a while, then moved on a bit and stopped again at Diben Bras. Here, the waves smash into honeycomb coloured cliffs. We tip toed across a pebbled causeway and climbed high up in the rocks to stand victorious, and watched the spectacle of fishing boats battle through criss-cross tides, seeking refuge in the placid harbour. At the port we observed boxes of freshly caught fish being landed and loaded into transit vans and couriered to the cannery.

The twisting coast road beckoned us on to Terenez where another harbour featured pleasure craft instead of fishing boats. We watched a grandfather punt a dinghy with his granddaughter on board, to a larger boat. They climbed on to the vessel and as he baled water from the floor space, she sorted the picnic bags they had brought with them. As we drove away, the old fellow pulled the cord to start an outboard motor and they puttered upstream. They were travelling parallel to us as our car climbed the hill that followed the shoreline. The boat disappeared upriver into a valley and we ended up back at Morlaix and then home.

We treated ourselves to galletes and cider for supper in one of the superb creperies in Huelgoat before turning in for the night. Tomorrow, we have a long day ahead as we plan to slice up the long journey back to Dieppe and the ferry to the UK.

If we had remained here, we could venture much further afield, perhaps south to Pont Aven. I have been there before. The small town has the charm of a Cornish village and celebrates traditional Breton festivals, where clogs and Celtic costumes are worn. The main event of the year is the Fête des Fleurs d'Ajoncs. The post-impressionist artist, Paul Gauguin had lived there and painted several of his masterpieces in the quiet backwater.

We could instead head to the west coast, south of Brest, where the terrain becomes much more rugged and testing, with sandstone peaks and countless beauty spots. It has far more to offer than we could cram into just a few days.

If we were heading home directly from here and catching the nearest ferry back to the UK, we would drive to Roscoff. It's less than 40 miles away and is a delightful port, nothing like many of the ferry ports that dot the shores of Europe. It's perfectly feasible to book a hotel in the town for a night, before or after sailing. Roscoff has lots of comfortable bars and restaurants, a botanical garden and lovely walks along the shoreline. The stone architecture reminds me of Scotland, which is probably why Mary Queen of Scot's came to stay when she was betrothed (at age 6) to Dauphin Francis, the soon to be King of France. Instead, we shall make our way along the Normandy coastline towards Dieppe, and spend a night somewhere new to both of us.

In the morning we left Brittany, knowing we shall return and spend a lot more time discovering the treasures that lie in these hills

NORMANDY

Honfleur

We plan to spend the night in Honfleur which is several hours drive from here. It cuts out around two thirds of the 330 coastal miles to Dieppe. I've heard so many good things about Honfleur it's about time I went to see what the fuss was about. We spent most of the journey on the motorway, bypassing Dinan which was a wrench: I know how beautiful this place is. It has a riverside port deep below the town itself. It's a magnet for tourists. There are many more beautiful places around here too. Head up towards Dinard and the roads lead to countless scenic locations. The coastal towns west from there will connect to the places we visited earlier in the week. The Pink Granite Coast is as pretty as its name suggests but were determined to get to Honfleur. Even the amazing Mont Saint Michel we can see just off the coast is not on our list to visit.

It was mid-afternoon when we arrived at Honfleur and instead of the jaw dropping beauty I was promised, I only felt head shaking disappointment. The traditional 18th century portside buildings are still there but the modernity of tourist trappings have overwhelmed them. The whole town was mobbed for a start. Traffic blocked every street, there was absolutely nowhere to park and hordes of people clogged the pavements and squares. A mock pirate ship and funfair seemed to be the key attractions. Families and clans of bikers surrounded every possible window and doorway of the bars, shops and cafes as we crawled through in a slow-motion log jam. I'm sure it is beautiful in the off-season when all the funfair rides have gone and the locals get their town back. But not today. There's not a chance that I was staying here overnight. Joy agreed. I want to continue our theme of charm and character not chaos and queuing. We were seeking leisurely, laid-back lingering, not legions of loud, loitering, landlubbers. I can get that in Largs during fair fortnight. It's a shame, the estuary of the river Seine flows by as it washes into the La Manche. There's a botanical garden nearby that would have been worth a visit too. Maybe an early springtime trip, mixed with a tour of the Normandy Beaches would be more suitable.

We hightailed it out of there, once we finally broke free of the yoke of gridlocked traffic, and headed across the river Seine to Le Harve via the stunning bridge that can be seen from miles around. Plan 'B' became Etretat on the Normandy coastline. It's the white cliff, coastal resort that inspired Claude Monet to create more than 50 paintings. This too was so busy that all the hotels were fully booked. The whole of France had decided to join us for a weekend along the northern coast. Plan 'C' was to try Fecamp. It's a bigger town than Etretat, but no less attractive for that. The harbour down the middle made it all the more enticing. Sadly, this too was fully occupied, but the wonderful receptionist in the Best Western created plan 'D' and phoned a hotel in a tiny place called Veulettes-sur-mer. They had rooms available. She warned us that although the town was charming, she had no idea as to the quality of hotel she was sending us to.

Veulettes-sur-mer

The road there was unbelievably twisty. It is called Coteau des Grande Dalles. We disappeared into deep ravines with hairpin bends that looked on the GPS display as if the road was a strand of tightly scrunched up wool. I would love to ride this stretch on my motorcycle. Gordon, the Garmin was going nuts trying to work out where on earth we were; he kept disappearing off the screen or doubling back on himself. He got his own back on us as we tried to find the hotel once we reached the centre. Despite Joy entering the exact coordinates, he forced me to drive up the hill and away from the town. He then demanded a right turn onto a 400-yard-long gravel track that ended at an electricity sub-station. We had to reverse before heading back down to

Centreville. This time we spotted the small hotel and parked up. 'Gordon' is going to end up being tossed overboard if he doesn't get his act together. The hotel was adequate, in that it was cheap, dry and quiet. I've seen makeshift flats in shelters for the homeless better furnished than here, but it was great to not be in Honfleur.

We have travelled 300 miles today. About 80 more than we anticipated. The walk along the sea front was pleasant but everywhere was closed and people had already gone home for the night. It's not the sort of place I would be happy to arrive at with my children for a fortnight's break, but the one night was good enough for the two of us. It was dark when we began to search for a place to eat. A small, busy restaurant welcomed us where the large empty one, attached to the town's casino did not. We had a bucket of moules and a bonfire sized pile of fries to help soak up the wine. The night was less than quiet and the central heating could not be turned down to anything lower than 'furnace'. Opening the window didn't help as the seagulls were having a protracted argument.

St Valery-en-Caux

It's Sunday morning and we were off again, along the coast to spend the day in Saint Valery-en-Caux. It's about a 20-minute drive towards Dieppe and turned out to be everything Honfleur no longer seems to be. The harbour area had boats six deep, stretching back upstream. There is a road bridge that has to be raised to allow boats to pass in and out of the haven. We wandered for hours picking out buildings of antiquity and others that are just beautifully maintained. It's not far to walk to the lighthouse on one side of the estuary, where we were followed by an elderly couple with a pushchair. I thought it was a very pleasant sight to see grandparents taking their offspring's baby out for a stroll in the sunshine. Well, that was until we reached the car park and they opened the door to an oversized camper van. It was not a child at all but a dinky, molly-coddled dog. This pathetic creature was wrapped up like a new born. When it was lifted down it had neither the strength nor will to move of its own accord. It just stood there, quivering and waiting to be carried into the warmth of the vehicle.

We spent all day in Saint Valery-en-Caux, apart from a short trip inland to visit the town of Cany Barville. Now this place is posh. We'd hoped to find a hypermarket that was open but that didn't happen, so we will have no cheap wines to take home. However, the town itself was a gem to wander around and we stumbled upon the 15th century watermill. It is set in a beautiful location and still operational, generating electricity. We also stopped for coffee in a sweet little café in the square, so the drive out was not wasted.

Back at Saint Valery-en-Caux we watched the boats coming and going, the road bridge was called into action more than once. The tide went out very quickly leaving one boat marooned in the mud while the crafts on the other side of the lock gently bobbed about in the calm water. Another highlight was a procession of vintage cars that trundled through the town. It was a rally where every conceivable mode of pre-war transport, with appropriately attired travellers, became the focal point of pedestrian attention. There was something happening everywhere today, and none of it disappointing.

Just as evening descended, we walked along the sea front once again and decided to patronise a casino we had spotted earlier. This was ostensibly just to use the toilet, as restaurants elsewhere were now closing up for the day. The bar was open so we chose to have a glass of wine while we were there. To our delight, there was a dance floor which was full of young and old alike going through their paces to Latin American rhythms. They knew all the right steps, and each couple went through their full repertoire with every tune. It's 6.30pm on a Sunday evening in a casino on a sea front in Normandy. Several of the young guys and girls were so enjoying themselves and dancing with such skill, it was hard to tear ourselves away in the end. It was so good to watch, Joy suggested we ought to take lessons when we get home. I changed the subject. It was time to eat. We found a small restaurant up a side street that served crepes and charged very little for the privilege. I love this town. It has so much character. It would serve well as a central point when exploring this part of the coastline.

It's been a lovely day. We have less than 30 miles and several hours in which to reach Dieppe for the late evening ferry back to Newhaven. To make the most of our scurry to the port we kept on the little back roads, hugging the shoreline as much as possible, instead of the more direct D925 to Dieppe. At Vueles-le-Roses the pebble beach is shielded by cliffs, not unlike Dorset. It reminded us of Sidmouth. There are little roads leading to sea fronts at St Aubin-sur-Mer, Quiberville and Pourville-sur-Mer. Each diversion lightened the mood as we knew in a short while we would be clanking across the ramp of the ship that would take us home.

It was an easy trip to plan. Easy because we had no fixed deadlines except for the ferry crossings. We could have changed our destination on any given day, which we did. Although we struggled after Honfleur there was never any panic setting in as there will always be a B&B or hotel that has a vacancy. Costs were kept low due to taking the ferry crossing from Newhaven and picking out modest hotels as best we could. Travelling like this is amazing fun. Without a tight schedule, we felt much more relaxed. It won't be the last time we do this.

Evreux

We are in Paris and waiting at the Gare St Lazare to take us back to Normandy. I had recently had some treatment for a back injury and was coming to the end of the recommended recuperation period. It was considered better that we take the train rather than drive to France. As long as my activities covered little more than bending my elbow or shuffling a few hundred metres on foot, it should be okay to get away for a few days. We chose Evreux for that very purpose. The journey so far was painless and the scenery as we sped away from Paris, delightful. A little old dear next to me snored gently and the lovely young lady opposite smiled sweetly as I ensured

I stayed comfortable. I never complain! For two reasons, we had booked to stay at a hotel situated directly opposite the station. First, it was of course, not too far to walk and secondly, it was the cheapest in town. Despite being aware of its location on a main thoroughfare, we took the risk for a quiet night's sleep. However, I have adopted the motorcyclist's habit of keeping a couple of pairs of ear plugs about my person. They certainly came in handy.

It was early afternoon when we set out to explore the town and get our bearings. Each corner and side-street offered a new vista. There are some old buildings that survived the Nazi bombardment during WWII when Evreux was extensively damaged. Records say that the town at one point, burned for a whole week. The shops in the precinct appeared to have few if any, familiar chain stores. There was certainly an absence of charity shops and 'pound' stores too. The Sales were on in some outlets which made the whole afternoon experience much more entertaining. The cafés looked inviting and we took our time to decide on which restaurant to secure for our evening meal.

We finally came upon the perfect place. It was a creperie in the Rue du Duc de Bouillon. From the exterior it resembled a shed but inside it was pleasant and intimate with a lot of artwork on the walls. The odd collection of tasselled covered tables had curio objects or vases in the centre. A tiny counter was tucked tight into the corner of the main dining room. None of the rooms were large. It was very homely, just like coming to tea at your eccentric aunt's terraced cottage. We returned at supper time. Three diners sat at another table and all acknowledged us as we entered. The proprietor came out from the kitchen, wiping her hands on her apron and smiled a warm greeting. No one here spoke English but we still got along fine. I ordered Pastis to show my Francophilia. The menu offered crepes or galettes with a choice of toppings. Ours arrived with just about everything from the list, including a scrunchy salad. We also received a pottery flagon, filled with locally brewed cider and a china cup from which to drink. I hope they don't expect me to sing Le Marseillaise. You can't get more French than this. It was a fabulous meal.

We might have enjoyed it more if we knew what the chatter at the other table was about. The three people tried to engage us but we could only smile pathetically. My French translation book was of little use. I managed to discreetly check-up a word or two but the conversation had long since moved on by the time I found a phrase that made sense. Other diners came and went and by the time we finished our coffee and paid, we were ready for a bit more of a wander in the streets before the sun finally set. We all shook hands, with smiles and good wishes as we left. "Bonsoir," I do understand.

It was very quiet in the streets, just the occasional courting couple hanging around the kebab shops and cigarette vendors. We sauntered around more back streets and made mental notes for a more lingering look in the morning. As we got closer to the centre of town, the bars and cafés were busy but we were happy enough to retire to our room. Shutters wound tight to block out the light and ear plugs in to block out any sounds. We slept well. Vive la France.

Taking out my ear plugs in the morning I congratulated myself on a piece of good foresight. The rush hour traffic was in full voice under our window. The aluminium shutters squeaked open and the sunshine blazed in to hail another beautiful day. After croissant and coffee, we followed the town map to the nearby commonwealth war cemetery. With this year being the centenary of the end of the Great War, it would be appropriate to pay respects to those who gave their lives so that we can wander about like nerdy tourists in shorts and tee shirts. It was a shorter walk to the cemetery than it looked on the map.

I clicked my camera at entrances to parks, gables, wrecked greenhouses and unusual foliage as we seemed to pass something remarkable in every street. The cemetery was very well maintained, like so many in France. This one was mixed with family graves and ancient crypts as well as rows of headstones of military personnel. The French soldiers' graves were marked with swords, and the Allies' with Portland stone. Engravings revealed Canadian, South

Africa and many other nations that contributed to the efforts of the Second World War. We wandered for quite a while here and checked out a few of the family graves and crypts. Very thought provoking and poignant.

As we ambled back into the town, crossing the river Iton, we came to one of Joy's favourite establishments, the Tourist Information office. On the notice board we zoomed in on a flyer for a puppet show. The next performance was at 2pm today. It's part of an arts and dance event week. Underneath that was another flyer entitled "Dance Spectacular" that the Academy of Dance was advertising, for this very evening. With these two events filling our agenda for today we decided to take a coffee break in the café next door and re-jig our plans.

The theatre where the puppet show was being held is located inside a college campus. The lobby of which was awash with mums and dads and very small, excited children. We were handed a ticket each at the door and went through to sit at the back to watch a short show entitled The Circus Comes to Town. It's not that I am in to puppetry, it's just nice to see what the locals do and be a part of what the community get involved in. We also agreed that we shouldn't have to worry about language problems because it is all about imagery. It can be fascinating even if the content is rubbish. I watched a puppet show in Lisbon not long ago. In that instance, it was an extremely clever concept with unique stage designs and props, but utterly awful in content and plot. I gave it 10/10 for originality but only 3/10 for content.

This show was very much like those oddball entertainment events that the school board put on back home when I was a kid. A bunch of mop haired arty types in dungarees making serious work of erecting a few props and lights and then putting on a threadbare show which would still enchant the children. Most of the show included silhouette shapes projected onto a screen, depicting circus characters and creatures arriving triumphantly on the stage, performing their specialist act and then leaving again. Even I can understand that narrative. There were amusing moments as the silhouette elephant blew away like a deflating balloon and a man shot from a cannon landing in a bowl of soup. We were very entertained and everyone enjoyed it. I liked it more than the play in Lisbon.

Wandering back towards the town we passed a derelict church adjacent to a whole cluster of buildings that used to be a monastery. The city has a long ecclesiastical history and was once within the domain of the kings of Navarre in Spain. In the 1300's, King Louis the Headstrong (no relation to Louis the Armstrong) married off his daughter Joan II to her French cousin Philip d'Évraux the Wise. By default, he became the King of Navarre. They had a son who succeeded them called King Charles the Bad and in turn his son, reigned as King Charles the Noble who finally ceded Evreux to France in 1404. Thirteen years later it became Scottish land when it was awarded to Sir John Stewart of Darnley for services against the English in the Hundred Years War. I love learning about key figures in history with unusually blunt nicknames. Joy had a few ideas about my nickname, should I ever become ruler.

We had plenty of time before this evening's performance and we made tracks for a little lane we spotted yesterday. The path led between some old houses, up a grassy hillside via lots of twisting steps that took us higher and away from the dwellings. It was not a difficult climb and my back was not complaining so we kept going. We soon reached a large clearing that gave views across the whole city. The surrounding meadow was vibrant with flowers and insects. Butterflies with patterned wings I'd not seen before, flitted around my feet, and bees were flying along, riding piggy back. A young couple were cuddling in the long grass nearby. If we hadn't appeared, I guess they might have been doing piggy back riding themselves. The view down the glen and across to the surrounding hills in the distance was worth the climb. The ivory white stonework of the Notre Dame Cathedral stands proud over the surrounding buildings, like a mother swan with her ugly ducklings. A cathedral has been here since the 4th century. The present building is a bit younger, probably 11th century. We found a bench, sipped water, sucked on a sweet or two and took in the peace and bliss of this moment. There was silence but for the insects, the swaying of the grasses and my ever-present tinnitus. Beautiful.

We made our way back down the slope and followed the crooked route to the cathedral itself. It's bigger than most football stadia. Outside you can get neck ache staring up at the detailed filigree skills of the stonemasons. Inside you get no respite as you strain to admire the ornate glass work and great organ.

The nearby museum was worth a peek. The basement boasts a Roman wall. A gaggle of school children listened intently as their teacher explained the artefacts in the glass cases. The art galleries too intrigued. The paintings and photographs on display slowed our pace in every room. Elsewhere, there are grand buildings that look more impressive from ground level. Some are half timbered and look like a Shakespearean chambermaid is likely to open a window to throw out the slops at any moment. Walking alongside the river a little further from the centre, we sat in the sunshine as ducks swam around and the cathedral loomed like a majestic backdrop in an idyllic Constable painting.

The theatre where the dance spectacular was being held is close to the college, so we had little difficulty in finding it. We arrived in good time and watched as excited parents and their offspring trooped through the glass entrance doors. Everyone was in smart attire. This is a very modern theatre. We were pleased we had changed out of our safari shorts and Hawaiian shirts. This should prove to be a wonderful experience. Inside, the auditorium is even more impressive. It has at least 500 tiered seats and a stage big enough to host a very large production. An elderly lady who spoke good English sat next to me and enlightened us as to what this whole event was about. It was a show put on between the College of Music and the Academy of Dance, to mark the end of the school year. The dean of the college was the conductor and the musicians and performers were either staff or students. The dancers had been picked from all years and classes at the academy.

The first performers to arrive on stage were utterly enchanting. This piece was entitled Little Steps. A score of tiny tots went through their routine with such pride and effort that I had tears in my eyes. They were fabulous. They tapped the floor, stamped their feet and tripped around in sequence to the simple tunes being played. The head tutor was on hand to join them from time to time and 20 minutes went by in a flash. The second part was performed by older children, up to perhaps 13 years of age. They danced all sorts of styles from classical, Latino and modern. It was all very tasteful and colourful, their costumes befitting of each theme. Joy and I were overwhelmed by it but the best, was yet to come.

Part three was taken from Delibes' Coppelia. This ballet always gets to me. Goosebumps and big smiles. The dancers were amazing for their age; mid to late teens. It was enthralling. The outfits were fabulous and the whole production so professional. We had just spent two amazing hours in the company of some very talented performers, and a whole theatre full of justifiably proud parents. We thanked the lady next to me for her informative help and we made our way to find somewhere to eat, leaving the parents and excited participants to celebrate such a wonderful evening's entertainment.

There was a fish restaurant just a short walk on the way back into town. We sat in linen table clothed comfort and ordered a bottle of Quincy and a sea food platter to begin. Sea bass for the main course and ice cream for dessert. It was all delicious. The waiter was a little curt to begin with, but then he relented and asked if he could practice his English on us. He said his Filipino wife spoke no French and nagged him mercilessly for speaking English so badly. We enjoyed some great banter as the restaurant began to empty. I ended the meal by ordering a Japanese whisky for a nightcap, and instead of pouring just the one shot, he virtually filled my tumbler. We had been chatting about whiskies earlier. It was a balmy evening and the wine and whisky made the shortish, giggle infused walk back to our hotel frivolously memorable.

Our short stay in France worked wonders for my recuperation. We made no effort to overdo anything except the indulgence of luxury and distraction. It made the perfect choice for a short break. The rail service is excellent and it takes less time to reach here than it can to get to some of the delightful, if awkward places, by train in the UK.

Back in Paris, we had a time to wander and do a little shopping before our train home. We walked to Rue la Fayette and joined the throngs in one or two of the major stores. As we waited to cross the road at Square Montholon I was approached by a young lad who said he noticed a gold ring at my feet. He picked it up and asked if it was mine. Of course, it wasn't. I told him so and said it was his lucky day and go enjoy his good fortune. He said he was an illegal immigrant, from Yugoslavia and therefore could not keep the ring as he could not possibly sell it. "Goodness" I said. "Yugoslavia? You must have left there before you were born. How did you manage that?" He then admitted to being Serbian but still insisted I keep the ring. He even tried to put it on my finger. As we tried to push him away a passing lady spoke to him in French. He turned tail and ran off across the road. She then faced me and apologised. She said she was a retired police officer and warned she would have him deported if he did not leave tourists alone. And people tell me Parisians are rude and dismissive of foreigners.

LOIRE

Touraine

We have returned to France by car. We are in the beautiful wine growing region of the Loire. It's a big family gathering and we have booked a château in the tiny village of Villeloin-Coulange, deep in the countryside. If we had come here directly from Evreux in Normandy, it would have been a gentle cross-country journey of around 200 miles. Instead, we came in a cavalcade of cars from the southern reaches of Wales, crossing the English Channel via the Euro-Tunnel. It's a long way round.

After a few days relaxing and exploring this area, Joy and I plan to move on to other parts of the Loire and take in a good sample of the different landscapes, culture and of course, the amazing wines this appellation is famous for the world over.

The convoy of three cars arrived at the château together, despite horrendous traffic congestion around Paris. The roads were not only gridlocked but confusing in the extreme. It's not a simple ring road like the M25. Lanes split, have ambiguous instructions and at one point all three cars diverted on to different junctions only to converge again several miles further along. Passengers were constantly phoning each other and checking where on earth each car was. At times the mayhem was frightening as vehicles careered from lane to lane to gain little advantage. Some motorcyclists with tiny children on board, holding on for dear life, as they filtered between the cars at speeds I could not even contemplate.

Once away from all the ring roads and motorways, the roads were a delight. The last part of the journey took us through open fields bisected by asphalt farm tracks. We all arrived together, unlocked the gates and collected the key to the front door. There was plenty of space for parking and just enough bedrooms for the dozen or so people now taking up occupancy. It's a very old building, idyllic even, at first sight. However, once we all had a giggle about the creaking floor boards, ill-fitting doors and archaic amenities, we had to set up a roster to ensure there was a little more functionality in getting chores done. Hot water, waste disposal, washing lines, food preparation and even bathroom usage needed to be addressed. Fortunately, there were no young children with us so we soon got it sorted. Once allocations were agreed everyone settled down to take in the positive things around us.

Joy's parents had suggested this treat. They love France as much as we do but don't get quite the opportunities to travel freely these days. It was a great way to get the family together. I'm all for variety, and this will give everyone the opportunity to experience a very pleasant escape from the rigours of working life back home.

Villeloin-Coulange

The village is situated in the Indre-et-Loire department that shares its boundaries with Loire-Cher, Indre and Vienne within the Central Loire Valley. In short, we are smack in the middle of the wine producing region of Touraine. The town of Touraine is about 30 miles north west of here. The nearest village of any note is Montrésor, less than 2 miles away. We are restricted in the village to two small shops and a church. Just down the lane is an arch over the road once part of a monastery complex but now a residential and business centre. It has turrets with candle-snuffer shaped roofs and tiny windows. More medieval buildings are tucked behind high walls. The short walk to the bottom of the valley reveals the river Indrois that runs alongside a converted railway station and other lovely cottages. The boundaries of the village are forested. Beyond these, wide open fields of arable land roll to distant hills. Footpaths beckon exploration, the crooked tracks lead through long grass into the woods. If ever a location was sought to re-create the image of Enid Blyton's Famous Five stories, this is it.

The grounds of the château are not without charm. The high boundary walls are centuries old and locked doors and bricked up gateways bear tell-tale signs of history. We found a small grotto and a statue or two among the long grasses and weeds that have been allowed to profit. The rose garden desperately needed some TLC but the bees still kept themselves busy. At the front, the balcony/patio was ideal for lounging and snacking on. We did have to keep moving the seating as the day wore on to keep in the sunshine, or out of it, depending on your proclivities. I don't think we will be complaining about that on Trip Advisor. We soon got into a rhythm and everybody was sorting out their priorities on where to go and when. It worked out fine.

We ate as a family at breakfast and in the evenings, and mixed and matched with places to visit during the day. My eagerness was to check out the surrounding countryside and the villages just a short distance away. I shall join the family by visiting a public château or two, and of course, why would I come here if I had no wish to sample the wines? Joy divided her time in favour of family members, which is understandable but we still found plenty of opportunities to do what we normally get up to on a trip to France, namely indulge.

Chenonceau

The drive to this lovely hamlet is a treat in itself. It's 20 miles north of our village and gave us the opportunity to note other places worth investigation as we sped along the empty lanes. Montrésor, for a start. It has a castle, medieval back streets and a creperie. As we passed Chemille-sur-Indrois, the river widens like a lake and has a restaurant or two within easy reach of lovely walks. When the D89 widened, we thought we had seen the last of the narrow lanes but within a mile or two were back on the single-track roads until Francuel. This is naked, rural France with no make-up, just beautiful countryside and not a cloud in the sky. A sign for the château took us along another narrow lane which resembled the access road to a farm, but once we crossed over the river Cher, we had arrived. The village is pretty enough for a visit but we have come here to look around the Château-de-Chenonceau. There's enough space in the car park for half of South Korea to arrive by coach.

The château is big, the grounds are beautifully maintained, and as Joy helped her parents to look around the rose gardens, I took a step to the perimeter wall to photograph the magnificent structure that straddles the river. This place has an incredible history. From the earliest of times this château has been involved in war, intrigue and the nefarious activities of kings, dukes and popes. The Medici's have left their DNA all over Europe but it's particularly in evidence here. The château became a popular gift to the mistresses of successive rulers and in 1560 Catherine de Medici held a party here to mark the occasion of her son Francis's ascension to the French throne. It was the first time France was to witness a spectacular firework display.

Bright flashes and explosions of a different kind came during the Great War of 1914-1918 as the château was used as a hospital. During the Second World War, the owners utilised the building that spans the river, to aid escapees from the clutches of the Nazis, north of the Cher and the Vichy to the south.

I took a gander inside the main building and marvelled at the paintings, baroque decor and accoutrements. I also soaked up the splendour of the gardens. Whilst Joy got on with visiting all the rooms in the rest of the castle, I checked out the wine cellars. I can vouch hand on heart, through personal experience, that they produce one of the most fabulous white wines in the whole of France. Armed with a couple of beautifully packaged bottles, I aim to do more empirical research on this delicious wine, just to make sure. When we finally left to get back to our own little château, we all agreed it was a very enjoyable and rewarding experience.

Montrésor

The following day, the sun was as bright as ever. Everyone but me piled into cars and headed off to the Zoo de Beauval, near St. Aignan. I had declined the invitation in favour of a walk into the countryside to find my own wildlife. I wished to take full advantage of the solitude and make my way through the forest, following the river Indrois, hopeful that I can reach Montrésor by lunchtime.

There are no sign posts, just instinctive decisions as tracks cross in the middle of head height cornfields and forested hillsides. As I walked along a dirt path, my thumping footsteps disturbed clouds of butterflies that had settled on the wayside. Tiny lizards gave me dirty looks before darting out of sight. Bees were busy, buzzards were swirling high in the sky and a fox totally ignored me as it trotted in front of a row of hay bales at the back of a glade. I could sing to myself (I only remember all the words to old Cockney Rebel songs) and let my senses synchronise in complete harmony with the natural surroundings. The path took me through the woodland and along the river bank for several hundred metres, and then petered out. It's not a big river, maybe 2 metres wide and knee deep in the middle. If I crossed, I would probably end up walking along the road that runs between both villages. I turned back for about half a mile and took the left track, up the hill through a cutting in the forest and met an asphalted lane.

It took 45 minutes out of my day but not a minute was wasted. I saw nobody. No one could complain about my bad singing or my elevated elation. I'm glad I brought along a full water bottle this was thirsty work. My face and arms were getting a bit of a tan as well. I didn't meet a single vehicle on that road. There are a few dwellings dotted about but not a soul appeared. The road went left and I crossed a steep field by way of a dirt track and came to a place called Blackford. At the summit I could clearly see the castle of Montrésor. I could discern a gravel track leading all the way through the woods at the bottom of the hill. Two farmers were doing something to a combine harvester at the side of a field, both waved as I passed. The track took me down into the forest, and continued all the way, passing a gravel quarry and ended at a road on the far edge of the village of Montrésor. I drank the rest of my water and trekked along the concrete bank of the river Indrois. To my left, the ancient buildings of the town, to my right well-maintained cottages with either pretty gardens or well stocked allotments.

This path ended in a large play park. I sat on a bench facing the river and a great view up to the small but impressive castle of Montrésor. It was built in the 11th century by the founder of the Plantagenêts, Foulques the Black, the Count of Anjou. He spent his life building more than 100 castles, plotting wars and assassinating his adversaries. Legend says he was feared by God and dreaded by the Devil himself. The scene today looked as captivating as a lover's smile.

I weaved my way over the river via a footbridge and found a cafe for lunch. This village is reputed to be one of the 'most lovely' in France. As long as the list comprises 200 such contenders, I won't argue with that. I shall return later with Joy so we can explore more of this beautiful setting.

Beauval Zoo

When Joy returned from her trip with the family, she updated me on the day's events. The zoo is situated just outside Saint Aignan, and plays host to over 10,000 animals. She said the entry price may seem a little steep but as the park is set in 35 hectares, she could have spent all day there and not seen everything. There are many paths throughout the grounds so it's not a cramped affair like some city zoos. The staff are committed to conservation and ensuring the habitat and enrichment programmes are of the highest standard. Every habitat was designed to cater for each species' particular needs and the animals all seemed at one with their surroundings. She was in awe at the size of a silver backed gorilla and laughed as an elephant played to the gallery by frolicking in his private lake. Orangutans, lions, red pandas, rhinos and giraffes all got a viewing. There was something around every turn, including wandering flamingos. There's also a tropical hothouse and equatorial dome.

Despite all her efforts to see everything she had missed the hippos, aviaries and cheetahs, to name but a few. Fellow visitors must have felt as exhausted as Joy's family, because everyone was leaving at the same time. As a result, traffic became congested and crossing the road back to the car park became nigh on impossible. Joy noticed a civilian had leapt out and began directing traffic and marshalling pedestrians safely across the road. It took her a moment to realise, it was in fact Ray, her brother in law, who was doing such a sterling job. Joy suggested he could have asked for tips!

My day by comparison was utterly devoid of any unnecessary human intervention.

In the late afternoon, when Joy and I returned to the village of Montrésor, we made straight for the castle. It's not anywhere near as grand as the white walled châteaux we see in the holiday brochures but it was worthy of a visit. We wandered around inside the grounds, soaking up the views from the top of towers and battlements, taking care not to misjudge the broken and worn steps here and there. Some barns inside the grounds are cluttered with broken carriages and artefacts from a blacksmith's workshop. The inner courtyard was a peaceful sanctuary. I'm sure Foulques the Black, found solace right here after dispatching his latest foe to a gruesome death.

There's much to be admired in the village itself and easy to visualise what it looked like before prefabrication reared its ugly fasciae. A narrow lane with half-timbered buildings that are now restaurants leads to the market hall. We could be in Ledbury or Ludlow. We passed a cottage with a hand written sign that said 'Miel'. An old chap was tending the garden. He spoke no English at all. I pointed to the sign. He led me right inside his house. In the gloom of his closed curtained living room he produced a tub of honey so large, I could have buried my head in it. We haggled. I came out with a smaller pot, more in keeping with my needs and gave it to Joy to keep safe until breakfast time. The two most popular restaurants here didn't win our custom. We stopped for supper in the tiny creperie and had galettes, followed by a crepe that I eventually discovered under a mountain of Chantilly, ice cream and chocolate sauce. We're certainly not in Ledbury.

Loches

While most of the family headed off to visit the château at Villandry to look around the famous gardens and sumptuous furnishings, I grabbed a car and took myself to Loches. It's 13 miles west on the D760. I parked the car on the edge of town so I could walk in to the centre via the riverside paths. It is a medieval town that attracts many visitors throughout the year. I did the right thing by parking so far out, as I could walk through tree-lined gardens and alongside the reed tangled river Indre right into the centre. As I passed the railway station, I took a peek at the timetable which told me it's about a three-hour journey from Paris.

I then spent an hour wandering through the backstreets admiring the buildings and pressing my nose against shop windows. It was market day and stalls lined the streets, selling all the varieties of foodstuffs, flowers, arts and crafts and clothing I have come to expect in any popular town in France. I'm always fascinated by the stalls that artistically display cheeses, fungi and cold meats. Wild boar inhabit the forests and the charcuterie stalls offer a dozen different versions of sausage and chorizo products. Tasting sessions are often encouraged. The lanes took me to the château du Loches, which stands high over the city. It's a beautiful example of fine French architecture. Joan of Arc was resident here, as well as Charles VII, who was helped to the throne by the lady herself. He was instrumental in getting rid of the English and ending the Hundred years war in 1453. About a 10-minute walk away is the Abbey Beaulieu des Loches, which was deemed one of the finest defences built by

Foulques the Black, the Count of Anjou. He was buried here in 1040, much to the relief of his surviving adversaries.

There are archways over some alleyways that lead to more bars and cafes. The sunshine brought patrons spilling out onto the pavement tables everywhere. I popped into a privately run wine merchants and spent far too long distracting the very helpful proprietor with questions about labels and blends that I had no clue about. I did buy an unusual white Bordeaux, made from Cabernet Sauvignon, which seems almost an oxymoron to even write. I also clinked a bagful of Loire's own superb wines when I left the premises, so his time was not completely wasted. Good job Joy had gone with the others today. I might have been dragged out of there much sooner than I would have wished for.

Many of the streets prohibit traffic so I could wander without disruption. My only issue was avoiding stopping at any of the busy bars because I was driving today. The buzz and ambience, along with the sunshine had a heady effect on my senses. This really is a nice little city.

I grabbed an alcohol-free lunch in a side café, watched over by an appreciative member of staff who was interested to know about my wine purchases. I didn't detect any smirking so I'm guessing I passed muster. I spent another hour wandering a little further afield, but kept within the town's confines. As the market stalls began to pack up, I strolled back through the streets to my car. These bags were heavy. I should have parked closer. I really enjoyed this city. It's very authentic in every way. It didn't disappoint at all. I hope Joy and her family like wild boar sausages and French cheeses though. I can't eat all of it!

Château de Villandry

While I was in Loches, struggling to find provisions for the whole family, Joy and the rest of the clan took a day trip to the Château de Villandry, just outside of Tours. Her father, Wyn, is a keen gardener and her mother, Rose had trained as a florist, so this trip was a special treat for them as the gardens there have a reputation for being amongst the best in all of France. The house was built around an existing fortress in the 16th century. Two hundred years later Napoleon Bonaparte acquired it for his brother, Jerome. In 1906 Joachim Carvallo, a Spanish doctor, arrived with his wealthy wife and they set about restoring and improving the gardens and grounds. It's a paradise for horticultural lovers. The flower beds are laid out in spectacular formation with box hedges, trimmed to perfection. The myriad designs must look amazing from above. The château is one of the most popular public attractions in France and receives more than 300,000 visitors a year. It was definitely a highlight for her mum and dad. I just hope I can keep Joy away from the garden centres back home until the memory fades.

The next morning, it was time to depart. Joy's parents and family headed back to the UK. We are staying in the Loire region. We have a few more places to visit yet. We headed for Saumur to begin a journey that follows the river Loire all the way back to Sancerre. This first step was on good roads and covered about 80 miles.

Before we reached our destination, we stopped at the Château de Breze. It's in the town of the same name, approximately 8 miles south of Saumur. The château has as rich a history as any in the Loire. In addition to the sumptuously furnished rooms and the drawbridge that crosses a dry moat, this gothic pile also boasts an underground fortress, comprising deep caves and a kilometre of tunnels. The cellars are well stocked with their very own brand of wines. We just couldn't resist this!

Saumur

Saumur is full of surprises. Sauvignon blanc grape gives way to chenin blanc as the dominant grape in this appellation. It is used in blends along with chardonnay and sauvignon blanc producing dry white wines, and it is also fermented to create rather high quality and therefore expensive sweet wines too. The buildings of the town are made mostly of materials quarried locally. The tunnels created by excavating the distinctive chalky limestone are now used to store barrels of wine during fermentation.

It's another beautifully maintained medieval town, sitting on the bank of the Loire River. The Château de Saumur dominates the skyline and can be seen from miles away, the centre of town is as picturesque as any. There's a museum dedicated to cavalry and military history. In 1940 the cadets from this academy defended the town against German attack in the Battle of Saumur. They hold military events at various times of the year but sadly, not today. The clouds were gathering, we should find an attraction that would not be hindered by the weather. We've already done a château. We need something different. We found it. If you like mushrooms, or to be more scientifically correct, all things mycological, there is a champignon museum within walking distance. It is built into the cliff side, and the tunnels, where 250 different species of mushrooms are propagated, were a delight to see. It's good for a family visit as there are plenty of opportunities for children to get actively involved, and for the adults, you can buy mushroom beer. The shop was quite busy.

My interest in mushrooms began a few years ago after watching a video presentation by Paul Stamets, probably the most renowned and revered mycologist on the planet. It's a fascinating subject and reaches beyond edible varieties. His research into the wider properties and ecological necessity of fungi is an education in itself. The visit here added to my understanding, as well as my recipe book.

Outside, the weather had turned drizzly but the city itself is still such a draw on the eye. We stayed until mid-afternoon, admiring the lovely setting the inhabitants of this town wake up to every day. We need to get a move on. If we head west from here, we would be following the flow of the Loire River into Angiers (Anjou country = rosé wines). However, it's east for us, on the

E85, through Tours, and onto Amboise. I hope there's a room available, we haven't booked anything yet.

Amboise

We followed the course of the Loire river and arrived in Amboise around tea time. It was a fabulous run. The river was so close to the road at times we could have thrown a net over the wall and trawled for fish. As we entered the boundaries of Amboise the bridge took us across the Loire. There's an island halfway which shows just how wide this river is. We found a room in a small hotel very close to the centre and used the rest of the daylight hours to walk around the streets and lanes. This place looks so medieval I felt I should be wearing chain mail and a codpiece. The famous belfry clock tower is located over a passageway and was being photographed by dozens of people that got in the way as we tried to squeeze by. The Château d'Amboise stands proudly above the rest of the buildings, overlooking the majestic river below. There were costumed jugglers busking in the squares and the atmosphere was delightfully relaxed. After the remote tranquillity of Villeloin-Coulange, this gentle increase in tempo was exactly what we were looking for.

We shopped a little, for trinkets mainly, and slumped in comfort in a restaurant, with a glass of wine in one hand and the menu in the other. We reflected on a wonderful, spontaneously evolving day that ended in this very lovely city.

In the morning we breakfasted on coffee, croissants and orange juice in typical French fashion while poring over the map to choose which route to get to Bourges. We had another impromptu walk around the lanes until we found where we had left the car and edged our way along the riverbank before turning right and taking the D61 south eastwards. The Loire curves north east from here and makes a big arc before it bends southwards, where we shall meet it again soon, I hope.

Bourges

We are leaving the district of Indre-et-Loire and driving through Loir-et-Cher. The river Cher might not be as well-known as the river Loire but it plays as important a part to the landscape and to viticulture as its neighbour. We last encountered it when we visited the château at Chenonceau, we now crossed it again at Montrichard. It's much wider here than Joy expected it to be. I'm cheating, I've been here before. The nine arches of the bridge, with the old Tollbooth at one end is a bit of a gem, especially with the castle walls and tower in the background. The castle, which is now a ruin, was another construction by Foulques the Black, whom we 'met' in Montrésor just a few days ago. Although it's a small town, other ancient buildings here bear some significance. The church was chosen for the marriage between King Philip V the Tall, and Joan the Lame, of Burgundy. I bet the wedding photographer had his work cut out that day! There's a lot of history everywhere we look.

The road, now the D796, follows the pattern of the river for several miles. We avoided the route through Vierzon, deciding instead to stay in open countryside. The slopes, vineyards and scenery are not spectacular, but reassuring like a cosy duvet. We passed through some notable wine growing places including Reuilly. The town itself may not be impressive but the name can be seen on wine bottles in every merchant across the known universe. We crossed the Cher for the last time, at St-Thorette. From the stone balustrade on the bridge, the water was shallow but still impressively wide. It was a lovely journey, but I seem to say that after every decision we made when driving through France. It can't be a coincidence.

Bourges soon came in to view. It's a more industrious looking city. We ambled through the town to the north side, parked up near the railway station and walked straight into the reception of the Hotel Berry opposite. A room door clicked open within minutes and we have a base for the next segment of our Loire extravaganza.

We are pretty much in the very centre of France now. Bourges is useful for a stopover place because it is easy to reach. A rail service can be made from Paris within 2 hours. The city of Orléans is just north of here and it provides easy access to the nearby wine region of Sancerre and Pouilly Fumé. Two rivers meet here and there's a canal, which made the town strategically important for transportation. It's been around since Roman times and has faced war, sieges and intrigue ever since. In 762 during the Aquitaine War Pepin the Short arrived with his Frankish Army and laid siege to the city. Once it toppled, the count of Bourges swore allegiance to Pepin and off they went to besiege somewhere else. I'm hoping during our short stop it remains peaceful.

In the 15th century Jacques Coeur became a notorious son of the city for his fraudulent activities by claiming to know the secrets of alchemy. He was training to become a goldsmith and gained the trust of a mistress of King Charles VII. He convinced royalty of his skills in creating precious metals from base elements, was appointed Grand Treasurer and even went to Genoa and convinced Pope Nicholas V of his attributes. He became the richest man in France. He went on to finance the French army who defeated the English in the squabble over Brittany which made him unbelievably wealthy. His downfall came when bragging got the better of him by claiming he had discovered the secret of the philosopher's stone. Everybody knows that was Harry Potter! His statue (Coeur's not Harry's) stands outside the palace of his name in the centre of the city.

By a strange coincidence, Monsieur Coeur was not the only Master of a Royal Mint who engaged in alchemy and the search for the philosopher's stone. Two hundred years later, a certain Sir Isaac Newton had the very same interest in converting base metals into gold and embarked on his own search for the elusive stone. He was also entrusted with the role of Master of the Royal Mint of England in 1699.

There's quite a bit of Bourges to see. We walked along the tree lined avenue and crossed the river Yèvre. The other river is the Auron. We hadn't gone 200 metres before Joy spotted the Jardin des Pres Fichaux and got her camera out. It's a pleasant little park, with well-kept paths, trees, hedges and shrubs. The avenue is straight and leads into the centre of the city. The stonework of the buildings began to look much older, and half-timbered frames could now be found between the less ancient structures. It had a quasi-modern/medieval feel about it. However, the road surface soon turned to cobbled and the old town reverted to the mostly medieval architecture. The cathedral to our left is a bit of a climb but we endured the pain to reach it. Maybe we have spent too much time in the car on this trip. The surrounding alleyways were not helping. There's a tempting shop just a few metres down each one. We will never reach the cathedral!

The cathedral is enormous. My interest however, was more focused on the restaurants and bars and more particularly, a café for a long cool drink. We sat in the open and watched other people huffing and puffing as they reached their goal of hitting the summit. It's not particularly high, everyone else seemed to be distracted by the side streets which made the straightforward walk so exhausting.

We spent the rest of the afternoon exploring until we ended up back at the hotel. I did reserve a table for dinner at a restaurant located in an open square. We had some time left before dinner so investigated the La Voiselle marshes. It's a five-minute drive away. There were a few people punting in the calm of the river. We admired the tidy allotments in the dachas along the gravel paths. It's very peaceful here and made a lovely change from the urban structures we had been surrounded by for the past few days.

Dinner was served in some style. Our waiter looked very much like Lurch from the 'Adams Family,' but he was most helpful as I tried to order everything in French. My steak was flawless, the French beans were tied together by a thin strip of carrot which looked like a tiny bundle of garlic-soaked twigs. We ordered a carafe of red table wine. I tried to insist on tap water instead of paying for a bottle. He eventually understood and brought us water in a carafe.

At the next table, a father and son combo, who only spoke to the waiter in loud gruff tones got less sympathy. They pointed at my plate and told him they wanted exactly the same. They called him back and said, "don't forget the water!" He returned with the meals, plonked them down unceremoniously and opened a bottle of Evian. He poured some into their glasses before they could complain. They looked crestfallen. The waiter looked across at me as he passed, smiled and winked. It was a lovely meal. The sun dropped below the horizon and the lights came on. The parasols were opened and we stayed as long as we possibly could, before our eyes dropped. Besides, the carafe of wine was now empty.

The reason we came here was not entirely just to stay in Bourges. I had been misleading Joy up to this point. The real purpose for ending our jaunt in the wonderful eastern reaches of the Loire Valley, was to see Sancerre, or more precisely, visit the vineyard and restaurant of the Henri Bourgeois company at Chavignol. Until now, I had not informed Joy of the extra curricula activity that was about to begin.

We had met Arnaud Bourgeois, the current owner of this prestigious brand, in Birmingham a couple of years ago. He was giving a presentation of his wares from the Loire and his vineyards in New Zealand. We had the good fortune to dine with him and discuss all things fermented. Joy took quite a shine to him, what with his Sacha Distel accent and he gave her his card and invited us to visit his vineyard and to call him if we were in the area. We didn't call, but we can accept his invitation to visit.

Sancerre

Sancerre is the epitome of sauvignon blanc at its very best. It's my humble opinion but few would argue against it. Across the Loire river are the vineyards of Pouilly Fumé, often recognised as the twin sister to Sancerre. They are hard to tell apart unless you've been practicing really hard (I've tried, believe me). It seems fitting that we should end our trip in the Loire with a visit to this appellation.

It took about an hour to get there in the car. The landscape for the most part is flat and unremarkable. The crops were mostly corn, wheat and sunflowers on both sides of the road. However, once we began to climb into the gentle undulations the arable gave way to pasture and then a few vineyards appeared. We could also see much farther into the distance until eventually we were surrounded by field after field of vines.

The centre of Sancerre has many narrow lanes with rows of cottages on either side. A busy square was ideal for lunch and a meander through the streets was achieved despite the rain that began to fall. The view from the ridge at the edge of the village, eastwards to the Loire river and the vineyards beyond was worth the trek all the way from Touraine.

Chavignol

We set off for the village of Chavignol, all of 3 miles away. As soon as we turned onto the road outside Sancerre the vineyards on every slope stood like armies in formation, waiting to do battle. As we drove along, a field of sunflowers, with their heads drooping looked like a vanquished enemy. As we approached the village, the names of the producers were ticked off like spotting celebrities at a film premier. Many of them had signs offering tours and 'degustation' but we had only one sign in mind. I had already called ahead and made a booking for a tour and wine tasting session. We pulled up at the gates and straightened our attire.

The next couple of hours were a delight to the eyes, ears, nose and palate. We know the wines well enough but to see and learn about everything that goes into creating such perfection was so gratifying. I would have felt we had missed the whole point of a visiting a wine growing region, if we didn't take in one tour and tasting experience. It's the same for anywhere. Be it Scotland for whisky, England for beer, Ireland too, and even Provence for the perfumes. Chavignol village is very small, the name conjures up images more so of goat's cheese. It's one of France's favourite. We tasted some Crottinde-Chavignol along with our wine. It was a most enjoyable afternoon. We left with the understanding as to why these premier wines are a touch more expensive than most. I'm sure I heard Joy say, "Because I'm worth it."

We had already checked into the hotel, and dinner in the family restaurant was a special affair and a fitting finish to our Loire experience. It was an exquisite meal. Our room was small but sumptuous, the dining room was meticulously laid out and the service superb. We had more goats cheese with our starter, lamb cutlets in a beautiful sauce and just enough room for dessert. Rosé wine and coffee provided the liquid requirements. I probably over did it with the wine but we don't have far to stumble to bed. I hope the low beam in the corner of my room doesn't cause a problem.

That's our Loire region sewn up. We set off early the next morning in the rain and headed for Calais. We can get the Eurotunnel crossing this evening, if we have no delays, and be on British soil by supper time. I hope Joy can do some of the driving. I've got a bit of a hangover.

PICARDY

We are coming up to the period commemorating 100 years since the end of the Great War. Joy has family connections to the battles that raged on the Western Front. Due to some very special circumstances we have been invited, along with her sister Meriel and husband Ray, to attend a memorial service in the cathedral in Amiens to mark the centenary of 'The Final Push' to end the Great War. Once that is over Joy's brother and both parents are scheduled to arrive to spend a few days paying our own respects by visiting a number of cemeteries along the Western Front.

Joy and I set off by car, crossing under the English Channel and took the relatively short journey to the town of Albert. It's an ideal location as a hub for many of the more well-known war cemeteries throughout Picardy and the Somme. We took the same route from Calais that I had ridden on my motorcycle the year before. At that time, Joy travelled with her folks by car to Albert via the main roads while I snuck a crafty diversion, taking the 'D' roads through small villages and other landmarks. It was my opportunity to re-visit the café at Quercamps and the village of Azincourt. It was much more entertaining than zipping along the toll roads.

Albert

We checked in to the Best Western Hotel. The owners remembered us, or at least the legend that is my motorcycle, and chatted for quite some time about our reasons for coming back. Joy's sister is due to arrive around lunchtime tomorrow, so we had the rest of this evening and the next morning to ourselves.

Albert is a terrific place in its own right. It has a depth of agonising war time stories beneath its busy, commercial façade. The Basilica of Notre Dame is the most visible and ideal place to start. The golden statue of the Madonna and Child that crowns the tower can be seen for miles. It became a focal point in both wars, the Basilica was destroyed in the First, and used as target practice by the Germans in the Second. We will later attend the place where the enemy had their big guns aimed at the spire and the fate that befell them.

The town was less than three miles from the front line and was occupied and retaken a number of times. There is a very informative museum that runs underground from the Basilica and emerges at a park several hundred metres away. With such close proximity to the fighting, it is no surprise that many war cemeteries can be found in all directions from here. It's like the moons of Saturn, ten times over. We checked out the local arboretum, which has some lovely features. The river Ancre splits into two, via a weir and waterfall in one corner. The two streams course through the park and join again on the other side. Among the trees and shrubs are compounds for chickens, pigs and sundry creatures. There are statues, a bandstand and some very interesting features along the walls where the museum exit is located.

The next morning, we returned to complete the trio of attractions by checking out the Basilica and then a walk through the tunnelled museum. There was plenty to take in. For lunch, we drove to the Tommy café, just outside Albert in the tiny hamlet of La Boiselle. The café is run by a British couple. It has a number of war time artefacts on display, some of which can be purchased. The service is friendly and the food wholesome. As we finished our salad, Meriel sent us a text to say they were close to Albert. Joy replied with our coordinates and ten minutes later they rolled up and ordered lunch themselves. This is like a military operation.

Amiens

It's the 7th August and we have a busy schedule ahead. We are meeting with the BBC at Amiens Cathedral at 5pm today.

This all came about when Joy applied for tickets to attend the Centenary of the Battle of Amiens at the Notre Dame Cathedral, to be held on 8th August 2018. To qualify for the ballot, it was necessary for applicants to write a few words about any member of the family that was involved in the 'Final Push' on that date 100 years ago. The organisation accepted her application but asked if she could expand on the details of her Great Grand-father's involvement. One of Joy's hobbies includes genealogy, especially of her own ancestry so she had a good deal of information to submit. Her article is reproduced here:

David Alfred Jones (Reg No 34502)

David Alfred Jones was born on May 5th 1889 in Ystradyfadog. His parents were Thomas and Annie Gwladies nee Fuge. Sadly, his mother died when David was only 3yrs old. His father later remarried and David had a step brother Hugh, and two half siblings Gladys and Arthur.

He worked as a railway porter on the Taff Valley Railway in 1911 and later was employed as a miner. At the time of his marriage to Rosina Gibbs on January 8th 1913 he was a collier. Their daughter Ethel May was born November 14th 1913 and their son, William Arthur was born in Pritchard Street Tonyrefail April 28th 1915.

When war broke out, he felt that he should join up. He came home one day and asked Rosina what she thought about him enlisting. She replied it was entirely up to him. Years later she stated that she always regretted those words and wished she had talked him out of it. He enlisted in the 14th Battalion Welch Regiment but died at The Somme on August 27th 1918.

His daughter Ethel once said that her last memory of him was as a small child, looking over the bannister and seeing him leave the house in his uniform. She never saw him again. The family tell a story that on one occasion his son, William went missing. He was finally discovered at the local train station. His mother wondered if he was looking for his daddy.

As a family we are lucky to have some of the letters that David Alfred wrote during his time away. On April 29th 1916 he writes, "The boy is a year old now. I hope to see him soon and wish him many happy returns of the day. I wish I was there." He ends his letter saying "I hope that by the end of this summer we shall be able to tell the tale of the Victory." Unfortunately, a year later he was still there. On July 21st 1917 he writes that he is planning to apply for a Sgt Major position. He ends his letter saying "I wish I was home right now I wouldn't mind how much it rained I'd be alright. It is awful weather here."

The following year on May 17th 1918 he wrote telling the family how hot it was in France. He said it would be lovely if on his return they could visit Blackpool. He is quite positive that Britain will be victorious stating "things are a long time coming to a head but they will come presently. We shall hear great news one of these days," He adds, "looking back at the time we got married it seems like only a dream. Out of that time we have been apart for most of it. But, when this lot is over there will be a difference, I am sure, because it will take a lot to get me to leave home again."

August 6th 1918, he is still hoping the war will end soon. He says he is in good spirits despite the rain and mud up to his knees. He writes that "things are looking much better than they did a few months ago. The papers are giving a good account of things in general now. I hope that this is the final touch to everything." His last letter home was written on August 8th 1918. Despite the difficult conditions he is excited as he is due leave in two weeks' time. "I shall be coming home in about a fortnight or three weeks' time. So, look out what a time we will have then." Sadly, he never came home. On August 20th he was able to send a field service postcard and we believe the next day he *participated in the Second Battle of the Somme. He had ticked the box to say he was well and would write as soon as possible. Tragically 7 days later he was dead. The telegram stated he had been hit in the back of the neck by a machine gun bullet whilst in the trenches.*

He is buried at Delville Wood cemetery and is fortunate to have a single grave. Sadly, neither his wife or children were ever able to visit his grave. However, his grandchildren and two further generations have made regular pilgrimages out of respect and gratitude for the sacrifice he made.

Somehow, the Times newspaper got a hold of this piece and asked her permission to use it in their coming supplement. Then, the BBC got wind of it and asked if Joy and Meriel would like to record an interview for a TV programme, due to be broadcast around the same day.

Ray drove the four of us to Amiens and we showed our credentials to the security guys as we met with Jonathan, the organiser of the VIP guests for tomorrow's service. A couple of panicking interns from the BBC followed by a camera crew and presenter of the show arrived. Joy and Meriel were bundled inside a blacked-out people carrier and with everyone else on board, they drove off. Ray and I headed for a chocolate shop/café and stuffed our faces with macaroons and other delights, expecting a long wait!

The girls were advised that they were heading for the cemetery where her Great Grandfather was buried. Well, that's not going to happen. His grave is in Delville Wood, some thirty miles away. The BBC had got it into their heads that not only was Sergeant David Jones buried in a nearby cemetery in Amiens but their programme director believed he was killed here. They had no idea where any cemetery was in Amiens, and neither did Meriel or Joy. The girls told them that the 'Final Push' stretched for scores of miles right across the Somme, not just on the outskirts of the city. The skies were clouding and light for filming was fading fast as the vehicle they were in was stuck in heavy traffic. The presenter, who was travelling with them asked if they could stand by any old gravestone and pretend their Great Grandfather fought and died right here. The girls refused.

Before Ray and I could finish our final piece of chocolate smothered fudge cake with Chantilly cream, the girls' sent a text to say they were back, and the chance of fame and fortune in the movie business was lost! The BBC were in a panic to find something to fill the slot they had badly planned this escapade for. It was so poorly organised. Joy was under the impression that the interview would take place in front of the cathedral, about the involvement of her Great Grandfather and his chums in the Welsh regiment, fighting in the Somme on 8th August 1918. The BBC had focused only on Amiens. The front line runs from the French coastline, all the way to Switzerland. Tens of thousands of Allied soldiers were 'sent over the top' at a given signal, on that day. Somebody didn't do their homework.

We had to feed and water the girls, as refreshment was in short supply in the blacked-out mini bus. Ray and I were not hungry. We spoke to Jonathan, who was doing a brilliant job organising everything regarding the logistics for the service tomorrow. He sympathised with the frustration and told us exactly where and what was expected of the four of us tomorrow. We left him with full confidence there would be no screw up with his responsibilities.

Sunset in Amiens, with the cathedral lit up, chiming bells, the buzz and the ambience was worth the drive from Albert on its own. It's a great city and has a wealth of history woven into its very fabric. Peter the Hermit, who roused the people of France, Germany and Italy to embark on the first Crusade was born here around 1050. A more recent resident with a penchant for inspiring travel of a more peaceful kind was Jules Verne who lived in Amiens until his death in 1905. All the history in between will have to be sought on a later visit.

The next day, we were dressed to the nines. Ray wore his military medals and the girls looked top notch for this very special and auspicious occasion. We decided to travel to Amiens by train, to save panicking with parking. On the journey we were joined by several passengers heading to the same event. A freelance journalist learned the circumstances for our presence and took copious notes. He promised to have the story told in one or two independent newspapers by tomorrow. He told us we had saved him a lot of shoe leather as he was under pressure to find a scoop by his Editor back in England.

We arrived early enough to find empty seats outside a coffee bar within view of the approach roads to the cathedral. Police bikes and casually dressed (armed) security services were everywhere. Scores of veterans turned up in uniform, medals flashing, backs straight and trouser creases sharp enough to cut paper. Older veterans too, dazzled in their finery. It was a proud day for everyone. We chatted with any number of people as they wandered in and out. The roads were blocked and cavalcades of limousines containing dignitaries were policed through many times. The service was being attended by royalty and politicians from all quarters.

We had been allotted a specific time to get through the strict security at the barriers. We were checked, double checked and searched at every key access point. Because we had **VIP** passes, we were escorted across the concourse towards a restricted entrance. Celebrity watchers in the crowd outside the barriers looked at us and screwed up their faces, murmuring "Who's that?" Jonathan came to greet us. We were shown to a section of private seating in the south transept.

The general public, with their allotted passes were shuffled to the pews that filled the nave. Several times we had to stand as dignitaries, ambassadors and members of the Royal family arrived to take their seats at the front. We could recognise politicians from Scotland and Westminster. There were military personnel standing at appointed places all around the cathedral. School children too, and any number of assistants working with Jonathan to make sure everything that had been meticulously planned would run perfectly. It did.

It was a beautiful ceremony. Beamed across the world by television. The readings, narration, songs and musical moments made the experience feel like we were on the stage of the most heart-warming, soul-searching and perfectly choreographed performance we had ever attended.

When the service finished Joy and I were ushered to a particular spot in the ambulatory. This is a cavernous arched hallway, behind and to one side of the altar. It was a nervous time. A few other couples had been allocated their own spot and we all waited in quiet anticipation. Nods, and comments into discrete comms devices by the security staff and organisers generated a flurry of stiffening of backs and focusing on the doors at the back of this hall. His Royal Highness, The Duke of Cambridge emerged, followed by the British Prime Minister, Theresa May, and several other dignitaries. Joy was introduced in person to them as they approached and we shook hands. I stood a little aside, this is Joy's gig. Each dignitary took it in turns to spend some time with us. The surprising thing was that instead of them asking who we were, they already knew. They had been briefed about Joy's great-grandfather and asked deeper questions about his life and Joy's efforts with her research. I was particularly taken by the presence of His Excellency, Herr Joacim Gauck, former President of the Federal Republic of Germany. He was such a nice pleasant man and he spoke easily with me for quite a while, as Joy and Theresa May nattered like old friends. I could picture myself enjoying a glass of Schnapps with him in the drawing room of the Reichstag on dress-down Friday! The dignitaries moved on to the next couple, rather like a speed dating session. The Duke of Cambridge was all the focus. I felt some pride for Joy to be here in front of him and the rest of the Heads of State, all because she penned that article on Sergeant David Jones.

I've been writing manuals and books for years, my employers barely paid me my wages let alone gave me the time of day! Then along comes Joy who pens a short note for a couple of tickets and gets invited to meet Royalty! I should sink into a sulk. Neither of us are celebrity chasers, although I did adjust Susan Penhalligan's tab on the back of her frock in Covent Garden once upon a time and I shook Ally McCoist's hand, but that's as far as it goes. But this was very special. It's certainly an indelible memory for all the right reasons. Sometimes, just sometimes, you make a decision to go somewhere and suddenly you get to witness this most poignant event much closer than you could ever imagine. I'm sure Sergeant David Alfred Jones and his colleagues would be proud that the efforts of his family in ensuring the 14th battalion of the Welch Guards, who gave their lives during the Great War have not been forgotten.

We thanked Jonathan profusely before we left the cathedral. He was absolutely flawless in the execution of his duties. As for the BBC? I can only think of execution.

Joy, Meriel, Ray and myself, joined throngs of attendees in the busy squares, and found a bistro to enjoy supper and a beer. What we saw of the city of Amiens in this brief encounter, was that it is well worth a longer visit. We were very pleased we didn't have to deal with the traffic getting out of here this evening though. The train journey back to Albert was much more pleasurable.

I don't think we can top that experience very easily.

Delville Wood

The following day the rest of the Welsh contingent arrived, Rose, Wyn and brother Gareth. A map was produced and we plotted where we would be heading for over the next few days. The first item on the agenda was where to eat that evening. There was unanimous agreement that it would be a small restaurant called Le Poppy. We've all eaten there before. It's 2 miles out of town and does not open every day. Today, it was 'ouvert'. It's a family run restaurant; the menu is simple but covers five courses. This was my choice: brawn style pate, white fish and garlic mash, bread pudding and custard, Mimolette cheese with crackers, coffee and a chocolate. Other options included soup, beef bourguignon, chicken, and several different cheeses. It's a fixed price of virtually nothing at all and includes a beer or carafe of wine, unless you're a soft drinks person. It's our 'go-to' restaurant, whenever we are in the area.

The following morning, we had an early breakfast at the hotel. Another fabulous spread for the 7 of us. By 9am were on our way to Longueval, and the site of the battle of Delville Wood. It was less than ten minutes' drive through tiny back roads. We stopped right alongside the cemetery gates and headed between the Portland stone headstones to lay a wreath on the grave of Sergeant David Alfred Jones. He is the grandfather of Rose. 925,000 soldiers perished in this region. That's almost the whole population of Glasgow, wiped out for reasons too futile and complicated to comprehend, even today. We also planted a pot of daffodils in the hope they would flourish each spring. Ray using an ice scraper from the car, and Meriel, pressing the mud down with the sole of her boot, gave the bulbs the best chance they could offer to keep Sgt Jones and his pals company long after we have left.

After a family photograph was snapped, we strolled through the rest of the cemetery and read various headstones and the notice boards telling of the events that happened here around one hundred years ago. We shared quiet moments for those who had fallen. It was not a morbid feeling at all, just an enveloping sense of respect, sympathy, pride and disappointment for all those young men that gave their lives in such an awful way.

Opposite this cemetery is a memorial ground, built on the battle field fought over by our allies from South Africa. Swathes of bare grass had been cut in the newly planted forest to allow folk to walk around and read descriptive signs, all with a story to tell. Pock marks where shells exploded and zig-zag channels revealed the lines where trenches had been dug. They give a glimpse into what it used to be like here during the hostilities. Now, the trees and lush grass hide the conditions the troops really had to endure.

Longueval

The tiny village of Longueval was not five minutes away. I walked it to stretch my legs. At the junction of the road, a large headstone stands, with a football on top. It is dedicated to the officers and men of the 17th and 23rd battalions of the Middlesex regiment. The footnote is a quote from Scotsman, Private Jack Borthwick, who played professional football for several clubs, including Cowdenbeath, Everton and Millwall. He was wounded in battle here at Delville Wood. The quote says "This is worse than a whole season of cup ties."

A small dog yapped at me as I passed a house, and at another, where a massive guard dog, with teeth like a rabid wolf wanted to rip out my throat. I marched on feeling victorious inside, at being able to do just that, as I caught up with the others. They had gathered for more photographs at a statue of a Scottish piper in the centre of the village. Everywhere you look, it seems, there is a reminder and a show of respect for what the British, French and Allied armies did to save this part of the world from German occupation. On the opposite road-side was a memorial for children who died in the conflict.

Mametz Wood

Our next point of call was not far away and found through winding country lanes. The gentle, rolling hills are not unlike Dorset but with walled off cemeteries appearing at random, between copses, clearings and meadows. This is the territory where much of the fighting actually took place. The history books tell us there's no randomness about the cemeteries. It's where outposts, battles, or strategic defences were contested. Down an asphalt track is the memorial to the Welsh regiments who fought in this sector, to regain a wooded area just across the valley. This is Mametz Wood.

The ridge behind the fiery red dragon, holding German-made barbed wire in its claws, overlooks the large expanse of what is now farmed fields. Enemy positions in the woods opposite this ridge, made for the killing field that picked off the soldiers ordered to run at them with little more than a rifle and petrifying screams. Today, looking across this perilous expanse, spelled out clearly to me, that those in command back in Whitehall had never even seen this part of the countryside before making the order to attack. The machinery I could hear rattling came from a couple of wood loggers, where once stood machine guns. It sent a cold shudder down my spine. In the silence in between cutting, I could hear skylarks. The very same birdsong that marks the polarity between heaven and hell in the poems of the Somme.

Lochnagar

We moved further on making our way to Lochnagar. We pulled up at a cemetery filled with iron crosses, which are often used as headstones for the German soldiers who lost their lives. Many of these, like British troops, had been hoodwinked into thinking that going to war was a heroic and romantic endeavour. A short war, that will repay them with peace and good fortune, once victory was achieved. All of these guys British and German, cousins in Teutonic blood lines, died horribly because three cousins by royal motherhood could not resist the desire for historical immortality.

Baron von Richthoffen (The Red Baron) was buried in this cemetery for a while. His remains since moved elsewhere. There are more than a few Jewish graves amongst the iron crossed squadrons.

At Lochnagar, the crater needs to be seen to be truly appreciated in its perspective. In 1916 the British tunnelled underneath this German outpost and planted mines. The wreaths of poppies people had thrown to the bottom of the near 30-metre deep crater look like bottle tops from up here. It's an almost perfectly symmetric cupped out, dry pond. From here we can clearly see the golden statue of the Madonna and Child atop the Albert Basilica. It was said that if the statue should fall in this war, all would be lost.

There is nothing else but flat fields of farmland all around. Today, the skylarks above were still giving their voice. It was an eerie moment. On July the 1st 1916 when the mine was detonated, it created the largest manmade explosion ever known and could be heard in London. The repercussions of this act sparked the extended slaughter of hundreds of thousands on both sides, along the Western Front. It has been said, Hell itself emerged from the hole that man had opened.

The remains of private George Nugent, of the Tyneside Scottish Northumberland Regiment, lay at the edge of this abyss undiscovered until 1998. A cross depicts the place he was found. His body now lies with his comrades at the military cemetery at nearby Ovillers. The duckboards that surround the crater have brass plates, with the names of many who had fallen, paid for by relatives who contribute to the upkeep of this remarkable site. Rose, the Granddaughter of Sergeant David Alfred Jones, saw to it that his name be amongst the rest, so that he may 'liveth forever.'

This was a morning so well spent. We had covered so much ground in such a relatively small area. Unlike the soldiers who spent months with hardly a yard gained, we have the freedom to drive on to wherever we wanted.

Beaumont Hamel

Our next stop on this tour was the Canadian memorial at Beaumont Hamel, not far from Auchonvillers. We were greeted by Canadian students, selected for a four-month secondment to act as guides. Vincent met us at the gate and chatted away amiably. More staff were on hand in the visitors centre and were very helpful and informative. There is no charge for any of the services here.

The grounds are pocked with shell holes and we can still see the vivid scars of trenches. A statue of a caribou represents the Newfoundlanders that served with the allied forces. The caribou is braying, as it faces across the crazy-golf like bunkers, made by exploding mines and shells. In the open space, sloping down towards the nearby woods is a solitary tree. It's just a stunted, mortified stick now; a halfway mark. It was known as the killing tree. When soldiers were ordered to rush the enemy, they were attracted, like magnets, for the possible cover this once proud tree could offer. Hundreds were mown down by the snipers and heavier guns hidden beyond the lines of trees farther on. A high-risk form of Russian roulette, perhaps. Maybe it was called Boche roulette.

The sun was hot today. Clearings amongst the manmade undulations inspire picnics rather than panic, but the sombre mood remains. One underlying theme amongst the soldiers in all these places was one of camaraderie and spirit. The spirit was maintained by humour. Those men would have had to have joked and bantered large doses of humour to keep themselves from sinking below the surface of sanity in this quagmire of madness. Sometimes, it's the only defence against the stupidity of war. The grounds and history of this site made it a very impressionable and educational visit.

Thiepval

We headed now for Thiepval. The largest monument in the district. Dedicated to some 72,000 soldiers of the British and Commonwealth forces. It was built by Sir Edwin Lutyens who also erected the Cenotaph in London and follows the same symmetric block formation as many of his grand designs. On the cold cream walls are listed the names of all who were lost around here but have no known grave, because they could not be individually identified. The monument dominates the landscape for miles around.

There's much to see and read at these war memorials. Each one can take an afternoon to absorb enough detail to give just a passable perspective. Every one has an aura, is poignant, dignified and was not in the least depressing or morbid. Afternoon tea was next on the agenda. There's plenty of small cafes in these villages, especially during the summer months.

After breakfast the following morning, we set up an operations room of our own and laid the map out on the empty table in the bar. There was full agreement that we should tour some of the sights west of Albert, particularly along the course of the river Somme. The main objective being the memorial for Australian troops just outside Fouilloy, a few miles south of Amiens. Gareth had done a little research of his own and found a place worth visiting before we get to Fouilloy. It's a peaceful countryside location not more than a 5-mile detour from the intended destination. This whole area, including the Somme valley itself, is a very nice alternative to the man-made features in which this region has become an unwilling victim. These tours require careful planning to avoid going around in circles.

Fréchencourt

We drove to an area of natural beauty at Le Puits Tournants, in the small village of Fréchencourt. It's off the D929 between Albert and Amiens. Here, the river L'Hallue feeds into marshes and creates wide pools where in some places, the crystal-clear water becomes brightly coloured. It looks as if blue and orange dye has been poured in somewhere upstream. The walk around the forested area, where paths lead is almost magical. The time available to us means we cannot explore them thoroughly. Birdsong, wildlife and obelisks pop up, and more isolated pools, for tranquil contemplation, give this place a delightful ambience, apart from the occasional cyclist bombing through. From here it was an easy drive south to pick up the threads of the memorial sites dotted along the Somme.

Fouilloy

We had to cross the river Somme itself to reach the Australian National Memorial near Villars-Bretonneux. This is an incredible place. The grounds are perfectly laid out with existing walls, that suffered many attacks during conflict. You can still see shell markings on the tower, but the site has been completely renovated and is among the very best of all to visit. The interactive museum is underground, in a light, airy series of rooms. I was so pleased we went to see it. The views from the top of the tower, right across the landscape for miles, are worth the trip alone. There is row upon row of headstones to the front of the complex. Allied soldiers share the soil with their Australian counterparts. I laid a wooden poppy between the headstones of two British lads, one Scot, one English who were inseparable as mates in life; now together for ever beneath the lawns.

There are other memorial sights dedicated to the Australian forces that fought on the Western Front. We can't do them all. Driving along the Somme valley trying to follow the river is very tricky as it breaks out into wide, scattered lakes, with dachas and villages popping up at random along the banks. We reached the First Australian Division Memorial at Pozieres, which has a very helpful guidance system with plates and landmarks that depicts how the battles to occupy the village, not a slingshot away, played out. Several soldiers were commended for bravery in this tiny enclave. An Australian, Brigadier Arthur Seaforth Blackburn led 50 men in four separate sorties to drive the enemy from a strong point on the highest hill on the Somme. His tactics and the unbridled bravery of his men won him the Victoria Cross. An English born soldier, Private John Leak took it upon himself to leap out of his trench and dispatched three hand grenades into the machine gun nest while under fire. He gained a reputation for being the last one to leave the front line and a most tenacious soldier. He was also awarded the V.C. and lived in Australia until he died peacefully in 1976.

Other places that attracted our attention were at Pérrone, Cambrai at Louvervalle and another cemetery at Pozieres, dedicated to 14,000 more soldiers that fell in these fields. This corner was believed to be where fighting was at its most intense. Le Tommy café is close by, another opportunity for a fine lunch and wartime souvenirs before heading back to visit more sites. Our tour took up the whole day. Many of these places are not far apart and can be reached by car within minutes. These were two very thought-provoking days. It's not only an excursion to read the headstones of relatives, if they were identified amongst the fallen, it's a deep and meaningful experience for anyone who has the slightest interest in history and how we came to be where we are as a nation or a group of like-minded countries. When so many innocents lost their lives in both world wars, so that we could enjoy peace and harmony for more than half a century, (which is a first for Britain) it is fitting and wise, that we should remember them. We are not done yet with the war memorials. We are only moving hotels.

Checking out of the hotel together the next morning the three cars headed eastwards. The final destination for memorial site visits will be in Belgium, but there are still a few more in France to see before we reach Ypres.

Vimy Ridge

It's around 40 miles from Albert to Vimy Ridge, depending on the route you take. I wasn't driving. On my previous visit I was on my motorcycle and arrived here via the pretty way. The Canadian National Vimy Memorial is like a private estate with a long tree-lined drive through perfectly maintained grounds. Joggers and cyclists lined the access road, dangerously at times, as traffic was busy in both directions. The car park was already filling up with coaches. Hikers and cycling groups were about to set off in all directions, while others prepared to visit the education centre or take guided tours through the tunnels and reconstructed trenches. The main attraction however, has to be the most awesome towers of blistering white stone I have ever seen. At first sight it looks like a skyscraper-high pillar, split down the middle and joined at the base.

The path to the foot of this wonderful piece of architecture was like walking towards a mountain that never gets closer. Like Thiepval it can be seen from miles around. It stands above all others in its style, taste, colour and magnificence. Statues, overcome with grief and sorrow portray the agony for those who lost loved ones here. At the base, a grieving mother and father (Greek God like) must be 6 metres from toe to head. As we climbed the steps to the tower, the statues now cling to the walls, looking up to the sky. At the top, the angels are carved from the white marble of the towers. It's very beautiful.

Names of those who died are engraved in all the surrounding edifices. At the rear, a lone mother looks down, mourning over the sarcophagus of the unknown soldier and, symbolically, all her children of Canada, who died during the war. It is as moving as it is stupendous. Ray disappeared way off into the meadow that stretches between the crest and the forest the Canadian army succeeded in taking back from the Germans. He now looked like a dot in the distance as he snapped away at the memorial. The scale of these towers is so difficult to capture on camera. We lingered here a while, taking it all in and reading the names of just a few of those fallen soldiers. The Canadian victory here was the catalyst that helped to spawn the effort to give Canada total independence as a nation, from the clutches of imperial subjugation.

At the visitor centre, Canadian students are available to help with the educational part of the whole package. They are so polite and helpful and so proud of their country. After asking lots of questions, one of the students invited us to take a guided tour. There was no charge. We walked along the now familiar pocked holes and mine craters that fashioned this landscape so crudely. Young, thriving trees, now stand where only a moonscape, squelched in disease ridden mud once dominated. We read the boards in the centre and took in the magnitude of the conflict as best we could, before stepping out onto the parade ground to await our guide, Maddie. A squabble of noisy, badly behaved French kids gathered next to us, with their inadequately trained parents. I muttered under my breath that this may not go well if they were walking through the trenches and tunnels with us.

With relief on all our faces Maddie said she was only taking the English-speaking group; her colleague got the short straw to take the French family. Maddie said she was pleased too. It was just the seven of us. Fabulous. It was an amazing excursion amongst the re-created trenches, minus the filth and knee-deep water the soldiers had to endure. We ended up at a point that was just 20 metres from the German trenches. It was said you could hear the enemy suck on his cigarette from this close. Stick your head up and a long bayonet could take your eye out, let alone a sniper's bullet.

The trip through the underground tunnels was mind blowing. Not a crouching, crawling affair but similar to the corridors you often find in cheap hotels, minus the wallpaper! It was dimly lit in those days. We know, we got a demonstration, and the quarters and meeting rooms were dank, small and hardly comfortable. Troops stayed down here for weeks on end; if they lived that long. Messengers had a life expectancy of 2 weeks, if they were nimble, we were told.

It really was an education. We emerged into the sunlight agog with the conditions this war had brought about in a soldier's life. Unforgettable and so worth the time.

We made our way out and on towards Belgium. Conversation never faltered for a moment. There was just so much to take in and far too much to discuss. We could start our own appreciation society for even this tiny corner of such a vast area that was so devastated by the events of 1914-1918.

BELGIUM

Tyne Cot

We are now in Flanders Fields, Belgium. Meriel and Ray knew of a cracking café at Hooge; another site of war graves and a mine crater, not 5 miles from Ypres. We had a lovely lunch in a themed bar with rows of polished and embellished shell casings around the walls, most are available for purchase. My smoked ham sandwich could have fed a platoon. We spent a while in the cemetery there before arriving at Tyne Cot. It's named after the Tyneside regiment that were based there. Cot is short for Cottage. It was a place of mass slaughter, brought about by irresponsible decisions by far away commanders and politicians. A comment made by one aristocratic leader summed it up when he finally visited the battle site to find out why their objective could not be achieved easily. "My God, what have I done?"

As you enter the grounds to the visitors centre a voice reads out the names and ages (if known) of every single soldier that was killed here. Inside, the names being read out were accompanied by a photograph of each victim on a screen. It was as solemn and heart rendering as you could imagine. There is much to read from the large displays depicting the developing debacle. Joy got a photocopy of details of her Great Grandfather here, printed off by the helpful staff. No charge.

The graveyard is a crescent of row upon row of marked gravestones. Many of the interred were 'Known only to God'. There are hundreds of thousands of headstones all across Picardy and Flanders but what is often overlooked, is that many of the graves contain more than one 'unknown soldier'. We were informed that some may contain six or more bodies. The scale of the avoidable tragedy can be too much to comprehend. The walls that stretched around the rear of this site list the regiments and soldiers who fell. You cannot take it all in. Ghoulishly, you search for names that match your own, chances are there will be one. Foolishly you try not to be affected. We departed just as a coach load of Belgians arrived. They blustered in like noisy football supporters. Oops. Don't say a word!

I don't know if this was the most poignant of military graveyards I have visited on this excursion, but it felt like it. Tens of thousands taken away from their families, just for the sake of a few metres of sodden turf. And the western world today wrings its hands at atrocities caused by others in far off countries as if butter would not melt in their mouths.

Ypres

We drove towards Ypres across flat, ideal allotment land only to be turned back because of road works. The place was swarming with hikers. We saw them when we arrived in Hooge. Apparently, it was national Walking Day in Belgium. We made our way by instinct to another access road into the town. Fortuitously, we could stop for a quick photo shoot at a French military cemetery. It had a more macabre memorial at the entrance than the others we'd visited. There are so many cemeteries within a ten-mile radius of here, it would be too easy to get way-laid for the rest of the week visiting them all. They all have a story to tell.

Ray and Meriel knew their way about in the town and we all followed easily to find the B&B they had booked for us. We could park up and relax for the next day or so. Joy found the Tourist Information office, which is in the Cloth Hall building in the centre. She then went in search of post cards, while I lingered outside a waffle bar. I watched enviously as children and adults emerged with smiling faces, partly obscured by either great slices of griddled dough or pyramids of ice cream, whilst Joy took her time picking up leaflets and stationery of no edible value whatsoever.

Even passing motorcyclists were stopping outside the waffle shop and throwing their crash helmets to one side and queued for the culinary reward. Joy and Meriel were nowhere to be found. My petted lip was obvious to all. I felt abandoned. I eventually found them in a book shop. The shelves, stacked with hundreds of choices on the subject of military matters, but there were a good many other interests covered as well. We window shopped for a while, taking a special interest in the displays put on by the numerous chocolate shops, as we made our way towards the Menin Gate. Ray and I were gasping for a beer by now. I mean, we are in Belgium. If we cannot have waffles, buns or chocolate surely, we can have beer!? My mind began to wonder what else can there be that we should acquire that's distinctly Belgian? If Joy even suggests hand-crafted lace right now, this could end in a blood bath.

We did check inside one bar but it was far too busy to fit us in. A guy told us there is another bar tucked under the ramparts not 50 metres away. That too was overcrowded, there was no room to even bend our elbow. Compromise was found in a tea room that served beer as well as coffee and cake. Two vacant tables were cleared of clutter and a truce resumed in our camp. Gareth and I chose the Passchendaele labelled beer. It was good. Ray and Wyn ordered a beer that came in one of those distinctly Belgian glasses. They were both smiling too I recall.

The main square is dominated by the Cloth Hall, a 13th century construction that had to be re-built after the war. It's a fantastic building with ornate spires and a clock tower, typical of the Belgian desire for decorated arches and icing cake adornments on all the gables. It's as if the architect had won a poker game with the ace of clubs and has celebrated by including the shape as often as possible. The hall was used for cloth storage in the middle ages and dozens of cats were employed to keep the rats from eating the fabrics. When the cloth was all sold and the hall empty, the cats were traditionally, thrown off the roof. Every year the festival of Kattenstoet revives this tradition with a carnival parade and a cat lobbing frenzy, but with only the stuffed fluffy or cartoon kind these days. The building houses the tourist information centre and the Flanders Fields museum.

The other buildings in the square itself have more than a slight resemblance to the narrow-gabled structures found in Dutch built cities. We have seen similar examples in Gdansk. The bars, shops and restaurants attract as many visitors as the memorials like the Menin Gate.

It was agreed to reconvene around 6.30pm so that we could head to the Menin Gate to get a decent spot to witness the playing of the Last Post which begins at 8pm each night. This was the key point of our trip to Ypres. It was less busy in the streets now and we could all congregate in a nice spot under the stone canopy of the Menin Gate. The crowd went silent as a platoon of young soldiers marched in to stand to attention and half a dozen veterans piped them in. Then a single bugle played 'The Last Post'. The sound reverberated through the arch and reached into every fibre. Tears were wiped back or left to trickle down faces. It was a solemn, captivating and deeply moving moment. When the bugler finished, you could hear a pin drop. Wreaths were brought and laid along the steps leading up to the roof of the Gate. The lump in my throat stuck there for some time as I reflected on all the war graves, memorials and of course, the service at Amiens that we had experienced in the lead up to this moment. It felt good to be at peace.

As the crowd dispersed, street traders lined the pavements back towards the main square. A chap at a stall was selling sketches and pictures of regiments and battle scenes, which were rather good. Meriel bought one for a keepsake. We strolled back across the square to take our seats in the rather nice restaurant Meriel and Joy had already wisely reserved for us. So that's where they disappeared to when I wanted my pocket money for a waffle! We ended the day weary but very happy. We have a whole morning and then some, before we head back into France for one more night and home.

Monday morning brought a crisp, cold air to match the whitewashed blue of the sky. I went for a brisk walk before breakfast and had to skip out of the way, more than, once as kamikaze cyclists sped past, heading for school, college or the workplace. We had a good breakfast, said our farewells to our hosts and headed off to spend some time in the city centre and take in the view of the river Leperlee from the ramparts. St George's Church is a must see, from the inside. Each chair has a hand-woven hassock, cross-stitched with the emblems of the many regiments that fought in the Great War. Brass plaques covered most of the wall spaces and we spent quite some time wandering around here absorbing the sentiments for those lost in battle.

The architect for this church was Sir Reginald Blomfield, a Devonshire man, who was commissioned to design the Menin Gate as well as several memorial and burial grounds in the area, including Tyne Cot. The church's purpose was to serve the needs of the local parishioners as well as the many pilgrims who began visiting the city after the Great War ended.

I found a cushion and then a plaque on the wall of this church dedicated to the forces of the Somerset Light Infantry. My own Grandfather was shipped to Ypres at the start of hostilities. He was a machine gunner and was wounded for his troubles. The resistance by these soldiers of the British Expeditionary Force, against all the odds, earned them a nickname from the Boche as The Old Contemptibles. He survived the war, re-enlisted after his recovery and was wounded again before the fighting ended. I was personally pleased to have been able to pay my respects to him and some of his comrades in arms.

The ramparts offer a lovely walk and in the summer breeze, it was a delightful stroll. At the waters' edge some goats were grazing on a grassy bank and at the confluence we spotted another military cemetery where headstones faced a beautiful view across the river. Ypres is covered in scars but it's a lovely city.

Langemark

We took a slight detour on our way to Poperinge and stopped off at the Welsh Memorial north of Ypres, at Langemark. We had all visited here before but since we are all together this time it was thought a fitting tribute that our war graves tour should include a family photograph with a fiery dragon. Hed Wyn, the famous Welsh language poet perished here during the battle of Passchendaele in 1917. There's a strong interest in the Eisteddfodau (festival of Welsh literature) in these parts and the Belgian owner of the Sportman bar, just along the road helped raise funds for the memorial. He also holds a monthly memorial service, which is well attended, especially in the summer months.

Poperinge

Lunch was planned to be taken in Poperinge before we return to France. This is a lovely little place, steeped in wartime history. I expected perhaps a toasted sandwich but we did not reckon on the La Poupee Tea Room and Restaurant. The plat-du-jour was unavoidable. How can we say no to carrot soup, followed by chicken Marengo on a bed of very tasty Spanish rice? The chocolate mousse dessert was so rich and creamy Meriel could not eat all of hers for fear it would clog her arteries. I was willing to take the risk myself and eat it for her.

The town has more to offer than a nice restaurant or two. It has a very dark war time history. It was under German occupation for some time. During that period, the daughter of the lady running the restaurant we ate in today, played courtesan to a German officer, and behind the complaints and scowls from other villagers she was passing vital information back to the Allies. Her bronze statue stands in the square. There's a museum for enthusiasts of all things military and 'The Shooting Post' is close by. This was the post that was used to stand deserters and conscientious objectors in front of for execution. A hologram, visible in one prison cell, made Meriel shriek when she peered through the spy hole of the door. It shows a condemned prisoner pacing around. Joy laughed so much she needed the toilet!

We have thirty miles to travel for our final stop on this epic journey. We will stay the night in St Omer and set off early in the morning to the village of La Coupole. We are going to visit the V2 rocket site that was the secret programme Nazi Germany had for their final throw of the dice to win World War II. After that, it's on to Calais for all of us and the Euro Tunnel back to England, and for some Wales.

PAS-DE-CALAIS

St Omer

The flat, straight roads through Belgium and into France took no time at all. Military cemeteries continue to dot the landscape. Crossing the border somehow felt like coming home. The minimalist aspect of the Belgian topography gave way to subtle changes in terrain and road surface as the French countryside enveloped us. The convoy stayed together all the way into the town centre, I was leading the way, probably because I'm so slow.

We found the Ibis Hotel easily enough. It was chosen for its proximity to the centre for Joy's parents' ease and for the fact there is suitable parking in the grounds for all the cars. The staff were helpful, young and fun. I sat at the bar as they practised their English on me, asking questions about London, Scotland and for some unknown reason, Norwich, while the others sorted their stuff in the rooms.

When Joy was ready, we took a stroll into the local area. We are now in the Pas-de-Calais district. From a geographical point of view, Joy and I have now reached all four corners of this country as well as the central marker that is Bourges for the purposes of this book. And we are not finished yet. St Omer has, like most towns and cities, been subject to sieges, burnings, war and re-alignment since the 7th century. It's been part of Flanders, Burgundy, Netherlands and was even under Spanish rule at one time. The English also interfered with the place on more than one occasion. Now, it's a peaceful haven. Small enough to be laid back and big enough to attract a lot of visitors to the bars and amusements in the old streets that survived urban renewal schemes.

There are lots of squares, most are bigger than usual but there is a small pedestrian precinct that has plenty of artisan shops. We walked around for quite some time before settling in the main square to enjoy the buzz of the weekend revellers. It's a good place for a stop-over if you're travelling from Calais down through France, and probably great for a weekend break too. It's got a quirky feel to it. One of its most notable sons was Charles Blondin, the acrobat who was the first to cross Niagara Falls on a tight rope. This sort of sums the place up. During the evening, after dinner, with the parents in bed, Joy and I returned to one of the bars in the alley next to Place du Maréchel Foch for a drink. We sat inside, a husband and wife duet were entertaining the patrons with a selection of songs from all over, in English and French. I asked for a glass of dry white from the barman. His reply was, "Sancerre or Pouilly Fumé?" Not fobbing us off with a cheap Pinot Grigio? I love France. We had a glass of both before we left for the night. Joy agreed, the Pouilly Fumé was beautiful. But the Sancerre still got the blue riband.

La Coupole

A few miles south of St Omer is the little known, but no less significant location, where Hitler's secret weapon to save Germany from defeat was built and launched. The site is deep in the woods that hid this enormous construction from enemy eyes. This whole project was undertaken without anyone in the area knowing what was going on. They were told it was to be an electricity generating station. It wasn't until we got to the centre of the site that we realised how incredible it was to have kept it a secret. The entry fee covers a walk through a re-construction of the defence and military hardware that guarded the site. It's imposing enough just making our way through the trees, up and over the incline. When we finally reached the bombed-out complex, it takes your breath away. The cold, grey concrete walls and ramps reminds me of the nuclear plant at Chernobyl. The magnitude is difficult to grasp until you stand someone in front of any part of the building. It's not completely in ruin, the railway lines, ramparts, causeway and equipment are all discernible, and the signs lead you around the whole of the complex, including the interior. Images, films and original workings explain how the enormous rockets were moved and loaded before launch. It brings the realisation of how lethal this weapon would have been if it ever got into full production. The rockets look more like NASA property than ordnance.

In many ways, this visit at the end of our tour of Picardy and Flanders was very fitting. The modern technology during the closing year of WWII, had leapt beyond trench warfare. The hundreds of thousands who died in those wars could have been a mere appetiser for the maniacs who want to master the art of killing thousands with just one shell. I personally, feel eternally grateful that my 1950's generation have yet to experience first-hand, anything like the devastation those that came before us had to suffer. We all gathered together prior to the short drive to Calais in separate cars and agreed that this particular reminder was a very poignant experience. Now, it was home time for all of us.

GRAND EST

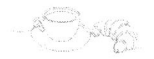

We have another famous wine growing region to visit. The Alsace runs close to the German border and for that reason, its grapes, architecture and landscape are close enough in comparison to cause some confusion to taste buds and perspective alike. We have decided to take the train from London again. There's a good railway network to the eastern regions that should reach the parts we are aiming for. We hope to cover as much ground as possible without resorting to hiring a car.

Nancy

The walk from the Gare du Nord to the Gare de l'Est is little more than 400 metres, if we choose the right short-cut. There's always road works outside the station so we were prepared to be forced to walk the long way round. Today, in drizzly rain we achieved most of the journey under cover. The Gare de l'Est is as busy as every other terminus in Paris. I'm less concerned about pickpockets than I am of ending up being carried on to the wrong train when a rush breaks out.

We found our reserved seats, stowed the luggage and sat opposite a Korean couple, who dozed for the best part of the journey. The train sped like lightning through the Paris suburbs, but still took 13 minutes to escape, and raced like a getaway car through completely empty countryside for the next two hours, without stopping. It's devoid of people, except for the occasional hamlet or farm. France is so big and empty! After a brief encounter with Champagne, we entered Lorraine and finally made a direct beeline for

Nancy. Joy assured me these are not the first names of the Three Degrees. She also reminded me they had a hit called 'Dirty Ol' Man'.

The first stop after more than two hours of high-speed action was our destination. Nancy-Ville is a fairly large station and has exits front, rear and to the sides. I had checked that our hotel should be found if we left by the rear exit. The Korean couple followed us to the surface. On the street I could see the small neon light of our chosen hotel. The Korean couple sidled away in search of their hotel. Two hundred metres and we were indoors. The rain had stopped and dusk had descended. It was 5.15pm.

Our room in this All Seasons hotel was small but perfect. A garret with Dorma window. Between the rooms and the lobby is a courtyard with a massive tree and several picnic tables. We can lunch there one day, if the weather is kind. We put our stuff away and decided to head out. As we left, the Korean couple came in, pleased they too had found their hotel.

Joy grabbed a local map off the counter and we headed directly to Stanislas Square. We needed to get our bearings, a glass of wine, a coffee and find a nice restaurant for dinner. There's a white stone arch with sculpted Roman figures at the top of Rue Stanislas which leads down the hill and into Place Stanislas. The square itself is beautiful. Stanislas is a strange name to give to a French landmark. It's named after the guy whose statue has pride of place atop a plinth in the centre. He was the exiled King of Poland (Stanislaw Leszczynski) who was given the title Duke of Lorraine by his son in law, King Louis XV in the early 18th century. There are neat, ornate and opulent buildings on all four sides facing the centre. Gilded wrought iron gates with fountains and statues adorn the corners. Restaurant awnings stretch over exterior seating along two sides of the square, which is the size of a football pitch. Every brick, cobble and railing are as clean as the day they were erected. No wonder this has been named a World Heritage site by UNESCO. Beyond one set of wrought iron gates (with gold leaf embellishments) is a façade, with clock and bells tolling a welcome, for Joy and I. We have hit the jackpot. Nancy is gorgeous.

We sat and stared at this square for ages. Families and lovers (I saw lots of kissing and canoodling) strolled hand in hand and as dusk fell, flash lights sparkled as cameras captured the images all around.

The shops in nearby streets all displayed designer labels, very few were the corporate retailers we see everywhere else. I bought a bottle of local wine to stow in our room for later consumption and we finally tracked down a lovely looking restaurant for supper. It was a struggle at first as many were bistros or brasseries with functional menus. We fancied something a little more special. This can be tricky because there's a fine line between what we class as top end to our tastes and pocket, and the outlandish prices charged by celebrity chefs and their Michelin starred money gobblers. There were two or three such places here.

We peered over the half-mast window blinds of Le Cap Marine restaurant. A girl was setting the tables and I beckoned her to the window. She unlocked the front door and took my request for a table for 8pm. We had time enough to dump my wine purchase back at the hotel, freshen up and check the map for where to explore tomorrow.

We arrived at the restaurant on time and were seated in a corner enabling us to observe everyone else. The décor was smart with light beech woodwork surfaces, crisp table linen and oversized wine glasses. The other diners comprised small family groups and intimate couples. Despite our poor grasp of French, we were well looked after and the waitress said it was fine as she wanted to improve her English. The wine list was the size of a telephone directory. I watched a grandmother at another table carefully select her choice from the list. She did her tasting routine before accepting the bottle. The waitress told me she knew nothing of wine before she came to work here and now never wants to leave because of that wine list.

I saw her point. I could have spent the next decade and a large fortune working my way through the choices. I settled for a bottle of Domaine du

Turner Pageot from Languedoc. It hit the spot. As they poured the wine, we were served an h'ordeuvre of lightly battered fish pieces with a small dish of soft mousse while we waited for our starter. My starter was truly delicious, l'escargot, arranged in a circle with a small, mouth-watering rissole over a puddle of a cheese sauce. I'm in heaven. The main course of pork medallions laced with a dark sauce, a tower of waffle-like pancakes with roasted parsnips stood no chance of survival. My dessert of 'tart,' pink grapefruit pieces with a syllabub and lemon mousse ice cream and vanilla sauce topped off a stunning meal.

I asked the wine waiter to choose an appropriate wine to accompany my dessert. I was brought a glass of Muscat which had tones of apricot jam and candy floss. The perfect start to our gastronomic adventures in Eastern France. The bill was very modest compared to the Michelin starred restaurants, and the attention to detail and service was wonderful. The chef and owner came over to express their thanks and said their intentions were to supply the best eating experience possible. They got our vote. "Merci Monsieur. Merci beaucoup Chef." What a way to finish our first day? We slunk back to our room like stray cats that found an open door to a sofa warehouse. My own wine bottle will have to wait until tomorrow to be tasted. I was as full as an egg.

Sunday was very quiet out on the streets. Well, at least until around midday, but after breakfast we slipped out of the hotel into brilliant sunshine and a clear blue sky. We returned to Place Stanislas, passing a boulangerie near the hotel that had a queue of customers reaching out through the door and past the display windows. It looked wonderful inside, with carefully laid out shelves of the most scrumptious breads, pastries, cakes, chocolates and tiers of gift box affairs containing all the items I've just mentioned. Small children were standing on tippy toes at the glass fronted counter with eyes as big as macaroons as they surveyed the amazing goodies on offer.

After taking in the relaxed ambience at Stanislas Square, we then moved eastwards towards the canal and the river Meurthe. The distinctive French architecture looking back at us from every angle. Barges lined up along the banks. Some freight, some private and others with big glass windows revealing decked-out dining rooms, for that cruise ship experience. There are plenty of things to see and do in this town. We entered a large park. It's not as big as Regent's Park in London but it has the same energetic personnel jogging around in groups, sweating off those pounds. A woman jogged along whilst pushing a pram. Several enthusiasts were vigorously exercising on the grass. It got me in the mood too. I popped a treacle toffee into my mouth and gave my jaws a good Sunday morning work-out as we strolled with almost the same conviction as this perspiring party of puffing plodders. There's a segregated area in the park with a large concrete stage facing a concreted, open space. This would be a great place for concerts, well away from houses and roads. They must make good use of it in the summer months. A nearby fun fair was all closed up and parents with tiny tots, strolled along the paths between the flower borders, gardens and trees. It was an idyllic Sunday scene. I half expected to see Claude Monet sitting at an easel.

Snaking through towards the oldest part of the city brought us back amongst grand buildings, walls and courtyards. Joy spied a lovely café, with kerb-side tables cluttered with folk drinking coffee, smoking and chatting with friends. It was barely midday but the place had already taken on that leisurely relaxed image depicted in fine French paintings. We agreed we might luncheon here after we explore yet another inviting passage and see what's around the next blind corner. We found more lanes leading to more distractions.

We passed a deli that had set up a ladened table outside. It was groaning under the weight of all the cheeses that could not fit on the shelves inside. A food market appeared in a lane between the walls of a church and an old building. Honey stalls, more cheeses, meats, spices, olives and a hundred other stuffed and marinated morsels of mouth-watering munchiness. I got stuck inspecting wines in tiny shops, and other fascinating fare. We should have brought a shopping trolley with us. We found a local crémant of some distinction and bought cheese, salami, bread, fruit and water. It was decided to give the café back at the kerb-side a miss, and instead picnic in the enclosed gardens of our hotel.

But there was yet still more to see and photograph. Antique shops were opening for the afternoon and tiny cafes were serving up piping hot espressos and mini cakes for the peckish. Tempting and torturing us at the same time. We did eventually tear ourselves away, and spread our items out on a picnic table in the sunshine. I opened the now chilled bottle of wine we had bought yesterday, laid out grapes, an apple, two wonderful cheeses (Munster and Cantal), salami and broke off chunks of soft, fresh bread. A bottle of water was in here somewhere.

Later in the afternoon we nipped into the railway station to check on where we might adventure to tomorrow. The screen flicked up; Strasbourg, Metz, Luxembourg, Luneville, Baccarat and Toul, (where our lunchtime tipple was produced). That's a nice list. We discussed them over dinner, all evening and right up to the very last minute the next morning.

We checked-out after breakfast. I'll miss the fresh orange maker in the breakfast room. It swallowed up a basket of fresh oranges. I watched my juices flowing into the glass through the Perspex window as the wheels mangled the fruit between two sprockets! Novel to see it working, fabulous to get your orange juice so utterly freshly squeezed.

Back at the railway station we stared at the departures board. The decision appeared in an instant. The next train to Luxembourg leaves in ten minutes. The train for Strasbourg departs an hour later. It all clicked into place. Luxembourg it is then. We climbed aboard and settled on the right-hand side of the train, as we expect to follow the course of the Moselle at some point. The carriage was not busy and the journey extremely pleasant. We passed through Pont-a-Mousson. It's right on the Moselle. Joy was delighted when I told her there is a massive factory there that produces sewage pipes! We passed the yard that confirmed my suspicions. Almost every manhole cover that you see on the pavements throughout France has the name Pont-a-

Mousson emblazoned on the lid. Every day is a school day. I'm sure she was trying to get her camera out but we had passed completely through the village before she could remove the lens cover.

Metz

When we arrived at Metz we decided to break the journey and have a quick look around. Our tickets were valid for such impetuosity. The Moselle splits into several branches as it flows through the city and reforms towards the outskirts to the north. Apart from the football team, I know nothing about Metz. They play in the same colours as Heart of Midlothian FC. I now know the Carolingian Dynasty was based here in the 8th century. They are known to have established the religious plainsong we recognise as Gregorian Chants, though I don't think it came from the terraces of Metz FC! It's a very old city with roots that can be traced back to 3,000 B.C.E.

We exited the station and after asking a couple of passers-by for directions, headed for the Basilica of St Pierre-aux-Nonnains. It was a very pleasant walk and a nice surprise to see clusters of pre-medieval buildings surrounding the church. The Chapel of the Templars was closed when we were here, but the 12th century building has murals on many of the walls. The Basilica is reputed to be the oldest church in France. It is built with tiny bricks and is very different to most religious piles we see. This was worth cutting the train journey for. We walked along the precinct that leads to the Metz cathedral, which is of the more predictable design and stonework. It too, has attractions worth taking a peek at. The expanse of stained-glass windows is said to be the largest in the world, some of which was the work of Herman von Münster. I never thought I'd see *that* name in the annals of history! There were plenty of options for lunch. We really had to make tracks back to the station and head to Luxembourg, so we bought some snacks from a food outlet and hoped the trains were still running.

It took about an hour from here to the centre of Luxembourg city. The tracks followed the Moselle until Thionville. It's is a wonderful river, very wide, placid and picturesque, with lots of locks along this stretch. The barges carrying freight ploughing the surface, are large enough for the captain to park his own car on deck.

Luxembourg

Outside the station at Luxembourg was not an enthralling sight. It's busy, chaotic even, and there's nothing grand about the Duchy at this moment. We decided to check out the hotels in the vicinity but the ones we could see looked seedy and run down. We tried a side street a bit further along. There are lots of neon signs along the walls. We realised why. It's the red-light district, all sex shops and sleazy bars. We made a swift exit. A few metres further up the road and around another a corner, an appropriate hotel stood before us. They had a room available and any anxiety we might have been experiencing melted away. We can now go and see what this city has to offer.

It has a divide between old and new. The new was where we were staying and the old is where everyone is attracted to; unless you want the sex shops of course! The divide is a gorge of about 15 metres deep and 300 metres wide. It's a natural fortress. In fact, the name Luxembourg derives from the Saxon word for little fortress "Lucilinburhuc" which makes it pre-Roman. The tiny country of Luxembourg has been around since the 10th century. Its strategic importance is due to being the dividing point of Frankish and Germanic territories. Linguistically, French, German and Luxembourgish are spoken.

Two road bridges breech the gorge and below us the houses, in nicely maintained parkland, look very pretty as we peered over the wall. The old city is lovely and deserves the moniker 'Grand Duchy'. Pencil thin towers stretch above the cathedral and ministerial buildings of ancient opulence face us, while the new city behind is dominated by modern steel and glass office blocks that look on with jealous malice. We took a short stroll down the streets where designer shops proliferate. Tomorrow we shall check out the rest of what this old city has to show us.

We found a busy Spanish restaurant thronged with happy chattering diners. It had just one table available. Whilst gorging on steak and fries, we got chatting to a group of guys from Cork, over here on a business trip. The banter was light and a lad at another table joined in, regaling us with tales of his recent trip to Mongolia. The evening developed into a large and happy family gathering.

We spent the next morning exploring the parts of the old city we had missed the previous evening. We earmarked a nice restaurant for lunch and agreed we should head back into France by mid-afternoon.

The river Alzette runs through the old city and gives the place a very country town feel. It's a bit like a layer cake as high walls over the embankments make the dynamic buildings very separate from the cottages and gardens down amongst the greenery. The back drop looks photoshopped. There are plenty of places to keep our attention here in the centre. It's all pedestrianised and became amusing when we kept emerging from one alley or another to find we were back where we started. There were soldiers standing guard at a building, opposite a café that specialises in hot chocolate. The high ceiling in the upper room of this café was arched with bare brickwork at each end. It gave it a cloistered university hall feel. It was cold outside, Joy suggested we should take the guards a hot chocolate to warm them up.

The lunch we promised ourselves in the Ristorante Mi & Ti proved to be an excellent choice. We sat on high stools in the window. The food took a few minutes to arrive but the wait was so worth it. It was a culinary delight. Four cheeses, four different cold meats and a dish of marinated cherries in a little extra sauce and fresh, crusty bread. The wine too was gorgeous.

The train journey back to Nancy was as much a pleasure as the trip up was the day before. There is a station stop along the way, at a place called

Frouard. The automated announcement on the train pronounced this in a purring French accent as Phwoarrrr. Maybe we should jump off there and see if it lives up to its name!

Toul

Over coffee in a café that looked typically Parisian, with ornate mirrors, a dado rail and posters of old newspaper stories hung in picture frames, Joy and I hatched a plan. We would not stay in Nancy but take a short journey to Toul and find a bed there tonight. Tomorrow, we will head further east and spend a few days in Strasbourg, deep in the Vosges region.

A short hop of twenty minutes by train, through a place called Liverdun, this journey was beautiful. It's autumn, the colours of the leaves have faded and begun to falter. Tree trunks are exposing their nakedness to the elements. Fortunately for us, the cruel winds of winter have yet to come. The train crossed the Moselle more than once. We had to keep swapping seats to get the best views. This river really is beautiful. Liverdun looked inviting. If Toul turns out to be a bit blunt we can just head back there. As the train rounded the next big bend, two low hills failed to hide the massive towers of a cathedral peeking above the rooftops of Toul.

A big cathedral means cafes and bars and hotels could be nearby. We walked along a country road from the station, dragging our cases behind us. It's not too far. There's no traffic. We came to a left turn that leads into the town itself. Within a few hundred metres we reached Le Hotel Lorraine. Inside, it is about as picturesque and undeniably French in style as you could imagine. Chintzy wallpaper, an old wooden counter and big iron keys hanging off hooks behind reception. We had to sign nothing. Just accept the chunky wrought iron key on a massive star shaped fob and head up two flights of spiral staircase to our lovely little room.

We were soon back on the street to check out the neighbourhood. We are already in the centre of town and there's a restaurant directly opposite our hotel. Around the corner is a crescent of shops with a café on the end. A warm smile and fresh Arabic coffee was served to perk us up. Narrow passageways disappear into terraced residential quarters in all directions. Many homes lie abandoned while others are well maintained as the residents try to keep life going in these decaying towns. The dwellings have so much potential that we could easily succumb to a pushy estate agent and buy a pile of rubble in the hope of reconstructing its former glory.

The cathedral Saint-Étienne, that we saw from the train is far larger than the city appears to merit. It was first constructed in the 13th century but has been derelict and neglected since the Revolution. Its architecture is pure gothic of the most flamboyant style. Looking at it now, if it were a ship it would be called a rusting hulk. Its importance arose from the increase in trade since Toul became a Free Imperial City around the 12th century. The walls that surrounded the whole town were needed many times, to defend the inhabitants and armies within. American forces were garrisoned here during the fighting in The Great War. It therefore played a significant role in the final outcome. Throughout every turmoil the Moselle continued to glide quietly by just beyond the walls.

By some happy coincidence we wandered into a winery where they store and sell their own wines. The proprietor was happy to show us, step by step, how their grapes are harvested, fermented and bottled. He admitted it was he who 'riddled' the sparkling wine bottles to maturity. Degustation was mentioned and our French is good enough to accept without further explanation.

It was not far to walk back to our hotel. Our room was so warm and cosy. High ceilings, Fleur de Lys patterns on the walls and curtains, and a window large enough to haul a grand piano up and pull it inside. It was a mere 8 paces from hotel door to restaurant entrance. A delightful brasserie. It was busy inside so the atmosphere was greatly enhanced. We had salmon hot pot and ice cream for dessert.

I was woken a couple of times overnight by a fellow guest who was snoring like a mating hippo. In the morning we deduced that the man with this affliction was the enormous guy sitting at a nearby table, swallowing a dump-truck sized load of food. When he left the dining room, with his wife in tow, he pushed through the saloon swing doors and just let them rock back, cracking his wife's knuckles as the two doors merged. He looked totally unconcerned. She was purple with pain and rage.

We checked-out, but were permitted to leave our cases safely under the spiral staircase until it was time to leave town. Turning back towards the centre we noted it was market day. It's really a market for the locals. There's little tourism here. Young mums with pushchairs and older folk were queuing to buy their groceries and knick-knacks. I think we were the only couple without a string bag. I really like the quiet, reclusive nature of these small cities in France. Everybody was friendly. They spoke whether we could understand them or not and always smiled.

The train back to Nancy was dead on time. We watched an old lady being assisted across the tracks by rail staff before we departed. She was seated next to us and spoke just enough English to bring a little conversation. This was a terrific excursion. We have covered quite a lot of territory and added another country in along the way. Our next location is a couple of hours east from here. As we stared from the window of our train, I looked across this peaceful, rolling landscape and said a big thank you to Lorraine and Nancy, for sharing their beauty with me. I won't tell anyone if they won't.

Strasbourg

It was almost 10pm and I had all but memorised the short walk from the station to our hotel. It took less than fifteen minutes. Opposite the apartment/hotel Sejours et Affaires is a very pretty and inviting restaurant with diners still inside enjoying their Sunday evening. We plan to join them. First, we will check-in, dump our bags and be out again in no time.

The hotel was all locked up and there was no one around. Lights were on in the lobby but the only way to gain access was to punch in a key code that secures the door. We searched through our papers. We don't have the code. There was no mention that the place would be shut at this time of night. A few minutes later a couple of lads walked up behind us, punched some digits on the keypad and the door opened. We entered too.

There was no sign of anyone, but we did see a notice board that had a telephone number written on it. It's all in French and we guessed it must be a help line. I was answered by a recorded voice, in French, that seemed to tell me that the offices were closed until Monday morning. I checked through our paperwork again and found only a copy of the email from the agency stating I could check in after 2pm on this day.

Joy was chuckling away. Our mishaps in the past include; arriving at a hotel in Lisbon, where no booking was logged. In New York, our documents and passports had gone off in the taxi we'd just arrived in from the airport. In another traumatic episode, our cases for the hold had to be abandoned at Gatwick airport due to the shuttle bus being held up in a road traffic accident, (we had to board the flight with our pockets stuffed full of underwear). We have had set-backs, such as a fire in the channel tunnel and volcanic ash over the Atlantic, but to arrive at a hotel to find it closed for the weekend was a new one.

We had no option but to go find another hotel to spend the night. We will sort it out in the morning. The receptionist at the Best Western around the corner spoke very little English but understood our plight. She offered a room at a knock down price and we fell on our feet with a lovely top floor suite with a balcony overlooking the city. We dumped our bags and set out in the drizzly rain to find somewhere to eat. It was now past 11pm. The pretty restaurant we noticed earlier had closed. We walked through the streets only to find kebab shops and a rather undesirable looking café still trading at this time of night. There was no other option but to eat at a McDonald's.

I bring Joy to France to savour the delights of French cuisine in the style that makes this country famous the world over, only to drag her kicking and screaming under the golden arches for a flannel burger and matchstick chips. We were starving by now. There were armed police officers in here. I'd better not jump the queue. They were in it.

We ate our meals inside and watched late night revellers come and go. Outside it was raining hard, but we soon returned to our unplanned hotel and settled down for the night.

In the morning, I popped across the road and bought fresh croissants while Joy brewed the coffee for breakfast. We took advantage of the rooftop views and collected a few photographs before nipping back to the original hotel to see if they were open.

The girl, now sitting at her desk, told us the agency ought to have emailed us details about the hotel reception closing at midday on Saturday and reopening on Monday. We should have been provided with the code for the exterior door and a location to find the key set aside for our reserved room. To compensate she offered us an upgrade to a family room which is much larger than the one we had been allocated. We had no complaints at all about this. The fault of weekend access confusion lay with the booking agency.

The rain has stopped and Strasbourg is all ours. It is the capital city of the Grand Est, formally known as Alsace. It looks beautiful even from the narrow street we were located in. The old city is surrounded by a ring of canals and channels, not quite Venice, but it is no less appealing. Alleyways ran like veins between cobbled arteries. We frequently slipped away from the shops along the boulevard and ended up in a courtyard or two.

The many delicatessens displayed mouth-watering foods which made passing by impossible without stopping. I could list a hypermarket's till receipt of items that I wanted to add to our basket. We stored what we did buy in our kitchen and headed out again, drawn through the chill yet dry air, like a magnet, towards La Petite France.

The brochures haven't lied. Some of the multi-storey, half-timbered buildings are over 400 years old. We must have snapped a hundred pictures before we even crossed the canal and headed towards the brick towers that line the banks of another river system. The converted wharfs, that once were tanneries and old storage buildings, are now restaurants, work-shops, offices and museums. Many have been painted in pastel shades, the Swiss/German architectural style is very evident.

Working our way slowly around, we climbed above the Vauban Barrage that regulates the flow of water through the canals and lingered on the rooftop esplanade. The views are captivating, as towers and church spires detract the eye from the grey canvas of the winter sky. We dawdled for so long my tummy began to complain through lack of pastries. The difficulty now is which café to choose from! Goodness knows what dilemma awaits when it comes to dinnertime.

We left the weirs, locks and canals behind us and wandered away from the tourist trail. We bought a few items from a cheap outlet run by a smiling Asian lad (I bought an Arabian teapot and Joy bought a toothbrush) and we stepped into a Moroccan café for pastries and coffee. We could have hired a hookah pipe to smoke if we wished. The family running this café were also very friendly. They smiled and waved us off when we left.

The Citadel Park would make for a very pleasant walk, maybe not on a rainy day but I'm sure it's busy during the summer. It was built in 1964 and surrounds the ruins of the old fortress, that was erected in 1681. Our friend Vauban, of course, was the architect for the defences of Strasbourg as well as the barrage we had just visited. We wandered all afternoon around the streets, until we were eventually drawn under the filigree architecture of the magnificent cathedral. The approaches to this quarter are rife with gift shops selling tacky trappings and printed tea towels, but it was exciting to see all the Christmas decorations draped over the balconies of the medieval buildings. The glow from the lighting in this twilight setting gave it a magical edge. It felt like Christmas already.

Inside the cathedral is yet another giant astronomical clock. The original was installed around the same time as the clock in Auxerre, except this clock has been replaced twice. It has dials, indicators, cherub statues and probably a giant key to wind it up at the back. It reaches the ceiling and, on the hour (while another clock face shows a different time half an hour later) it chimes, squeaks and sets into motion several characters that are strategically placed for such events. Along with dozens of other people, we looked up until our necks cricked. It displays accurate times for eclipses and much more besides. It resembles a giant steam boiler, and I wondered quietly if it had been made in the Glasgow shipyards. I half expected to find a brass plate stamped with John Brown Engineering! Joking aside, it is a very impressive piece of equipment for its time.

It was time for us to head back and prepare ourselves for the evening meal. I calculated that the cathedral frontage was facing away from the location of our apartment, so I guided Joy in the opposite direction. One hour and fifteen minutes later we were still nowhere near any familiar sign or our hotel. I had a printed map, a Google map on my mobile phone and Gordon the Garmin GPS with me. Still I could not find our way back inside the close-knit circle of the old city. Yet, we were still inside a canal complex. Perplexed, despite the still attractive yet new territories we were exploring, I wanted us to be back in the warmth of our room. We passed some nice restaurants, sometimes twice. I tried to blame Joy for this. I think she was wreaking revenge for all the blame she has to take for previous deviations. She was obviously, subtly motioning me down the wrong alleys and over the wrong bridges just to make me look foolish. Well it worked.

We finally spotted a familiar looking road and were home. In reality, it's ten minutes from our hotel to walk to the cathedral. I will say no more on this subject except, we saw parts of the city that few tourists would think about straying into, yet all were a pleasure to explore.

We returned to La Petite France and opened the door to the Little Venise Restaurant, which in true Alsace style, was a mixture of French, German and Swiss in every way. Joy chose a chicken dish cooked in Riesling whilst I had pork on a king-sized mattress of sauerkraut. Alsace wines, being predominantly white, come in several grape varieties. We shall try a different variety each night and Joy can elect her favourite at the end of the week. Tonight, it was Silvaner. We had no room for dessert but since 'apfel strudel' was not listed anyway, I did not sulk.

We strolled back through the deserted alleyways with an air of absolute serenity. The feeling of being blessed with such good fortune as to be here in this beautiful city was not ignored. The central heating had worked wonders in our room and we slept without pause until the new day dawned.

Tuesday was marked down as Veterans Day. The French equivalent of Remembrance Day in the UK. Many of the shops were closed but there was still plenty to entertain us. In Kleber Square, several market stalls had appeared. One was selling old advertising prints and posters. A woman was speaking in broken English to the stallholder and asked, "Do you focus on the artist or the product you are selling?" The stall holder mentioned something about appreciating the skills of such-and-such an artist, but the other woman was not accepting her half-hearted response. She argued something about the importance of "becoming at one with your subject." She suggested that the stallholder should follow her ethos because, she insisted "When I sing, I become Ella Fitzgerald and only when I become Ella Fitzgerald, do I feel I am doing justice to her work."

I had to see what this woman looked like. I peeked through the canvas partition of the adjoining stall expecting an elegantly dressed diva with the deportment of a diamond voiced songstress from the golden age of jazz. What I saw, was a batty old bag in a grubby overcoat having a bad hair day. Snigger. I think she was Belgian.

We wound our way towards the cathedral once more. It was almost midday. Crowds were filtering through the doors, most probably to witness the performance of the aforementioned clock. Outside, an elderly Romanian woman in a wheelchair was whizzing around cutting in front of people and waving a paper cup at them. It looked like a cross between dancing on ice and Grand Theft Auto. Folk had to dive out of the way to avoid getting run over.

We went inside and waited in the corner for the bells to signal midday and the entertaining routine of the clock to begin. The performance was rather limp and disappointing. A few clangs and a bit of movement by one bit and then, nothing. To the left however, people began to gaze upwards as a video recording was flashed on a large screen. It told the story of the clock in three languages. I have no idea what it was talking about because the magic was lost in the detail. Absurd detail. I would not recommend buying the DVD. Unless you have insomnia.

We shuffled out with many others. Only the diehards remained, like dyslexic train spotters at an abandoned track. Outside, the wheelchair woman had gone, her shift over. She was replaced by Romanian wheelchair man. I cannot vouch nor deny if it was the same wheelchair they used.

The afternoon was spent very productively. We shopped and drank hot chocolate, and returned to the cosy warmth of our hotel room until supper beckoned. It was taken in a rather nice Pizza restaurant where the Muscat grape performed the part of the Joy's Alsace wine challenge. Her opinion leant towards the Silvaner we had the night before.

Basel, Switzerland

We had all but covered the focal points of Strasbourg for now, so we took a day trip to Basel in Switzerland. It's about 75 minutes away. It was quite exciting to arrive in another country. There was no passport control, but security officers took aside several travellers as we waltzed through without hindrance. We checked with the bank in the station about the currency here. Apparently, we can buy goods in Euros but will receive the change in Swiss Francs. Credit cards will be charged in either currency.

Well, we tested that out. We were like shopaholics despite the notion that Switzerland is much more expensive than France. I found a fabulous pair of boots that had my attention straight away. The label said: '50% off'. We wandered from shop to shop all the way down to a bridge that crosses the Rhine. This iconic river holds as much reverence for me as the Danube or the Neva. Today the clouds were high enough to allow clear visibility to the horizon and we took many photographs from the bank, above the hill by the cathedral and on the bridge itself. Non-motorised wooden ferries, called Fahri, transport people across the river by use of a steel cable. It might have been fun as the river is rather wide but at this time of year, it's far too cold for that malarkey. We crossed by means of a bridge.

After sharing lunch in a department store café on the opposite bank we headed back through the narrow lanes towards the station and up the hill. The town hall (Kanton Basel Stadt) deserves a mention as the frescoes and brickwork are amazing. Not surprisingly, there are more narrow lanes and shops to be found. Many of the buildings here are so photogenic, we were both in danger of getting RSI in our index fingers. Small bars, specialist shops and delightful guest houses proliferate. It's a beautiful city. In the 7th century the city fell under Frankish rule as it was already within the boundaries of Alsace at that time. So, in some respects, we may not have left France after all. However, it was destroyed during an invasion by the Magyars in the 10th century and again by an earthquake in 1356. It became Swiss in 1521. In 1938 a chemist named Albert Hoffman first synthesised the hallucinogenic drug LSD in Basel. We were about to embark on a trip of a different kind, as we had tired ourselves out with all these steep hills and made for the railway station and home.

On the way back, the guard on our train was a somewhat large guy with long, lank, neglected hair. He did not look fit. His bulk made it difficult to walk without rocking sideways, like Humpty Dumpty in a railway uniform. He didn't come through the carriages to check tickets but he did make a swift beeline for the chocolate vending machine at the next station. The bulges in his uniform reminded me that I might have problems packing all our purchases in the limited space we have in our suitcases. Another holdall seems the only answer. Thank goodness we are not travelling by air.

For our evening meal we finally got a table at the pretty restaurant across the road from our hotel. The red gingham table cloths and heavy wood furniture fitted perfectly with the bare walls and low arches. I had escargot to start, followed by fish, and concluded with a gorgeous chocolate mousse on a sponge base and fresh cream. Joy seemed to enjoy her steak and crème brûlée. Her grape tonight was gewürztraminer.

Obernai

Thursday, time for another away day. There's a gorgeous boulangerie just around the corner from our hotel that has a wide choice of breads and pastries available all day. They must be baking constantly as there is always a fast-moving queue no matter when you turn up. We scuttled back to the railway station for the second day running. This time, a local service took us to Obernai. It is located on the eastern slopes of the Vosges mountains and is smack in the midst of the Alsace vineyards. The names of the towns in these parts all sound very Germanic, despite the region only being annexed by our Prussian cousins during times of military conflict. Most of the village names end in 'Heim'. Obernai was named Oberehnheim during those periods, which was its original name in the 13th century. It is one of the 9 imperial towns of Alsace, an alliance which freed these towns from empirical authority of the nobles. The traditional costumes worn by the town's women during pageants and festivals were copied from Marie Antoinette who liked to dress as a simple shepherdess when attending country fairs at Versailles.

Obernai is just wonderful. It has so much character. The main thoroughfare is lined with beam framed buildings that bulge and sag due to the ravages of time and yet are all in excellent condition. Virtually every single one of them demands a photograph. Today is market day. The streets are lined with several score of stalls. Some sell the usual garments and foods while others have a somewhat curious line of stock. Mattresses. It must be a mattress mecca because there were at least half a dozen vendors embedded amongst the stalls.

The market reached into several side streets as well as the main square. Even the church grounds were set up for trade. The market has been going since the 11th century. It really is impressive for its size and the quality of wares on show. We grabbed a couple of bargains. A woolly hat for just a few Euros. Joy got herself a very nice woollen top from a stall where the chap kept apologising for speaking such poor English. He was such a nice man. He would not accept it was our fault for not understanding his native tongue.

We walked back towards the railway station laden once more with goodies, taking a circuitous route along ramparts that encircle the old town. There are battlements here too. It's all very beautiful. We munched pastries and drank fluids while waiting for our train to take us to our next destination for the day.

Colmar

On the journey to Colmar, the vineyards just kept gliding past as we nipped from village to village. I particularly like the names of Gertwiller and Gottwiller. Apparently, the village of Barr is also worth a visit but we didn't find that out until after we had returned to Strasbourg.

We had to change trains at Sélestat, which gave us time to grab some lunch. There's not much here but a café annexed to what looked like an old folk's home. It was more than adequate. We sat and watched the locals come and go. Several old dears from the home came and ordered plat-du-jour and took a glass of red wine with it too. Very sweet.

Our connection to Colmar arrived and departed on time and we were soon walking the fair distance from Colmar station to the town centre. The park on the right was preparing itself for Christmas, and trees and other temporary buildings were being erected for the festivities. In the town itself we were enlightened by the architecture. The shops are laid out in more modern style than Obernai but the history books record that Colmar as a town dates back to Carolingian times, those, of the Gregorian chant fame. The Emperor Charles the Fat, held a Diet here (this is not a pun) in 884 C.E.! Colmar is another town that joined the imperial alliance together with Obernai. Its tempestuous history includes occupation by the Swedish army during the Thirty Years War, and was held by Germany in 1945 until the U.S. 6th army liberated it to become French once again.

We clicked away merrily as we strolled for over an hour. The hardest part as usual, was deciding which café was the most likely to secure our custom for afternoon refreshment. We chose a bar this time. The restaurant area looked fabulous. It was all gingham soft furnishings and Austro/Swiss décor on the walls. We had coffee and a glass of Riesling. In this Hansel and Gretel cottage bar, it was one of those moments when you could just sit there until closing time. Joy declared that Riesling was the superior Alsace grape for her palate. Few would argue that.

We have more to explore. These lanes and the medieval buildings seem to be on all sides and around every corner. An American lady approached me and asked if I would take her photograph as she posed in front of a statue. No problem, but she turned her back as I aimed her camera, to reveal a logo on her waterproof jacket. 'Baltimore Running Club'. She told me it was to impress her husband who was back home in Baltimore. I suggested she must have worn out quite a few pairs of running shoes to have reached this far.

Joy and I made our way back to the railway station and in the twilight of the afternoon skies we caught the train to Strasbourg. It was a great day's exploration. Where would she like to go tomorrow, I asked. Germany? We could almost walk there. We got back before the sky had pulled on it's all enveloping shroud and headed for the Halles shopping precinct just across the canal, and C&A. We really do need another holdall.

We edged towards La Petite France proper and sat in a classical, cellar restaurant with all the hallmarks of history and quality. We dined well. The décor and ancient clock that was free standing against one wall added to the ambience. A young couple arrived with a baby in a cot that was so wrapped up it could have withstood an arctic gale. They set the cot down beside their table and staff stopped and cooed at the silent mite every time they passed. The parents, proud as they should be, enjoyed their meal without disruption, and so did we! It was a fitting end to a very culture filled day.

When we exited the hotel on Friday morning, I spotted a tucked away restaurant called Beaujolais, which at first glance just looked like someone's living room. Squinting through the blinds I judged it to be the ideal place for our finale this evening. The waitress, setting up for the day, let us in and accepted our request for a table for 8pm. She was Cuban and spoke virtually no English. But by now we could at least feel confident to book the table in French. Well, we hoped we did.

Our next target was to pay some respects and find some war graves, which are located on the north side of the city. We walked along the busy roadside for a short while and then cut through a wooded park and back to a thoroughfare. This led us to a graveyard that was filled with headstones for French, German and Islamic victims of WWII. The headstones over the Islamic graves were very distinctive. It was well laid out and thought provoking. Billboards at the main entrance explained the purpose and history of those that have fallen.

This graveyard was not on our map however. We still have some way to go for the cemetery we were looking for. About a mile further along is the Jewish graveyard, which is the last resting place for civilians, who have passed away without the expedience of war. But there is also a section set aside for those who suffered terribly at the hands of the perpetrators of the holocaust. There is a large memorial inside the gates with many names listed. Yet even more poignantly are individual gravestones in cold grey slate that identify who and where these poor victims fell. Death camps in Eastern Europe were mentioned, and on some stones, a note to say the survivor of said camp perished shortly after living through the horror. There is a washroom available here so that visitors can cleanse at least their hands if not their minds as to how abominable humans can be to humans.

We paid respects and wandered slowly back. In a park a woodpecker was busy knocking his head against a tree not 10 metres away. Joy reminded me that some woodpeckers have a tongue so long it wraps around their brain to protect it from bashing against their skulls when head banging tree trunks. Eventually, we came to the city walls. These are severely scarred with the legacy of wars. Railings and bars block the tunnels that were bored into the concrete and rock. Evidence of the garrisons that utilised this semi-natural defence against intruders. It's quite eerie walking along when there is no other soul about. Some of those padlocks on the barred off dungeons don't look disused. Joy was equally taken by a huge 'insect hotel' that was placed alongside a row of allotments. Some of the plots had dachas suggesting a more pleasant place of refuge away from the crowds, for insects and human inhabitants alike.

We spent the afternoon exploring more of the shopping area, Galleries Lafayette got a look in but not through our wallets. I spotted a woolly hat, very similar to the one I bought in Obernai, this one was marked up at 20 times what I paid for mine. We returned to C&A because I had bought a pair of jeans the day before that were a little too tight. It must be all the Alsatian food I'd been tucking away.

The final dinner of the trip. The restaurant we booked this morning turned out to be a superb choice. The menu was written in scroll lettering on a chalk board, and since it was in French, we could not decipher a word. The host did his best to recite each line but he may as well have been reading a bus timetable. We just pointed and hoped for the best. The wine option was easier. However, they served no Alsace wine only Burgundian. Well, the place is called Beaujolais so I should have known, idiot. They only served wine by the glass which made it even easier as I could select from the table covered with recently corked bottles. I plucked a gorgeous white for Joy, she said so, and a perfect red for me. At €5 a large glass, this proved to be a brilliant idea.

The food was exquisite and the other diners in the room created a delightful atmosphere. The Cuban waitress was floating about smiling all the time. A French girl also served at the tables, dressed in black with a white apron, and flirted wickedly with everybody. I had a delicious dessert wine with my pudding which topped off the whole evening. We all shook hands and were waved off the premises, filled to the brim and not even empty of wallet. It was the absolute perfect ending to the week.

Saturday morning, and we had to vacate the room before the receptionist arrives. Our train departed at 9am. We had already packed our extra, recently purchased holdall with breads and pastries and soft drinks. Our shopping booty fitted in somewhere too. We left Strasbourg on time, next stop, Paris. A group of lads behind Joy were sitting at a table playing cards. They were off to the international rugby match in the Capital. They did have beer with them, just a couple of small bottles which when emptied they put back in their storage bag. There was little more than moderate chatter all the way. I got another glimpse at Champagne as we sped through the countryside between Reims and Epernay. Every rail journey on this trip has been an absolute pleasure.

HAUTE-DE-FRANCE

Lille, Christmas Shopping

It's early December. We had planned to take the ferry to the Hook of Holland, and spend a few days in one of the many Dutch towns that hold a Christmas market. It transpired, that timings of crossings, connections and accessibility to these towns is not as straightforward as we had hoped. So, at the last minute, we resorted to type and booked the Eurostar direct to Lille. It seems fitting that the journeys we have indulged in to create this book, should end with a trip to a Christmas market in France.

We had been to Lille before and liked it so much that we promised to return. We booked an apartment at the Sejours et Affaires, the same hotel chain we enjoyed when we were in Strasbourg. The hotel is sandwiched between both the International station and the domestic terminal of this lovely old city. We hardly had to put a foot outside the station to reach the reception desk. It is also situated right next to a hypermarket. Our room on the 11th floor offered views across the city and down onto the platforms of the Gare Lille Flandres. I could play train spotter as we sipped tea. There was little or no noise penetrating the thick safety glass from up here.

It was mid-afternoon as we wandered out into the biting cold. Since our last visit, much of the upgrading of the squares, pedestrianised streets, the campus around the international railway station and the adjacent shopping centre has been completed. It's looking good, but it took quite a while for us to get our bearings. The changes since our previous visit made it appear like a whole new city. In fact, several restaurants and cafés have changed their names and even had a makeover. I was keen to find the bar which had a railway theme, including a train that rolled over tracks suspended from the ceiling. The train has been shunted into sidings somewhere and the window dressing and whole interior has been upgraded to 'classy wine bar,' replete with young, bearded flashy waiters and smartly apparelled waitresses. We did dally. It's very nice but the price for wine and coffee all but wiped out tomorrow's food budget!

Lille has a smashing city centre. There are plenty of alleyways, open squares and shopping options in every direction. It's all on level ground too. A giant Ferris wheel dominated the skyline, and carousels and grottoes had been erected in so many nooks along the precinct. The baubles and lights were tastefully done, and the shops and restaurants had spent a lot of time making their premises look festive and inviting for us consumers. It was beginning to feel a lot like Christmas.

As dusk coated an ever-darkening sky, the lighting and atmosphere in the streets glowed brighter. Folk gathered in cafés and bars to warm up from the intensifying cold. Joy stood in front of the church in the centre as the bells tolled the hour. It was less of a cacophony, just gentle melodic chimes in keeping with the scene around us.

A visit to the old part of the city is essential, particularly down Rue-de-la-Cleff, where the narrow streets lead to more narrow streets and passageways snake to bars, artisan shops and restaurants. Lille is like a Tardis. It doesn't look very big on the map nor when you begin to wander out from the centre, but there always seems to be one more square, beyond the one you've just left. I should recommend the tourist board of Auxerre take a look at what Lille has achieved by developing these narrow streets and turning them into a honeycomb of juicy attractions.

As far as restaurants are concerned, we had plenty of choice, and the ones we did dine in were exemplary. L'Orange Bleue was arguably the best restaurant we had dined in for a long time. The exposed brick walls, white linen table covers and unhurried ambience made for a delightful experience.

The menu was simple and balanced, we were never pressurised, even after we'd finished our coffee.

In the same district, is another fantastic restaurant named after a recipe for pastry. It's called Le Pâte Brissee. They have a lovely signature dish which comprises, chicken, creamed potato, cheese and sundry sumptuous morsels, blended with the guile of a culinary craftsman. Joy ordered this the last time we were here. I ate it! The waitress had mixed up the order. We returned here one lunch time and asked if they still served it. Joy was smacking her lips in anticipation. Yes, they do, but only in the evenings now. They were fully booked that evening. Joy was inconsolable.

We wrapped up warm after breakfast and stretched our legs with a wander away from the precincts, towards the river Deule and the Citadel de Lille. This is protected by a moat created by a combination of canals and a river. The pentagonal fortress was built around 1670 and was crowned, the Queen of Citadels. The architect was Sébastien Le Prestre deVauban. We could have guessed that. We have encountered his works all across France. His structures were deemed almost impossible to breach. This citadel is now the headquarters of the 'corps de reaction rapide' made up of several nations working closely with NATO as an emergency defence resource. The grounds around the perimeter have a rambler's walk, more rugged than the park in Strasbourg, but as we are in the depths of winter, we'll take their word for it. We strolled for a while alongside the peaceful flow of the river. Our feet were already beginning to ache and the cold crept into our bones. We soldiered on.

Even after two trips to Lille I can say we've not exhausted possibilities for further exploration. It's such a laid-back place, but with so many constituent parts. Even Primark got a look in as we ventured into the Euralille shopping mall. There is a large war graves cemetery nearby, which is well worth visiting. Lille was liberated from German occupation in September 1944 by the combined efforts of British, Canadian and Polish forces. Of course, there are also churches, museums and street entertainment, no matter what time of the year. We did our best to patronise all the attractions to some degree, but it's December and priority must be given to Christmas.

The Christmas market is laid out in a square near to the central precinct. It was quite busy for most of the day, but nothing like the chain gang shuffling at Birmingham's German market. Nobody here was drunk either. Several stalls sold mulled wine and heated cider but it was all imbibed by moderate and sociable consumers. The other stalls were selling the usual Christmas curiosities and decorative pieces and some sold artisan jewellery. There are plenty of options from the numerous food outlets, so we won't go hungry. I could have made myself quite sick alternating between galettes, noodles, chocolate treats, candy, nougat and buns. I sampled a few.

The whole city is a mecca for lovers of mussels. The Aux Mussels restaurant had a table available for supper, if we would like to wait for thirty minutes and sip some wine. I think we could manage that. I was served a bucket of mussels, steamed in garlic and escargot sauce. Joy had a white wine accompaniment with her pile. It was such a struggle. We sat there for ages picking up shell after shell and the bottom of the bucket never seemed to appear. Joy eventually gave up. They had her beaten. It was touch and go for me too. These might have been smaller molluscs than some but these little critters made up in numbers what they lacked in size. The Aux Mussels restaurant's reputation lives on.

Bloated, we strolled through the night air and back to the hotel. It had been a lovely day as there was so much more to enjoy than just the market. Before lights out I counted the trains that were now stabled in the sidings outside the station below our window. Late night passengers quietly boarded their local services to leave for home.

Breakfast was easy. Carrefour's is right next to our apartment, so I could slip out for pastries and croissants whilst Joy made the coffee.

We had already ticked off several names from our Christmas list courtesy of the previous day's shopping and Carrefour's amazing choices. Our cases were going to be overloaded once more if we were not careful. Not least with the wines that were a fraction of the extortion we suffer in the UK. We even bought cheeses here. The choices are mouth-watering and that's just for one particular type. Mimolette for example; there were five grades of this fine quality cheese on offer in the same display case. I could have filled a family sized trolley just with cheeses. There were several cabinets stocked with various foie gras and pâtés and row after row of assorted biscuit treats. The French seem to be a race of very discerning shoppers. Our Christmas Day table will have a distinctly Francophile look about it this year.

We chose to explore more outer reaches of the city centre this morning, before plunging recklessly back into the shops. We took a walk towards the redbrick clock tower at the Porte de Paris. The Beffroi de Lille is part of the city council offices and can be seen from miles away. It's the tallest civil belfry in Europe and was constructed after the original belfry was destroyed during the Great War. The Triumphal Arch, just 100 metres away, marks the original boundary of the city back in 1400. The Arch was completed in 1692 in memory of the Sun King, who's army captured Lille, making the city forever French. It's incredibly impressive just walking around the perimeter as it sits in the centre of a roundabout surrounded by commercial properties, reminiscent of Edinburgh's Georgian quarter. We meandered onward, enjoying whatever attracted our attention. We even took a wee peek inside a motorcycle showroom, which goes to show that Joy has many interests!

We came to Place de la Republique, which in the summer would be a magnet for visitors and picnickers. The fountain had been emptied for the winter but there was still a throng of people here enjoying the open space. A busker with a saxophone was all that entertained today. The familiar tune had Joy humming along. The Palais de Beaux Arts museum is here, with paintings and sculptures by all the famous names as well as a few local starlets. My particular interest was drawn to the Lille born artist Louis Joseph César Ducornet, born with severe physical deformities in 1806, who painted with a brush between his toes. The metro trains stop here and the walkway under the road is interesting, if neglected. It has several strange sculptures hanging from the ceiling. We never had cause to use the subway system, but it would certainly be useful to reach all the parts if walking proved a bit tiring. Most alleys and street corners had something interesting to distract us.

Back in the centre, the posh shops were busy trading. Galleries Lafayette is such an attraction with its magnificent, modern Christmas tree outside the front doors. But with C&A close by it was no contest as to where my pennies will disappear. I found several essential items of clothing I needed to add to the few I bought in the Strasbourg branch a couple of weeks ago!

We next ventured to the cathedral. It was completed in 1999, so has modern aspects compared to the ancient buildings in other cities. It was commissioned to replace the Collegiate Church of St Peter which was destroyed during the French Revolution. It is interesting enough inside, with lots of stone hearths. In each alcove, protected by iron gates, was a large stone plinth with icons and carved markings representing some saint or other, and detailed floor designs around it, like a hearth. I think it was erected to celebrate the patron saint of fireplaces! There was also a nativity display for those willing to pay to see it.

We wandered back to the market and stood under the Ferris wheel once more. It was dusk by now and time to pay the Ferris man. I'm not overly keen on these rides. Scary antics on quaking machinery in travelling funfairs as a kid come back to haunt me. But this was very pleasant. We made several revolutions as we clicked the cameras at every conceivable target until they turfed us off.

Our final dinner was booked at La Fossetta, an Italian restaurant that we had eaten in before. It was so good the last time, we wanted an encore. It was bustling and frenetic inside, we could well be in Little Italy in New York. The male waiters are disgustingly handsome and smooth. They looked after us as if we were regulars. Which we would be if we lived here. We had a fantastic time. I ate a perfectly cooked steak titivated with a fig sauce. Other diners came and went and many were turned away. There was no room at this Inn! It's surprising to me that this city has so many wonderful restaurants, yet, this modern high velocity Italian restaurant just keeps the punters coming in droves. I ordered home-made nougat and ice cream for dessert. The perfect finale.

We left there late. It was a fantastic meal and I honestly believe it ranked at least equal to the best restaurants I have been fortunate to dine in. I told them so and they seemed genuinely pleased to hear this tribute. I sincerely meant it. We ambled back to our apartment having satiated our desires for a blemish free trip to Lille, for Christmas shopping and fine dining. It could not have been better.

Now we have to try and get all the goodies in our suitcases before heading home tomorrow. We had brought the emergency shoulder bag we purchased in Strasbourg and it did the trick. The advantages of having no luggage limits on the Eurostar paid off yet again. The rains came down at night. The howling winds reached gale force, and horrible screaming sounds emanated from the metal grills, that lined the roof-top above our room. The ear plugs I had packed came in handy after all.

The time we spent in Lille ended with a few minutes waiting at a tiny departure gate at the International station. Our train came in dead on time and after a minute or two of queueing to have our passports checked we were settled into our carriage as the train gathered speed to take us all the way back to England. 90 minutes later we stepped out into the London sunshine and another very pleasant cabby drove us to Marylebone station and the train for home.

FINAL NOTE

Making as much use of the railway network in France is key, for ease of mobility in this large and diverse country. Utilising the Eurostar to reach French terminals is the quickest for people with easy access to London or Ashford in Kent. Interconnecting stations from Paris or Lille are simple enough, the hardest part is trying it for the first time. Once achieved the opportunities are endless. Car hire fills in the gaps for the more remote places. The train certainly takes the strain.

During our travels, I made frequent mention of Tourist Information offices and joked about Joy's obsession with seeking them out as soon as we arrived anywhere. Also, her fixation with buying postcards and her endless search for stamps. The information offices are usually very well staffed and we gleaned so much more by 'dropping in' to see what was going on during our stay. With regards to postcards, Joy is an eager subscriber to 'Postcards of Kindness,' a social group who write to guests at care homes throughout the UK. She usually jots a few notes of what we are up to and posts them to the homes for the residents and staff to enjoy. The popularity of these communications has opened a whole new dimension for her, and more importantly, the people she sends them too. I'm told her readers have as much fun learning of her adventures and antics as we had of experiencing them.

On our journeys around France, we have either stayed in, visited, or passed through, more than one hundred towns and cities. We have reached the very corners, and touched the borders of Italy, Spain, Germany and Belgium. We have skirted the beaches of the Mediterranean and the rugged cliffs of the Atlantic coastline. We journeyed to the very heart of the country, and yet we have hardly scratched the surface. We covered many aspects of French life; the food, wines, chateaux, mountains, war graves, hospitality and history, yet we doubt we will please everybody. There will always be a town that was missed, a wine that was ignored or vital landmark that went unnoticed. The only reply I can give is to make a note and try to experience it on a future visit. There is so much more to France than many people give it credit for. I'm just a visitor, who turned up one day for a day trip to Calais and wanted more. Writing this book was my attempt to bring some of the amazing places and delights that I've experienced into the open. I hope these pages brought some additional insight, an enhanced historical perspective, a little humour and not least, a degree of entertainment. But most of all, I hope it inspires the reader to take another look at France and perhaps the inclination to go and see for themselves some of the places beyond the big cities and resorts that grab all the headlines.

ACKNOWLEDGEMENTS

When I read through the acknowledgements provided in other books, I'm always amazed at the number of people who are showered with blessings and credits by the author. It's not untypical to count 20 or more individuals that have provided help and support in getting a story perfected, proofed and fact checked. Then they go on to thank editors, companies, specialists and gurus for their contribution in helping to keep the author sane. I have no such deep well to draw upon, but I am very pleased for the help and support I received in ensuring the contents of this book could be presented in the way it now looks.

I am indebted to my good friend Andrew Sear who took painstaking steps to run a magnifying glass over every word, and for his talent in spotting ambiguities and vagueries on my part. I would also like to thank Dave Barr, a Canadian domiciled Scot and Michelle Turnbull, who have always encouraged me to continue writing and to get my musings up there for a wider audience. I must also thank Bill Munn who was part of the team that harassed me for essays to break up their monotonous days and lunchtime lulls.

I wish to thank Jonathan Greensted of the Government Department for Culture, who was so professional and helpful in the arrangements for our wonderful day spent at the memorial service in Amiens Cathedral. It was a special day in its own right, but the lengths he went to, to ensure we were so well looked after on such an auspicious occasion demands extra thanks and respect.

Writing this book, from the notes I made during each trip, has been a labour of love for me. Travelling as we have done has been such a rewarding experience. We are certainly all the richer for it. I'd like finally to thank Joy for her unfailing faith and support, not to mention patience and tolerance with my ideas, antics and mischiefs. Of course, I am grateful to you the reader who has reached this far. I sincerely hope the contents of this book has enlightened and entertained.

ABOUT THE AUTHOR

Born and raised in Somerset Eddy Smyth moved to the Home Counties in 1972 and followed a career in personnel in the manufacturing industry. His skill in assessing and appraising people led to specialising in personal development programmes for executives and highly qualified engineers. Relocating to Scotland in the mid 80's he worked in the fast-expanding IT sector in 'Silicon Glen,' advising Chief Executives on recruitment processes and writing scores of manuals, guides and operational policies. His understanding of people in the work place, drew attention from international corporations as they began start-up operations and then, subsequent closure of the same factories during that frenetic and hostile economic period. He returned to England to spend the rest of his career employed within the rail industry where he not only preferred working with 'real' people but could utilise the opportunities to indulge a lot more in his hobby of travelling for leisure. Now retired from full time work he can concentrate on his travel writing as well as visiting all the places he only dreamed about during the industrious years.

His passion for travel, love of wines and an eye for the obscure can be found in all his writings as he continues to explore places and countries, with or without his motorcycle and bring those experiences to life for others to share.

Printed in Great Britain
by Amazon